WITHDRAWN

IL PASTOR FIDO

A CRITICAL EDITION OF
SIR RICHARD FANSHAWE'S
1647 TRANSLATION OF
GIOVANNI BATTISTA GUARINI'S
IL PASTOR FIDO

BY
WALTER F. STATON, Jr.
AND
WILLIAM E. SIMEONE

OXFORD
AT THE CLARENDON PRESS
1964

Oxford University Press, Amen House, London, E.C.4

GLASGOW NEW YORK TORONTO MELBOURNE WELLINGTON
BOMBAY CALCUTTA MADRAS KARACHI LAHORE DACCA
CAPE TOWN SALISBURY NAIROBI IBADAN ACCRA
KUALA LUMPUR HONG KONG

PRINTED IN GREAT BRITAIN

PREFACE

THE present edition of Fanshawe's translation of Guarini's *Il Pastor Fido* has a double purpose: first, to provide students of the history of European drama and of the history of literary criticism and taste with an accessible English version of Guarini's play and, second, to make more available to students of seventeenth-century English literature the most important unrepublished work of Sir Richard Fanshawe.

Renaissance Italian drama, important for its influence on other Renaissance drama and for its aid in interpreting Italian Renaissance criticism, has been too little accessible to English readers. A series of translations like Lacy Lockert's of seventeenth-century French drama is greatly to be desired for sixteenth-century Italian drama. Until such a translator appears, however, the present edition of Fanshawe's translation of *Il Pastor Fido*, taken together with T. E. Lord's translations of Politian's *Orfeo* and Tasso's *Aminta*, will supply the need for one segment of that drama.

Much of Fanshawe's work has had modern editing: his translation of the fourth *Aeneid* edited by A. L. Irvine (Oxford, 1924), that of the *Lusiad* by J. D. M. Ford (Cambridge, Mass., 1940), and his shorter poems and translations by N. W. Bawcutt (promised for 1963, but not yet issued). While some of Fanshawe's work remains unedited, most notably the translation of Hurtado de Mendoza's *Querer por solo querer*, the present edition of his most popular and in many respects his best work closes the principal gap.

Our manuscript has been read in part by Professors Emerson Marks and Ralph Nash, both of Wayne State University, and *in toto* by Professor G. Blakemore Evans of the University of Illinois. We are grateful for their very helpful suggestions. We are also grateful to Mr. Alan Cohn of the Southern Illinois University Library for his efforts on our behalf beyond the call of duty.

As for the division of labour, while we have co-operated closely throughout, Mr. Simeone is principally responsible for the section of the introduction dealing with Fanshawe and for the textual introduction, Mr. Staton for the section dealing with Guarini and for the critical notes; the rest of the work was done jointly.

While this book was still in proof there appeared Nicoletta Neri's *Il Pastor Fido in Inghilterra con il testo della traduzione secentesca di Sir Richard Fanshawe*, Università di Torino, Pubblicazioni della Facoltà di Magistero, No. 21 (Torino, 1963). This is a photographic reprint of the 1647–8 edition with an introduction and notes.

W. E. S.

Carbondale, Illinois   W. F. S.
May 1964

CONTENTS

PLATES

INTRODUCTION

PART I

BATTISTA GUARINI'S *IL PASTOR FIDO*

FOR two hundred years after its composition, Guarini's *Il Pastor Fido* provoked admiration and imitation among cultivated people all over Europe. First published in 1590, the play had gone through twenty Italian editions by 1602; the seventeenth century saw forty more, and the eighteenth century swelled the total to over one hundred. Six different French translations, the first appearing in 1595, went through a total of twenty-five editions; five English translations, the first appearing in 1602, went through a total of thirteen editions; other versions appeared in Spanish, German, Greek, Swedish, Dutch, and Polish, as well as in several Italian dialects and in Latin. Praised extravagantly by critics as diverse as Voltaire, Rousseau, and William Schlegel, Guarini's play served as a model for a long list of dramatists. Of the host of Italian imitators, Guidobaldo Bonarelli is the only one of much merit. Notable among the French are D'Urfé, Racan, Hardy, and Mairet; and among the English, Samuel Daniel and John Fletcher.

While the day of its great popularity is doubtless for ever past, *Il Pastor Fido* is of interest to modern English readers for three reasons. In the first place, the play, though not great, is rather good; in Fanshawe's translation it is much better and more readable than many English plays of the same period that are printed and read relatively often. In the second place, Guarini's play is important to an understanding of the evolution of European literary taste and style. Its popularity in the seventeenth and eighteenth centuries indicates that, though it was written in the late Renaissance, the play contains elements that became fashionable in the succeeding age; consequently, it is not surprising that *Il Pastor Fido* figures frequently in modern discussions of the development of baroque art, seventeenth-century decadence, neoclassicism, and the like.

Thirdly, Guarini and his play have a good deal to tell us about late Renaissance dramatic theory and practice. In his three essays on tragicomedy and in his voluminous notes to *Il Pastor Fido*, Guarini has probably written more fully and more explicitly about his art than has any other Renaissance dramatist. A generous selection from *Il compendio della poesia tragicomica*, the most important of the essays, is translated in Allan Gilbert, *Literary Criticism* (1940). Included in the present edition are translations of the introduction to the notes, which contains a brief summary of Guarini's main critical positions as well as a few new statements, and of some extracts from the notes themselves, material which has not been printed even in Italian since 1737. This criticism, taken together with the play that gives it meaning, has considerable interest for students of sixteenth- and seventeenth-century English and French drama.

Il Pastor Fido, although it has affinities with several dramatic genres, is primarily associated with pastoral drama. The pastoral eclogue, from which the drama ultimately derives, had been a relatively unimportant literary type in classical times, but it enjoyed an enormous vogue among Latin-writing Renaissance humanists. Passing into the vernacular, it rapidly drew into itself a rich complex of ideas and significances of native and Christian as well as classical origin, and formally it branched from the more or less strict eclogue pattern into the lyric, the novel, and the drama. Eclogues, which had generally been written in dialogue form anyway, began to be staged in various Italian courts in the late fifteenth and early sixteenth centuries. These acted versions passed in the course of the sixteenth century from simple dialogues to more elaborate plots under the influence of such mythological dramas as Politian's *Orfeo*, of Sannazaro's highly successful depiction of the pastoral setting in his verse-prose medley, *Arcadia*, and of various other literary developments. At the courts of the Estensi in Ferrara a series of literary men gave impetus to the development of the pastoral drama. Giraldi Cinthio's *Egle* (1545), Agostino de Beccari's *Il sacrificio* (1554), Alberto Lollio's *Aretusa* (1563), and Argenti's *Lo sfortunato* (1567) all point the way toward the apogee of the dramatic pastoral, Tasso's *Aminta* (1573).

The *Aminta*, besides being a work of considerable literary merit, has special importance for the present discussion as the principal stimulus for Guarini's *Il Pastor Fido*. Its plot concerns the unrequited love of the shepherd Aminta for the frigid, chase-minded shepherdess, Silvia. Aminta saves Silvia from rape by a lustful satyr, but the shepherdess, instead of being grateful, flies scornfully from her rescuer. Later the distraught Aminta, being told that Silvia has been devoured by wolves, casts himself over a cliff. At this point

Silvia, who has really escaped the wolves, relents and goes to find
Aminta's body. But Aminta's fall has been miraculously broken,
and a messenger describes the blissful union of the two lovers. At
the end of Act I the chorus had sung yearningly of the Golden Age,
when love was not bound by law, and the concluding thought of the
play is that it would have been better if Aminta had been gratified
immediately without enduring frustration and misery.

Present at the first performance of Tasso's play in 1573 was the
future author of *Il Pastor Fido*. Battista Guarini, a descendant of the
famous humanist, Guarino da Verona, was born at Ferrara in 1538.
After studying at Padua, he became professor of rhetoric at the
University of Ferrara in 1557. About 1564 he returned to Padua to
become a member of Scipio Gonzaga's coterie, called 'the Academy
of the Eterei', a period of his career to which he alludes in *Il Pastor
Fido*, v. i. He entered the service of Alfonso II d'Este in 1567 and
served on many diplomatic missions, which took him as far as
Poland. He was made a cavalier in 1568 and secretary to the Duke
in 1585. After leaving the Duke's service in 1588, Guarini held
various posts in various Italian states. The latter part of his life was
filled with honours for his literary attainments, but also with savage
family quarrels. He died at Venice in 1612.

Guarini began the composition of *Il Pastor Fido* about 1580. A
painstaking craftsman, he put his work through an endless series of
revisions and submitted it to several friends for criticism and correction. By 1586 the plot had attained its final form, but the author
continued to polish his style until the time of publication in 1590.
The play was never so popular on the stage as in the study. It has
been questioned whether the 1585–6 Turin performance for which
the prologue was written actually took place; the first performance
which can be clearly established was at Crema in 1596. In November
1598 Duke Vincenzo Gonzaga sponsored at Mantua a very lavish
production, which should probably be considered the play's official
première. In 1602 an elaborate illustrated edition, the twentieth,
with corrections and notes by the author as well as an accompanying
treatise on tragicomedy, was issued by G. B. Ciotti at Venice.

At first glance *Il Pastor Fido* appears to be deeply indebted to
Tasso's *Aminta*, but this indebtedness should not be exaggerated.
In the first place Guarini intended to emphasize his rivalry with
Tasso by writing a few parallel scenes, and in the second place most
of the elements of both plays were in common use by earlier writers

of pastorals. The opposition between chastity and love, for instance, is as old as Euripides' *Hippolytus* and had been used by Giraldi Cinthio in *Egle* and by Beccari in *Il sacrificio* as well as by many other writers. Tasso presents the opposition in his opening scene in a dialogue between Silvia, the chaste shepherdess, and the older, worldly-wise Daphne, who punctuates her speeches with the refrain, 'Change, change your mind, little fool that you are!' Guarini uses for his opening scene a similar dialogue between Silvio, the chaste hunter, and the rather colourless confidant, Linco, who likewise reiterates a refrain: 'Leave, leave the woods, leave following beasts, fond boy, and think of love!' Guarini was challenging Tasso with this scene, but he was right in thinking that Tasso had no proprietary right to the theme. Guarini likewise challenged Tasso with a chorus about the Age of Gold, the fourth in *Il Pastor Fido*, in which he uses the same subject, the same metrical pattern, and even the same rhyme words as appear in the first chorus in *Aminta*, but draws the opposite moral. Guarini's conclusion, moreover, 'True joy is a thing that springs from Vertue after suffering', is purposely contrasted with Tasso's, 'Would that the flavourings of our delight should not be such grievous torments.' Other similarities, like the presence of a lustful satyr in both plays, are mostly the stock-in-trade of many pastoral plays, and in this instance the differences between Guarini's and Tasso's satyrs are far more important than their likenesses.

Like most such challenges, Guarini's challenge of Tasso proved unfortunate in that it has tempted critics into a facile contrast of the two poets. The *Aminta* is certainly better poetry; we hear in Tasso's plea for freedom to love an authentic heart's cry, and the world-weariness of Daphne, 'The world grows old and in growing old it saddens', strikes a sympathetic chord in the modern sensibility. Such appeals are lacking in Guarini's play. Apart from this, however, the two men are artistically very much alike. The main artistic effort of both is to achieve classical unity without sacrificing Renaissance variety, and both use the same means to this end. In *Gerusalemme liberata* Tasso imposes the Homeric kind of plot unity on Ariostan material, using as much liberty in introducing extraneous episodes as classical precedent will allow. Unity of the Homeric sort he achieves after a fashion, but his episodes lack Ariosto's narrative verve. What gives his epic the variety the Renaissance craved is rather his sensuously lyrical passages. The *Aminta* like-

wise achieves the classical unities of time, place, and theme. Short
as it is, however, it has not the sort of unity through lack of happen-
ings that we find in the tragedy of Alcyone and Ceyx sketched in
Scaliger's third book, or, for that matter, in Racine's *Bérénice*. On
the contrary, *Aminta* is full of exciting events. But it is the lyrical
passages rather than the events that give the play interest.

Il Pastor Fido is much the same. Guarini works out as complicated
a plot unity as classical precedent will allow, using a double plot of
the *Andria* type climaxed by a powerful *Œdipus*-type recognition
scene. Indeed, his double plot is more skilfully managed than in
Terence's *Andria*. His sub-plot, the Silvio–Dorinda plot, has
stronger characters and therefore more vitality; it is more tightly
tied into the main plot; and its resolution is more artfully contrived
—Silvio's change of heart is caused by his own act, the shooting of
Dorinda, which act is in turn caused by the very passion for hunting
that had caused his initial coldness. Moreover, along with plot unity,
Guarini has achieved thematic unity as well. The central idea of
the play is the power of love to transform the human soul. This idea
underlies the miseries of Arcadia and their cure; it is revealed in the
gentlemanly behaviour of Mirtillo toward Amarilli in Act III, as is
emphasized by the third chorus; it appears again in Mirtillo's offer
to sacrifice himself for Amarilli, an act foreshadowed by the third
chorus; and most importantly it appears in the transformation of
Amarilli from the fearful girl of Act IV, scene v, to the brave one
of Act v, scene ii. As for the celebrated unities of time and place,
Guarini observes them naturally, without apparent effort and without critical comment.

Thus Guarini has succeeded in imposing the classical sort of
unity on a rather diversified plot. But the desire for variety is not
satisfied by the variety of incidents in his plot. As with Tasso it is the
lyrical passages in Guarini's play that attract our attention. Thus an
important development like Silvio's wounding Dorinda with an arrow,
which would be a main point of interest in playwrights like Beau-
mont and Fletcher, is overshadowed by the lavish descriptions of the
boar-hunt and the extraction of the arrow, the chorus of shepherds'
hymn of praise, and the echo scene. So dominant indeed is the lyrical
emphasis in *Il Pastor Fido*, with the antiphon in the opening scene,
the incantations of the priests, and the ballet of the blind-man's-buff,
that the play verges on opera, and it is hardly surprising that it has
inspired a number of musical settings, including one by Handel.

Controversy has also obscured somewhat Guarini's critical position. Even before *Il Pastor Fido* appeared in print, it was attacked by a professor at Padua, Jason de Nores, in *Discorso intorno . . . la commedia, la tragedia ed il poema eroica* (1587), mainly on the grounds that the mixture of tragedy and comedy destroyed artistic unity and that poems about rude shepherds cannot provide moral instruction for city-dwellers. Guarini replied to De Nores's attack in *Il Verato* (1588); De Nores countered with *Apologia contro l'autor del Verato* (1590); Guarini rebutted with *Il Verato secondo* (1593); other critics joined the controversy on both sides; finally Guarini summed up his position in *Il compendio della poesia tragicomica* (1601) and restated it further in the annotations to the 1602 edition of his play.

Throughout the whole of this controversy Guarini's position is more consistent than most modern writers have supposed. His main answer to De Nores's complaint about the impossibility of uniting tragedy and comedy is that the artist may so shape the tragic and comic elements as to allow them to blend:

Art observes that tragedy and comedy are composed of heterogeneous parts, and that therefore if an entire tragedy and an entire comedy should be mixed, they would not be able to function properly together as a natural mixture, because they do not have a single intrinsic natural principle, and it would then follow that in a single subject two forms contrary to each other would be included. But art, a most prudent imitator of nature, plays the part of the intrinsic principle, and while nature alters the parts after they are united, art alters them before they are joined in order that they may be able to exist together and, though mixed, produce a single form. (Tr. in Gilbert, op. cit., p. 512; cf. Appendix I, p. 176.)

What Guarini means is abundantly clear from his 1602 annotations. In those on I. iii and I. v, for example, he points out that Corisca and the Satyr are treated comically so that their villainous roles do not give too tragic a tone to the play.

On the related question of whether the tragicomic form was recognized by the ancients, Guarini cites as many classical precedents as he can find, but his main answer is that tragicomedy is a new form—in fact, a better and more refined one, as befits a better and more refined age:

From this results a poem of the most excellent form and composition, not merely corresponding to the mixture of the human body, which consists entirely in the tempering of the four humours, but much more noble than simple tragedy or simple comedy, as that which does not inflict on us atrocious events and horrible and inhumane sights, such as blood and deaths, and which, on the other hand, does not cause us to be so relaxed in laughter that we sin against the modesty and decorum of a well-bred man. And truly if today men understood well how to compose tragicomedy (for it is not an easy thing to do), no other drama should be put on the stage, for tragicomedy is able to include all the good qualities of dramatic poetry and to reject all the bad ones; it can delight all dispositions, all ages, and all tastes—something that is not true of the other two, tragedy and comedy, which are at fault because they go to excess. (Tr. in Gilbert, op. cit., p. 512.)

To De Nores's complaint that a fable about rude shepherds cannot instruct sophisticated city-dwellers, Guarini replies at length that shepherds of the past had a complete society with kings and priests as well as commoners. (See Gilbert, op. cit., p. 530, and Appendix I, p. 176.) But his main answer is that art exists not to instruct but to purge—tragedy to purge pity and fear, tragicomedy to purge melancholy. (See Gilbert, op. cit., p. 522.)

Not so controversial but equally important in Guarini's critical thought are two other ideas. The first is his advocacy of a plot based on complication or 'tying the knot' and denouement involving reversal of fortune through revelation. The theory is a combination of Donatus' commentary on Terence and of Aristotle's praise of Sophocles' *Œdipus*, but its practice leads to a formula for a complicated plot, bringing some characters near death, followed by a surprise happy ending that is very little reminiscent of the ancients. The second is his notion of decorum, according to which each character conforms to an ethical principle which is his informing trait, or as Guarini says his 'architectonic': thus Mirtillo's architectonic is faith, Amarilli's chastity, Corisca's unbridled lust. (See note on ll. 3681–6 and Appendix I, p. 175.)

Guarini's theory and the play which seems written to exemplify it were the fruit of Renaissance thought and experience, but they point more clearly than almost any other Renaissance production to the succeeding age. In 1606, according to Jonson's *Volpone*—

> All our English writers,
> I mean such as are happy in the Italian,
> Will deign to steal out of this author, mainly:
> Almost as much as from Montagnié:
> He has so modern and facile a vein,
> Fitting the time, and catching the court-ear!

And in France pastoral tragicomedy imitated from Tasso and Guarini was the dominant dramatic form during the first quarter of the seventeenth century. But long after writers ceased to imitate Guarini directly, the literary qualities he stood for continued to please: the tendency toward opera, the surprise happy ending, the refined avoidance of brutality and bloodshed, and the employment of courtly characters representative of chastity, lust, good sense, and the like. Such things lived in European literature for nearly two centuries, and when they died Guarini and his play did not survive them.

PART II

FANSHAWE AND HIS TRANSLATION

THOSE who knew Sir Richard Fanshawe, Guarini's translator, described him as a man who would be attracted by the sententious morality of *Il Pastor Fido*. Charles I and the Marquess of Ormonde called him an honest and able man. When Sir Edward Hyde heard that Fanshawe had been made a prisoner after the battle of Worcester in 1651, he said, 'I wish he were at liberty, for upon my word he is a very honest, excellent man.' (*CSP, Clarendon*, III. 34.) More certain than any of these gentlemen of his excellence was Fanshawe's wife, Ann, who held him up to their children as an example of a perfect courtier. She described him as a handsome man, of gracious and wise countenance, with clear and distinct speech. His only exercise was walking, and this he usually did with book in hand. He 'was cheerful in his conversation, his discourse ever pleasant, mixed with the sayings of wise men and their histories, repeated as occasion offered . . .'. Argument he regarded as an uncharitable habit, and he had no use for factions. 'He would never be drawn to the faction of either Party, saying he found it sufficient honestly to perform that employment he was in. His conversation was so honest that I never heard him speak a word in my life that tended to God's dishonour or encouragement of any kind of debauchery or sin.' He kept a hospitable house because he thought that hospitality 'was wholly essential for the constitution of England. He loved and kept order with the greatest decency possible'. (*Memoirs*, ed. H. C. Fanshawe, 1907, pp. 3–5.)

Keeping order with any decency at all could not have been easy through much of Fanshawe's life. For if his internal weather was

serene, the weather outside was not. In 1643, when Charles I
raised his flag at Oxford, Fanshawe rode to the University to enlist
in the King's cause. For the next few years he and his wife, a cousin
whom he married in 1644, led a nomadic life. They were with the
Prince of Wales when they had to retreat, 'more dead than alive',
to the Isles of Scilly and then to Jersey. Before 1651, when Fanshawe was taken prisoner, he journeyed from England to Ireland, to
Spain, to France, to Holland, to Scotland, always in the futile and
weary effort to defeat the King's enemies at home. Fanshawe's
capture at Worcester ended the game, and for the next seven years
he was completely cut off from the Royalists in exile on the Con-
tinent. Then, in September 1658, he learned that Cromwell had
died. The next month he crossed into France. As a reward for his
devotion Fanshawe heard from Charles II that 'if it pleased God to
restore him to his kingdom', Sir Richard would reap his share of the
general happiness.

After the King returned in 1660 Fanshawe was given diplomatic
assignments to Portugal and Spain. In 1661 he went to Lisbon to
make arrangements for the King's marriage to Catherine of Bra-
ganza. The Portuguese, who knew Fanshawe as the translator of
their national epic, were pleased with the ambassador's conduct.
Upon returning to England he thought he would remain there in
positions of honour, trust, and some profit. Instead, he returned
to Lisbon in 1662, and then in 1664 he was named ambassador to
Spain. This embassy had two principal aims, a peace between Spain
and Portugal and a commercial treaty with Spain. Fanshawe ac-
complished neither. An English historian has remarked that only
a person with the finesse and unscrupulousness of a Mazarin might
have succeeded. Fanshawe's embassy ended in his recall, but as he
prepared to leave Madrid in June 1666 he took fever and died.

Always incidental to his serious affairs, Fanshawe's literary career
began when he was a student, in the twenties, at Jesus College,
Cambridge, and at the Inner Temple. Though he pursued his literary interests through most of his life, whenever he could find time
for them, most of his poetry and translations were probably done
in the thirties and forties. Of his literary production Fanshawe's
original poetry is a small part and its themes are usually topical.
An ode, for example, praises a 1630 proclamation by Charles I,
commanding the gentry to reside in the country. Another poem,
in both Latin and English versions, describes the Escorial in Spain,

its college, its convent, its libraries, its palace and pantheon. Still
another, also in Latin and English, entitled 'The Escuriall of the
Sea', extols the almost finished warship called *The Soveraigne of the
Seas*, the greatest man-of-war of its time. Besides a number of lyrics,
Fanshawe also wrote a lengthy poem in Spenserian stanzas called
'A Canto of the Progresse of Learning', a rather confusing allegory
on the decline of learning since ancient times. Almost all of his
original verse was printed with *Il Pastor Fido* in 1648. By that time
Fanshawe's talent for such composition had all but dried up.

His talent for translation lasted longer, and he exercised it, con-
ventionally at first, in turning Latin verses into English. His youthful
translations done in the literal mode include the englishing of the
metrical portions of Boethius' *Consolation of Philosophy* and of
several of Martial's epigrams. These have never been published.
In the paraphrastic mode of translation, which Fanshawe was one
of the first to use, he translated the fourth book of the *Aeneid*,
published in 1648, and selected poems of Horace, published in 1652.
Of his translations into Latin, the most notable is his version of
Fletcher's *Faithful Shepherdess*, *La fida pastora*, published in 1658.
There are finally the translations from the Spanish, Portuguese,
and Italian that are the most impressive parts of Fanshawe's literary
work.

Fanshawe's translations from the Spanish include two sonnets of
Bartolomé Leonardo de Argensola and eight sonnets of Luis de
Góngora. The translation of one of the Góngora sonnets, 'A Rose',
is often printed in anthologies of seventeenth-century verse. A much
more ambitious but now forgotten translation from the Spanish,
made when Fanshawe was confined to England by the Republican
government and published in 1670, is that of Hurtado de Mendoza's
play, *Querer por solo querer*. His major translation from the Portuguese is the *Lusiad* of Luís de Camões.

Fanshawe's principal translation from the Italian is, of course, the
present work, *Il Pastor Fido*. A reasonable guess as to the date of its
composition is 1643-4. The principal evidence for this date is
John Denham's remark in July or August of 1647 that he had
written the commendatory verses for Fanshawe's translation 'two
or three years since'. (See *Poetical Works of Denham*, ed. T. H.
Banks, p. 59.) Now, three or four years since, i.e. through most of
1643 and all of 1644, both Fanshawe and Denham had been with the
King at Oxford. (See Lady Fanshawe's *Memoirs*, p. 24, and *Works*

of Denham, p. 9.) In March of 1645 the two poets parted company, Fanshawe going with the Prince of Wales into the West. It is possible, of course, that Fanshawe made his translation prior to his going to Oxford, but the relative leisure of his two-year stay there in the midst of an otherwise busy period of his life would have provided an excellent opportunity for undertaking a 5,500-line verse translation. It might also be argued that since Fanshawe published the work at his first opportunity after joining the King's cause (he did not get to London after the events described above until January 1647 and the work was entered in the Stationers' Register in June of the same year) he wrote it for publication and that, had he finished it before 1643, he would have published it earlier.

Two English translations of Guarini's play earlier than Fanshawe's are known, sample scenes from each of which are contained in Appendix II. The earlier, done by an anonymous relative of Sir Edward Dymocke and prefaced with commendatory verses by Sir Edward's friend and travelling companion, Samuel Daniel, was printed first in 1602 and again in 1633. Probably this is the production Denham refers to in his verses to Fanshawe:

> Whiles this restored work at thy command
> Casts off the blemish of an artlesse hand.

The fact is that a more incompetent translation can hardly be imagined. Dymocke's relative makes gross blunders in the sense of the Italian and condenses by about one-third, apparently skipping the more difficult passages; he translates into unmetrical blank verse with little felicity of wording. The most interesting thing about this translation is that it strives noticeably to preserve the more obvious rhetorical figures of the original. A second English version, done by Jonathan Sidnam in 1630, is contained in B.M. Add. MS. 29,493, probably in the hand of a copyist with a few corrections likely to be in the hand of the translator. Sidnam is considerably more accurate than his predecessor and attempts with fair success to reproduce the metrical effect of the original; his principal defect is that he fails to produce a reasonably good quality of English verse.

Fanshawe's version is not only greatly superior to both of these but is a notable achievement in translation generally. In his frequently cited prefatory poem, 'To the Authour of this Translation', Denham describes Fanshawe as a pioneer, who is taking 'A new and nobler way . . . / To make Translations, and Translators too'.

This new and nobler way, according to Denham, calls for a calculated degree of freedom. While he condemns changing the characters' names, modernizing the setting, or altering the plot, Denham frees the translator from following his original word for word and line for line or from preserving the metre of his original and even recommends brightening the original's dull passages.

Fanshawe is perhaps a shade less free than Denham describes him, but on the whole the description is accurate. Metrically, Fanshawe ignores completely Guarini's unrhymed, freely mixed eleven and seven-syllable lines, a verse form which became standard in Italian pastoral drama with Tasso's *Aminta*. About ninety per cent. of Fanshawe's translation is in five-stress couplets, the rest being mostly in four-stress couplets. It is possible that Fanshawe was imitating Fletcher's *The Faithful Shepherdess*, which has a similar verse mixture. But more likely he found five-stress couplets congenial to him (he uses them frequently in his other work) and varied them for special effects. In any case, his rhymed verse seems a quite suitable English form for pastoral drama. By ignoring Guarini's verse form, however, Fanshawe does lose the effect of occasional short lines: the refrain, 'Poor, but content!' at ll. 1680, 1689, 1700, for example, buried in five-stress lines, lacks the single-line force of the Italian, 'Nuda sì, ma contenta'.

But the change of metre gives an advantage that more than compensates for this slight loss, that is, compactness. Denham observes,

> Nor are the nerves of his compacted strength
> Stretch'd and dissolv'd into unsinnewed length.

Because of the nature of the two languages, 'unsinnewed length' seems always to be a problem in translating from Italian to English. Thus Fairfax, who translates Tasso octave for octave, frequently completes the thought of his original in five or six lines and is forced to add two or three more of invented matter. Sidnam, following Guarini line for line, resorts constantly to expletives' feeble aid. Note, for example, ll. 20–23 of the passage from Sidnam's version included in Appendix II B:

> O nature too imperfect then,
> That dost contend against so stricke a lawe,
> O lawe too too seuere, that dost
> Oppose the rules of nature.

This is a line-for-line translation of Guarini's

imperfetta natura
che repugni a la legge!
oh troppo dura legge
che la natura offendi!

but it certainly seems wordy compared with the Italian. Fanshawe's

Nature too frail, that do'st with Law contend!
Law too severe, that Nature do'st offend! (ll. 2496–7)

by ignoring the syllable count keeps close to the number of words in the original. This is a quality of Fanshawe's translation that shows up quite clearly in the broad view. From reading long passages of Fanshawe one gets an impression of 'compacted strength'; from Sidnam in the aggregate the impression is definitely of 'unsinnewed length'.

A subtler liberty than this metrical one is what we believe Denham means by

Wisely restoring whatsoever grace
It lost by change of Times, or Tongues, or Place.

Guarini's style makes very heavy use of the figures of word-repetition —anaphora, anadiplosis, homoioteleuton, &c. Fanshawe ignores at least half of these figures, presumably because they were out of fashion in his age, and substitutes others, mainly alliteration. A clear example of this occurs at ll. 2486–7. The Italian original reads,

Che giova a te, cor mio, l'esser amato?
Che giova a me l'aver sì caro amante?

Dymocke's relative (Appendix II A, ll. 6–7) preserves both the anaphora and the polyptoton in these lines:

What bootes it thee my hart to be belou'd?
What bootes it me to haue so deare a Loue?

But Fanshawe deliberately avoids these figures and substitutes chiasmus:

what avails it me
To have thy love? T' have mine, what boots it thee?

A more flagrant liberty is the one Denham describes:

Foording his current, where thou find'st it low
Let'st in thine own to make it rise and flow.

On occasion Fanshawe departs so far from his original that we may say he has written his own poem. For example, Guarini makes Corisca say:

> usiam mentre l'abbiamo.
> Godiam, sorella mia,
> godiam, chè'l tempo vola e posson gli anni
> ben ristorar i danni
> de la passata lor fredda vecchiezza;
> ma, s'in noi giovinezza
> una volta si perde,
> mai più non si rinverde.
> Ed a canuto e livido sembiante
> può ben tornar amor, ma non amante.

Both Dymocke's relative and Sidnam seem to have misunderstood this passage (see Appendix II A, ll. 98–102 and B, ll. 145–56), which means literally: 'Let us use it [i.e. beauty] while we have it: let us enjoy ourselves, my sister, let us enjoy ourselves, because time flies, and the years, of course, can repair the damages of their cold old age when it has passed: but if in us youth is once lost, it never grows green again: and to a hoary, white appearance, love can return, all right, but not lover.' Fanshawe's version is:

> Let us use it whilst wee may;
> Snatch those joyes that haste away.
> Earth her winter-coat may cast,
> And renew her beauty past;
> But, our winter come, in vain
> We sollicite spring again:
> And when our furrows snow shall cover,
> Love may return, but never Lover. (ll. 2593–600)

Fanshawe not only ignores the emphatic repetition of 'godiam' and the careful antithesis of 'vecchiezza' and 'giovinezza' in this passage, but he makes much more explicit the barely hinted-at comparison of earth and human life, even to the point of adding his own metaphors, 'furrows' and 'snow'. None the less, Fanshawe's liberty here is by no means irresponsible improvisation in the manner of Harington and other Elizabethans. In the first place, Guarini has called special attention to this passage by his use of rhyme, a rare practice in *Il Pastor Fido*. Fanshawe, for whom rhyme is the norm, calls attention to the passage by shifting to four-stress lines. In the second place, Guarini's note on the passage indicates that he is imitating Catullus' Epode v:

Vivamus, mea Lesbia, atque amemus,

. . .

Soles occidere et redire possunt:
nobis, cum semel occidit brevis lux,
nox est perpetua una dormienda.

Fanshawe's phrase 'snatch those joys' suggests an equally famous
classical poem on the same theme, Horace, Book I, Ode xi:

Dum loquimur, fugerit invida
aetas: carpe diem, quam minimum credula postero.

By such equivalences Fanshawe remains true to the poetic effect of
his original, even if he sometimes tampers with its literal sense.

The passages quoted above are, we believe, on the whole typical
of Fanshawe's translation. Sometimes, in translating proverbs,
stichomythic passages, epigrammatic lines, Fanshawe is lucky and
finds an almost perfect English equivalent for his original. Thus, in
Act II, scene ii, Guarini has

Sil. Che cosa è questo amore?
Dor. S'i' miro il tuo bel viso,
amore è un paradiso;
ma, s'i' miro il mio core,
è un infernal ardore.

Fanshawe translates:

Sil. What is this Love?
Dor.   When I behold thy eyes,
It is the light of Paradise.
But my own heart consider'd well,
It is the very fire of hell. (ll. 1518–21)

On the other hand, in about half a dozen instances, which are
recorded in the Critical Notes, he seems to have misunderstood the
Italian, and in a similar number of instances, also recorded, he adds
matter completely unwarranted by the original. More serious than
these failings, however, are a few instances in which he misses
Guarini's poetic direction. Perhaps the most glaring is one of the
most celebrated passages in the play, Amarilli's apostrophe to
Decency:

Santissima onestà, che sola sei
d'alma bennata inviolabil nume,
quest' amorosa voglia,

> che svenata ho col ferro
> del tuo santo rigor, qual innocente
> vittima a te consacro.

A possible literal rendering might be: 'O most holy Decency, who art the sole sacred deity of a well-born soul—this amorous desire, lanced now with the steel of thy holy rigour, as an innocent victim, I consecrate to thee.' Fanshawe's

> Vertue, which art
> The bindingst Law to an ingenuous heart,
> This inclination which in me I feel,
> Lanc'd with the sharp point of thy holy steel,
> To thee I sacrifice.   (ll. 2500–4)

badly misses the strong aristocratic and religious overtones of the passage.

Such failures, however, are exceptional. In general Fanshawe's level is so high that, were his original more highly esteemed, he would certainly stand in the front rank of English translators.

TEXTUAL INTRODUCTION

THE first edition of Fanshawe's translation of *Il Pastor Fido* was printed by Ruth Raworth and entered in the Stationers' Register on 8 June 1647:

Entred . . . under the hands of Sʳ NATH: BRENT and Master WHITAKER warden, a booke called *Il Pastor Fido written originally in Italian & now newly translated into English &c* (salvo iure cuiuscunque).

This edition, because it has the authority of having been printed from manuscript, serves as the copy text of the present edition. The second edition of 1664 and the third of 1676, as we shall presently show, have no such authority.

The title page of the 1647 edition is as follows:

IL | PASTOR FIDO, | The faithfull Shepherd. | A PASTORALL | Written in Italian by *BAPTISTA* | *GUARINI*, a Knight | of ITALIE. | And *now Newly* Translated out of | the ORIGINALL. || [Ornamental device.] || LONDON, | Printed by *R. Raworth*, M DC XLVII.

Coll.: 4° A⁴, (a)², B–Z⁴, Aa–Ff⁴.

A1ʳ: [Blank]; A1ᵛ: [Portrait of Guarini]; A2ʳ: [Title page]; A2ᵛ: [Blank]; A3ʳ: To the most Illustrious and most hopefull PRINCE CHARLES, *Prince of WALES*. [first dedicatory epistle]; (a)1ʳ: To the Authour of this TRANSLATION [commendatory poem by John Denham]; (a)2ʳ: *The Scene* ARCADIA. *THE SPEAKERS*.; (a)2ᵛ: *ALFEO. F.* [illustration]; B1ʳ: IL PASTOR FIDO. THE PROLOGUE, Spoken by ALFEO, a River of ARCADIA.; Ee4ᵛ: FINIS. Ff1ʳ: *Presented* TO HIS HIGHNESSE THE PRINCE OF WALES, At his going into the West, *Ann. M. DC. XLV. Together with CESAR'S COMMEN-TARIES*. Ff2ʳ: *Presented* TO HIS HIGHNESSE, *In the West*, Ann. Dom. 1646; Ff4ʳ: FINIS. [Errata]

The year after Ruth Raworth published the first edition, she assigned the rights of the book to Humphrey Moseley. The transaction is recorded in the Stationers' Register under the date 6 February 1647/8:

Assigned over unto him by vertue of a note under the hand & seale of RUTH RAWORTH, & subscribed by Master LATHAM warden a booke called *Il Pastor Fido, or the faithfull Sheapard &c, translated into English by Mʳ Fran.* [sic] *Fanshaw, with divers other poems annexed thereunto by the same author* . . .

Moseley reissued the play in 1648: that is, Raworth's sheets, sig. B–
Z⁴, Aa–Ff⁴. New to the issue were the poems mentioned in the Stationers' Register, placed after Raworth's Ff gathering. Also new to
the issue was an initial quarto gathering, hereafter referred to by
sig. *A, of which the second leaf only is signed A2. *A1ʳof this added
gathering is his new title page:

IL | PASTOR FIDO | The faithfull Shepheard | WITH | An ADDITION
of divers other | POEMS | Concluding with a short Discourse | OF THE
LONG | CIVILL WARRES | OF | ROME. | To His Highnesse | THE
PRINCE OF | *WALES.* || By *Richard Fanshawe,* Esq. || HORAT. *Patiarque
vel inconsultus haberi.* || LONDON: | Printed for *Humphrey Moseley,* and
are to be sold at his Shop at the | Princes Armes in S. *Pauls* Church-yard.
1648.

*A1ᵛ: [Blank]; *A2: [Device, prince's badge with initials C. P. and
motto] TO THE HOPE AND LUSTRE Of Three Kingdomes,
CHARLES Prince of *Wales,* Duke of *Cornwall,* &c [second dedicatory
epistle signed Richard Fanshawe]; *A3ᵛ: *The Printer to the Reader.;*
*A4ʳ: An Index of the severall things contained in this Booke.

The collation of the preliminaries of Moseley's issue varies among
the copies, but the normal form seems to be the following: 4⁰
*A⁴ A⁴ (a)².

After the Ff gathering in Raworth's edition, Moseley annexed the
matter mentioned on his title page in twelve new gatherings: Gg–
Rr⁴. Gg–Qq3: [Fanshawe's additional poems]; Qq4–Rr4: A Summary Discourse of the Civill Warres of *Rome,* extracted out of the
best Latine writers in Prose and Verse. To the Prince His Highnesse,
upon occasion of the preceding Odes.

The following copies of the first edition, including both 1647 and
1648 issues, have been used in the preparation of the present edition:

> 1647: University of Illinois.
> 1648: University of Illinois.
> 1648: Newberry Library.
> 1648: New York Public Library.
> 1647: University of North Carolina.
> 1648: Southern Illinois University.

The 1648 printer apparently believed that the *Pastor Fido* had been
more carefully printed than the poems which were added for his
1648 issue, for he wrote in his address to the Reader (*A3ᵛ), 'Thou
wilt meet in the *Additionall Poems* with *many* literall Errours, and in

Pastor Fido with *some*.' Indeed, the number and nature of variants due to stop-press correction indicate that the 1647 edition of *Il Pastor Fido* had been rather carefully printed.

In 1664 the second edition of Fanshawe's translation appeared:

IL | PASTOR FIDO: | THE | Faithful Shepheard. | With an Addition of divers other | POEMS, | Concluding with a short Discourse of the long | CIVIL WARRES | OF | ROME. || *By the Right Honourable* | *Sir* Richard Fanshawe *Knight*. || HORAT. | *Patiarque vel inconsultus haberi.* || LONDON, | Printed for *A. Moseley*, and are to be sold at the *Princes* | *Arms* in St. *Pauls* Church-yard. 1664.

Coll.: 8° A⁸, *B⁴, B–U⁸ X⁴.

A1ʳ: [Blank]; A1ᵛ: [Portrait of Guarini]; A2ʳ: [Title page]; A2ᵛ: [Blank]; A3ʳ: [First dedicatory epistle to Charles]; A5ʳ: [Index]; A6ʳ: [Second dedicatory epistle to Charles]; *B2ᵛ: [Commendatory poem by John Denham]; *B4ʳ: *The Scene* ARCADIA. THE SPEAKERS.; *B4ᵛ: *ALFEO. F.* [illustration reduced]; B1ʳ: [Prologue]; O4ᵛ: FINIS.; O5ʳ: [Two poems to Charles]; O8ᵛ: [Blank]; P1ʳ: THE Additional *POEMS*.; U6ᵛ: *A Summary Discourse of the Civil Wars of* Rome.

It is clear that this edition was set from a copy of 1647/48. In the first place, there is general agreement between the two editions in the composing of the choruses, the play of blind-man's-buff (III. ii), the echo scene (IV. viii), and other unusual passages. Secondly, there are no variants in 1664 that are not attributable to the printing house. Finally, 1664 contains five variants which appear in identified uncorrected formes of 1647/48. On these points, see the Textual Notes.

The third edition of the play was published in 1676, ten years after Fanshawe's death. Its title page is as follows:

IL | PASTOR FIDO: | THE | Faithful Shepherd. | With an ADDITION of divers other | POEMS: | Concluding with a short | DISCOURSE | OF | The Long Civil Wars of *ROME.* || By the Right Honourable, | Sir *RICHARD FANSHAWE*, Knight. || *Patiarque vel inconsultus haberi,* Horat. || *London*: Printed for *Henry Herringman*, at the Anchor | in the Lower Walk of the *New Exchange*. 1676.

Coll.: 8° *⁴ A–V⁸ X⁴.

*1: [Blank]; *2ʳ: [Title page]; *3ʳ: [First dedicatory epistle to Charles]; A1ʳ: [Second dedicatory epistle to Charles]; A5ᵛ: [Commendatory poem by John Denham]; A7ʳ: [Index]; A8ʳ: *The Scene* ARCADIA.; A8ᵛ: *ALFEO. F.* [illustration]; B1ʳ: [Prologue]; O4ᵛ: FINIS.; O5ʳ: [Two poems to Charles]; P1ʳ: THE *Additional POEMS.*; U6ᵛ: *A Summary Discourse of the Civil Wars of* Rome.

It is clear that the copy-text for this edition was that of 1664. Using new sheets, the compositor followed the 1664 edition line for line, page for page. In both editions, for example, B1^r has 20 lines ending with the word '*birth*'; B3^r has 16 lines ending with the word '*fights*'; K4^r (wrongly signed K2 in 1676) has 22 lines, and the catch-word is 'Their'. Each edition has 200 pages for the text of the play. Most of the errors of 1664 are repeated in 1676, and the latter contains no variants from 1664 which are not attributable to the printing house.

In 1692 there appeared what the publishers called a second edition. It is not a new edition but a re-issue of 1676; what is new is its title page:

IL | PASTOR FIDO: | THE | Faithful Shepherd. | With an Addition of divers other | POEMS: | Concluding with a short | DISCOURSE | OF | The Long Civil Wars of *ROME*. || The Second Edition. || By the Right Honourable, Sir *Rich. Fanshaw*, Knight. || *Patiarque vel inconsultus haberi*, Horat. || *London*, Printed for *Richard Bently*, *Jacob Tonson*, | *Francis Saunders*, and *Tho. Bennet*. 1692. 8°.

As Fanshawe translated the play, it was never performed. An adaptation of his text by Elkanah Settle was performed in 1677 at the Duke's Theatre. Settle, knowing no Italian, relied entirely on Fanshawe's work. In his stage version, Settle retained the five acts, though all are much shortened. Act I is cut to three scenes; Act II to three scenes; Act III to one scene; Act IV to three scenes; Act V to one scene. Moreover, the prologue and all the choruses at the end of the acts are missing. The Satyr is also gone. But Settle did add a character named Sylvano, a discontented shepherd, and another called Dorco, Sylvano's attendant. Settle has rewritten much of Fanshawe's translation, but some of Fanshawe's lines, such as Corisca's *carpe diem* speech, Settle has kept with only slight variation. Settle's adaptation was published again in 1689 and in 1694.

An eighteenth-century version of Fanshawe's translation, 'made by an ingenious Gentleman who would not permit us to prefix his Name', was published in 1736. This is Fanshawe's text with minor changes made chiefly to regularize the metre and to make the diction more modern or more elegant. Fanshawe's 'kicking Gyant' becomes 'restless Giant'; his 'thridding back' becomes 'running back'; his 'Empale ye triumph' becomes 'Circle ye triumph'; his 'belches up a smell' becomes 'utters up a Smell'. When the publishers say, 'In this Edition we have chiefly follow'd the Translation of Sir *Richard Fanshaw*', they mean that the revisions of the anonymous Gentleman worker were superficial.

The present edition is based on the 1647/48 edition. Along with substantive variants in the other seventeenth-century editions, all deviations from the copy-text have been recorded in the Textual Notes except the following: modernization of the long 's' and of ligatures involving consonants, regularization of roman 's' at the end of italicized possessive nouns, regularization of speech tags, and treatment of speeches that break a metrical line, where we have followed twentieth-century rather than seventeenth-century practice.

The editors have endeavoured to convey along with Fanshawe's text a fairly accurate idea of Guarini's original. To this end, Fanshawe's deviations from a literal translation of the Italian have been recorded in the Critical Notes when they seemed important or interesting. In the whole course of our work we have consulted on various points ten Italian editions of *Il Pastor Fido*, but in this part of it we have used only two, the 1602 Venice edition and the 1950 edition of Luigi Fassò. The references in the Critical Notes to the Italian text, therefore, are to these editions. Where these differ, we have generally resolved the differences on the basis of Guarini's notes, but, in the one instance in which we could not do this, we recorded it (note on ll. 4570–3).

NOTE ON THE ENGRAVINGS

THE portrait of Guarini and the picture of the river-god, Alfeo, which appeared in all the seventeenth-century editions of Fanshawe's translation, were copied apparently from engravings in the 1602–5 Venice editions of Guarini's play.

BIBLIOGRAPHICAL NOTE

THE principal early edition of *Il Pastor Fido* is that issued by G. B. Ciotti at Venice in 1602. A very elaborate edition of Guarini's *Opere*, including all the tracts by Guarini and others in the controversy over *Il Pastor Fido*, was issued in four volumes at Verona by Alberto Timermani in 1737; this is probably the most useful edition for the scholar. Two editions have appeared in the twentieth century: *Il pastor fido e il compendio della poesia tragicomica*, a cura di Gioachino Brognoligo (Bari, 1914) and *Opere di Battista Guarini*, a cura di Luigi Fassò (UTET, 1950); on the inaccuracies of these, however, see Walter F. Staton, Jr., 'The Annotazioni to Guarini's *Il Pastor Fido*', *Italica*, xxxvi (1959), 135–6. An English translation of excerpts amounting to about half of *Il compendio della poesia tragicomica* is in Allan Gilbert, *Literary Criticism* (New York, 1940), pp. 505–33.

On the life of Guarini and the composition of *Il Pastor Fido*, Vittorio Rossi, *Battista Guarini ed Il Pastor Fido* (Torino, 1886) is definitive. The most influential criticism is De Sanctis's in *History of Italian Literature*, tr. J. Redfern (New York, 1931), II, 672–84. Recent critical articles are Mario Marcazzan, 'Il Guarini e la Tragicommedia', in *Romanticismo critico e coscienza storica* (Firenze, 1947), pp. 87–99, and Ferruccio Ulivi, 'La Poetica del Guarini e *il Pastor Fido*', *Humanitas*, vi (1951), 88–103. Arnold Hartmann, Jr., 'Battista Guarini and *Il Pastor Fido*', *Musical Quart.* xxxix. 415–25, deals with the musical settings of the play. Madeleine Doran, *Endeavors of Art* (Madison, 1954), M. T. Herrick, *Tragicomedy* (Urbana, 1954), and Bernard Weinberg, *A History of Literary Criticism in the Italian Renaissance* (Chicago, 1961) treat Guarini's critical theory.

Of the many works on pastoral drama, three are especially important: Jules Marsan, *La pastorale dramatique en France* (Paris, 1905); Walter Wilson Greg, *Pastoral Poetry and Pastoral Drama* (London, 1906); Enrico Carrara, *La poesia pastorale* (Milan, 1909). While each of these is concerned primarily with one national literature, all three give fairly extensive treatment to the Italian origins.

The best edition of Lady Fanshawe's *Memoirs* was edited by H. C. Fanshawe (New York, 1907). Cf. also H. C. Fanshawe, *History of the Fanshawe Family* (Newcastle upon Tyne, 1927). Materials on Fanshawe's official life are in the *Original Letters of his Excellency Sir Richard Fanshaw, During his Embassies in Spain and Portugal* (London, 1702), and in the *Report on the Manuscripts of J. M. Heathcote, Esq., of Conington Castle*, Historical Manuscripts Commission (London, 1899).

Commentary on Fanshawe's translation of *Il Pastor Fido* may be found in: Walter Wilson Greg, *Pastoral Poetry and Pastoral Drama* (London, 1906); Geoffrey Bullough, 'Sir Richard Fanshawe and Guarini', *Studies in English Language and Literature presented to Karl Brunner* (Vienna, 1957), pp. 17–31.

BAPT· GVARINI THE AVTHOR OF PASTOR FIDO· ÆT· SVÆ· LXIII

Not mars' is this, but learn'd Apollo's knight:
Of Italie the glory, and delight.

F: Cross sculpt: ·

I L

PASTOR FIDO,

The faithfull Shepherd.

A PASTORALL

Written in Italian by *BAPTISTA GUARINI*, a Knight
of ITALIE.

And *now Newly* Tranſlated out of
the ORIGINALL.

LONDON,
Printed by *R. Raworth*, M DC XLVII.

To the most Illustrious and most hopefull
PRINCE CHARLES,
Prince of WALES.

SIR,

Whilst I had the honour to serve your *Highnesse*, I did it (how weakly soever) with that fidelity and dutifull affection to your Person, which found your gracious acceptance, together with some encouragement from your own mouth to hope a new and more fixt relation to you in the future; the onely suit I was bold to make: as having ever esteemed that to serve your *Highnesse*, would of it self be an abundant reward for having served you.

In the mean time I hold my self bound to pay your *Highness* some tribute of my hours of vacancy, presenting to your Princely view for the present this *Italian Pastorall*, into which the no lesse wise then witty *Guarini* (having grown unprofitably grey in *Travell*, *Universities*, and *Courts*, as out of the fifth Act, where he personates himself under the name of old *Carino*, may be collected) infused whatsoever of excellent so eminent *Schools* could teach so apt a *Scholer*. His scope therein being, to make *a Dernier effort* (as the French call it) or generall muster of the whole forces of his Wit before his Princely Master (the then *Duke of Savoy*) and withall to insinuate and bring into that awfull presence, in their masking clothes (as I may say) such principles of Vertue, and knowledge *Morall*, *Politicall*, *and Theologicall*, as (peradventure) in their own grave habits, out of the mouthes of severer Instructers, would not have found so easie admittance to a Prince in the heat of his youth, heightned with the pomp and flatteries that attend on Greatnesse, and with the glorious triumphs and felicities of his royall Nuptials then celebrating: though this was the same *Charles Emanuel* who proved afterwards in his riper yeers, by his Councels and by his Prowesse, *the Bulwark* indeed *of Italie*, against the puissance of the *great Henry* of France himself, your Highnesse most renowned Grandfather.

Your Highnesse may have seen at *Paris* a Picture (it is in the Cabinet of the *great Chancellor* there) so admirably design'd, that, presenting to the common beholders a multitude of little faces (the famous Ancestors of that Noble man); at the same time, to him that looks through a *Perspective* (kept there for that purpose) there appears onely a single portrait in great of the *Chancellor* himself; the Painter thereby intimating, that in him alone are contracted the Vertues of all his Progenitors; or perchance by a more subtile Philosophy demonstrating, how the *Body Politick* is composed of many *naturall ones*; and how each of these, intire in it self, and consisting of head, eyes, hands, and the like, is a head, an eye, or a hand in the other: as also, that mens *Privates* cannot be preserved, if the *Publick* be destroyed, no more then those little Pictures could remain in being, if the great one were defaced: which great one likewise was first and chiefest in the Painters designe, and *that* for which all the rest were made.

Just so our Authour (exposing to *ordinary view* an Enterlude of Shepherds, their loves, and other little concernments, with the stroke of a lighter pencill) presents through the *perspective* of the *Chorus*, another and more suitable object to his *Royall Spectators*. He shews to *them* the image of *a gasping State* (once the most flourishing in the world): *A wild Boar* (*the sword*) depopulating the *Country*: *the Pestilence* unpeopling the *Towns*: their gods themselves in the mercilesse *humane Sacrifices* exacting bloody contribution from *both*: and the *Priests* (*a third Estate of misery*) bearing the burthen of *all* in the *Chorus*, where they deplore their *owne* and the *common* Calamitie. Yet in the *Catastrophe*, *the Boar slain*; *the Pestilence* (but this was before upon that miserable composition with their Gods) *ceased*; *the Priests* above all others *exulting* with pious joy: and all this miraculous change occasioned by the presaged Nuptials of two of Divine (that is, Royall) extraction; meaning those at that time of the *Duke of Savoy* with the *Infanta of Spain*, from which fortunate Conjunction hee prophesies a finall period to the troubles that had formerly distracted that State: *So much depends upon the Marriages of Princes*.

I am not ignorant (*Sir*) that this famous *Dramatick Poem* must have lost much of the life and quicknesse by being powred out of one vessell (that is, one *Language*) into another, besides what difference may be in the capacity and mettle of the Vessels themselves (the *Italian* being transcendently both copious and harmonious), and besides the unsteadinesse of the hand that powres it; And that a *Translation* at the best is but the *mock-Rainbow* in the clouds, faintly imitating the true one: into which *Apollo* himself had a full and immediate influence.

Yet because it seems to me (beholding it *at the best light*) a *Lantskip* of these Kingdoms, (your *Royall Patrimony*) as well in the former flourishing, as the present distractions thereof, I thought it not improper for your Princely notice at this time, thereby to occasion your Highness, even in your recreations, to reflect upon the sad *Originall*, not without hope to see it yet speedily made a perfect *parallell* throughout; and also your self a great Instrument of it. Whether by some happy Royall Marriage (as in this *Pastorall*, and the case of *Savoy*, to which it alludes) thereby uniting a miserably divided people in a publick joy; or by such other wayes and means as it may have pleased *the Divine Providence* to ordain for an *end of our woe*; I leave to that Providence to determine.

To the Authour of this
TRANSLATION.

Such is our Pride, our Folly, or our Fate,
That few but such as cannot write, translate.
But what in them is want of wit, or voice,
In thee, is either Modestie, or Choice.
Whiles this restored work at thy command   5
Casts off the blemish of an artlesse hand.
Secure of Fame, thou justly dost esteem
Lesse honour to create, then to redeem.
Nor ought a Genius lesse then his that writ,
Attempt Translation; for transplanted wit   10
All the defects of air and soil doth share,
And colder brains like colder Climates are:
In vain they toil, since nothing can beget
A vitall spirit, but a vitall heat.
That servile path thou nobly dost decline   15
Of tracing word by word, and line by line.
Those are the labour'd births of slavish brains,
Not the effects of Poetry, but pains.
Cheap vulgar arts, whose narrownesse affords
No flight for thoughts, but poorly sticks at words.   20
A new and nobler way thou dost pursue
To make Translations, and Translators too.
They but preserve the Ashes, Thou the Flame,
True to his sense, but truer to his fame.
Foording his current, where thou find'st it low   25
Let'st in thine own to make it rise and flow.
Wisely restoring whatsoever grace
It lost by change of Times, or Tongues, or Place.
Nor fetter'd to his Numbers, and his Times,
Betray'st his Musick to unhappy Rimes,   30
Nor are the nerves of his compacted strength
Stretch'd and dissolv'd into unsinnewed length:
Yet after all (lest we should think it thine)
Thy spirit to his circle dost confine.

New names, new dressings, and the modern cast,   35
Some Scenes, some persons alter'd, had outfac'd
The world, it were thy work; for we have known
Some thank't & prais'd for what was lesse their own.
That curious hand which to the life can trace
The ayrs, the lines, and features of a face,   40
May with a free and bolder stroke expresse
A varyed posture, or a flatt'ring Dresse;
He could have made those like, who made the rest,
But that he knew his own design was best.

JOHN DENHAM.

The Scene ARCADIA.

THE SPEAKERS.

SILVIO, Son to *Montano*, & contracted to *Amarillis*

LINCO, An old man, servant to *Montano*

MIRTILLO, In love with *Amarillis*

ERGASTO, Friend to *Mirtillo*

CORISCA, A wanton Nymph, in love with *Mirtillo*

MONTANO, The chief Priest, Father to *Silvio*

TITIRO, Father to *Amarillis*

DAMETA, An old man, servant to *Montano*

SATYR, An old gotish fellow in love with *Corisca*

DORINDA, In love with *Silvio*

LUPINO, A Goat-herd, servant to *Dorinda*

AMARILLIS, Daughter to *Titiro*

NICANDRO, Chief Minister to the Priest

CORIDON, In love with *Corisca*

CARINO, An old man supposed Father to *Mirtillo*

URANIO, An old man Friend to *Carino*

MESSENGER.

TIRENIO, A blind Prophet.

CHORUS of $\begin{cases} \textit{Shepherds.} \\ \textit{Huntsmen.} \\ \textit{Nymphs.} \\ \textit{Priests.} \end{cases}$

ALFEO. F.

IL PASTOR FIDO.

THE
PROLOGUE,
Spoken by ALFEO,
a River of ARCADIA.

If from old Fame, and peradventure not
Believ'd at all by you, or else forgot,
O' th' Amorous Brook ye heard the wonder ever,
Which to pursue the coy and flying River
Of his beloved Arethusa, *ran*   5
(O force of Love!) piercing the Ocean,
And the earth's hidden bowels, to that Isle,
Where underneath the huge Etnean Pile
Upon his back the kicking Gyant lies,
Spitting despightfull flames at hostile Skies,   10
And leaves it doubtfull to the world that's under,
If heav'n at him, or he at heaven thunder:
That Brook am I. Though what you have been told
Ye may, your eyes ye cannot doubt. Behold!
Leaving my loved Nymph, and thridding back   15
That well known way where I had made a track
Through the great waters, I in person rise
And view (with tears of gladnesse in mine eyes)
That ancient and that venerable earth
From whose cold entrails I receiv'd my birth,   20
Not thrall'd and plundred (as of late) but free
And beautifull as it was wont to be.
O my deer mother! O Arcadia, known
By me thy son, though so long absent! owne
Thy deer, and (being improv'd by travell) now   25
Thy great ALFEO, *and as fam'd as thou.*
These be the streets once so renown'd, these be
The woods where the old russet honestie

Did live and die: unto this onely nook
O' th' iron world, when she her flight had took   30
From sinfull men, the golden age retir'd.
Here (that which elswhere is in vain desir'd)
Freedome unstrain'd, and from suspicion free,
Flourish'd in peace and sweet securitie.
An unarm'd people had for their defence   35
A wall of Vertue, and of Innocence,
Stronger then that whose living stones were layd
About great Thebes, whilst he that built it playd.
For when tumultuous war flam'd most in Greece
And other her more warlike Provinces   40
Arcadia arm'd, to this blest part alone,
This Sanctuary, there was never known
The least Alarum, the least sound to come,
Or of a friends, or of an en'mies Drum.
An so much Corinth, Thebes, Mycene hop't   45
To triumph o're their foes, as they were propt
By this good people, and their care were held,
Who were the Care of Heav'n, whom heav'n upheld.
A blessed mutuall bulwark they did prove;
Those to these here, and these to those above: 50
Those fought with weapons, and these fought with Pray'r.
Nor though each here a shepherds habit ware,
And bore the name; yet either in his meen,
Or exercises, was the shepherd seen.
But some would place themselves as spyes to prie   55
Into the Starres and Elements (the high
Secrets of Heav'n and Nature) others here
Were wholly giv'n to chase the fearfull Deer:
Others, whom glory had inflamed more,
T'encounter with a Bear, or tusked Bore.   60
Some swift in running, some were terrible
At Barriers, some in wrastling did excell;
One threw a dart, another drew a flight,
Both hit with cunning the intended white.
Some one thing, some another did affect,   65
(Each as his minde and fancie did direct)

---

60. *T' encounter*] 47/48 (*c*); *T' ncounter* 47/48 (*u*).

The sacred Muses Most, Virgins of yore
In high esteem, though now despis'd and poor.

   But how transported hither where the Po
Falls into Dora, is Arcadia now?   70
This is the cloyster surely, this the cave
Of ancient ERYCINA, *and that brave*
Aspiring Temple yonder is the same
Was consecrated to great CYNTHIA'S *name:*
How then remov'd? What new-come power can so   75
Transplant a Land, and all the People? O
Royall INFANTA, *but a child in age,*
Yet ev'n already as a Matron sage!
The vertue of your Name, power of your Blood
Great Catherina (*now 'tis understood*)   80
Wrought this; from that great House descended, which
New Kingdoms daily, and new worlds inrich.
Those great effects which we as wonders view,
Are naturall and usuall things with you.
As by that Sun which from the East doth rise,   85
So many excellent varieties
Are brought into the world, herbs, flow'rs & trees,
So many beasts, fowl, fish, in earth, ayr, seas:
So by the living Sun of your bright eyes
(*Which in the now more worshipt West did rise*)   90
New Provinces from every Clime about,
New Realms, new Laurels, and new Trophies sprout.
Low as my bottome then I bow to you,
Majestick Daughter of that Monarch, who
Enjoyes an Empire, so August, so great,   95
That Phœbus *in it doth both rise and set:*
And Wife of him, to whose brest, hand, and wit
Heav'n did the wals of Italie commit.
But Alpian rocks are needed now no more,
Bulwarks, nor horrid cliffes to stand before   100
Fair Italie, securer in your guard
Then in those hils which have her entrance barr'd.
That bulwark so invincible in war,
You make soft Peace's Temple, where from far
Men come to worship her. Long live as one   105

Yee Royall pair; this fair Conjunction
Presages Christendome again shall boast
Those many Eastern Scepters she hath lost.
This is a field worthy of none but you
(Magnanimous CHARLES*) and a field trodden too*   110
By your brave Ancestors. This Land is great,
Great are your names, great bloud in you is met;
Great your designes, your minds, and your aspects,
Great off-spring too, and deeds the world expects.

But whilst I prophesie, and Fate prepares   115
Circles of gold to crown your silver hairs,
Disdain not (mighty Souls) *this flowry wreath*
Gatherd on Pindus by those Maids that breath
Life in dead men. Poor offring (I confesse)
Yet such as, if Devotion it expresse,   120
Ev'n Heav'n it self disdains not: And if from
Your smiling heav'n a fav'ring gale shall come,
This Lute which from its gentle warbling strings
Sending still Musick to your ears, now sings
Soft Loves, and pleasing Hymeneall Rites,   125
Shall turn a Trumpet to proclaim your Fights.

ACTUS PRIMUS.

SCENA PRIMA.

Silvio, Linco, *With Huntsmen.*

Sil. Go you that lodg'd the Monster, as y' are wont
Amongst the neighb'ring sheepcoats, raise the Hunt.
Rowse eyes and hearts with your shrill voice and horn;
If ever in Arcadia there were born   130
A shepherd, who did follow *Cynthia*'s Court
As a true lover of her rurall sport,
Within whose Quarry-scorning mind had place
The pleasure or the glory of the Chase,
Now let him show that courage and that love,   135
By following me, where in a little grove
To Valour a large field doth open lye,

That dreadfull Boar, I mean, that Prodigy
Of Nature and the Woods, that huge, that fell,
And noted'st Tyrant that did ever dwell   140
And reign in Erimanthus; the fields mower,
The mowers terror: Go you then before,
And do not only with your early horn
Anticipate, but wake the drowsie morn.—*Exeunt Hunts. sounding.*
We, *Linco*, will to prayers, this perilous Chase   145
(Heav'n being our guide) we may more boldly trace.
'That work which is begun well is half done,
'And without Prayer no work is well begun.
   Lin. Thy worshipping the Gods I well commend,
But not thy troubling them who do attend   150
The Gods: The Priests as yet are all asleep,
To whom day springs yet later, where the steep
Surrounding hils a short Horizon make.
   Sil. To thee whose heart is hardly yet awake
The whole world sleeps.
   Lin.   O *Silvio, Silvio,*   155
Why did frank Nature upon thee bestow
Blossoms of Beauty in thy prime, so sweet
And fair, for thee to trample under feet?
Had I thy fresh and blooming cheek, Adieu
I'ld say to beasts, and nobler game pursue.   160
The Summer I would spend in feasts and mirth
In the cool shade, the Winter by the hearth.
   Sil. How's this? Thou art not *Linco* sure; for he
Such counsell never us'd to give to me.
   Lin. 'Counsell must change as the occasion doth: 165
If I were *Silvio*, so I'ld do insooth.
   Sil. And I, if I were *Linco* would do so,
But as I am, I'll do like *Silvio*.
   Lin. Fond youth, for a wild Beast so far to roame,
Whom thou must hunt with danger, when at home   170
One's safely lodg'd!
   Sil.   Dost thou speak seriouslie?
How neer is it?
   Lin.   As thou art now to me.
   Sil. Th' art mad.
   Lin.   Thou art.

Sil.   In what wood doth hee rest?
Lin. Silvio's the wood, and Cruelty the beast.
Sil. Mad I was sure!
Lin.   To have a Nymph so fair,   175
(Rather a Goddesse of perfections rare)
Fresher and sweeter then a Rose new blown,
Softer and whiter then an old Swans down,
For whom there lives not at this day a swain
So proud 'mongst us but sighs, and sighs in vain: 180
To have, I say, this matchlesse Paragon
By Gods and men reserv'd for thee, nay, thrown
Into thine arms without one sigh or tear,
And thou (unworthy!) to disvalue her?
Art thou not then a beast? a savage one?   185
Rather a senselesse clod, a stock, a stone?
Sil. 'If not to be in love be cruelty,
'Then cruelty's a Vertue: Nor do I
Repent, but boast, I lodge him in my brest
By whom I've conquerd Love, the greater beast.   190
Lin. How couldst thou conquer (silly Idiot)
Whom thou nere try'dst?
Sil.   In that I try'd him not.
Lin. O hadst thou try'd him *Silvio*, and once found
In mutuall Lovers what true joyes abound,
I know thou'ldst say, O Love, the sweetest guest,   195
Why hast thou been an alien to this brest?
Leave, leave the woods, leave following beasts, fond boy,
And follow Love.
Sil.   *Linco,* I take more joy
In one beast caught by my *Melampo,* far,
Then in the love of all the Nymphs that are.   200
Keep they those joyes unto themselves alone
That finde a soul in them; for I finde none.
Lin. No soul in LOVE (the world's great Soul)? But fool,
Too soon (believe't) thou'lt finde he is all soul:
(Perchance too late;) for 'hee'll be sure before   205
'We die, to make us all once feel his power.
And (take my word) 'worse torment none can prove,

197. *Leave, leave*] 47/48; *Love, leave* 64, 76/92.   207. worse] 47/48; worst 64,
76/92.

'Then in old limbs the youthfull itch of love:
'All tampring then will but exasperate
'The sore. If Love a young man wound, he straight   210
'Balms him again, hope holds up sorrows head,
'And smiles revive him, if frowns strike him dead.
'But if an aged man those flames endure,
'Whose own defects his own repulse procure,
'Then, then the wound is unsupportable   215
'And mortall; then the anguish is a Hell:
'Then if he pity seek, it is a curse
'To go without it, and to gain't a worse.
'Ah! hasten not before th' appointed day
'The curse of dayes; for if when thou art gray   220
'Thou learn to love, 'twill breed a double sense,
'Of thy youth's pride, and age's impotence.
Leave, leave the woods, leave following beasts, fond boy,
And follow Love.
    Sil.   As if there were no joy
But these Chimeras in a Lovers head,   225
Of strange Eliziums, by his feaver bred!
    Lin. Tell me if in this jolly month of May,
When earth is clad in all her best array,
In stead of bladed fields, brooks uncontroul'd,
Green woods and painted meads, thou shouldst behold   230
Bald fields and meads, brooks bound with Ice, the Pine,
The Beech, the Ash, the Oak, the Elm, the Vine,
And Poplar, like inverted Sceletones,
Stand desolate, ratling their naked bones;
Wouldst thou not say, Nature is out of tune,   235
The world is sick, and like to dye in June?
Now the same horrour which thou wouldst receive
From such a monstrous noveltie, conceive
At thine own self. 'The all-disposing Heav'n
'To ev'ry age hath proper Humors giv'n: 240
'And as in old men love absurdly shows;
'So young men enemies to love oppose
'Nature and Heav'n. Look *Silvio* round about,
Examine the whole Universe throughout:
All that is fair or good, here, or above,   245
Or is a Lover, or the work of Love.

Th' all-seeing Heav'n, the fruitfull Earth's a Lover,
The Sea with love is ready to boil over.
Seest thou yon Star of such excelling hew,
The Suns Postillion? That's a lover too: 250
Nor is exempted from her own son's laws,
But feels that passion which her beauties cause.
Perchance this very hour too shee did part
From her stoln sweets, and Him that keeps her heart.
Mark what a wanton eye she has! In woods   255
Rough Bears, the crook-backt Dolphin loves in floods,
And sluggish Whales; That little bird which sings
So sweetly, and so nimbly plyes the wings,
Flying from tree to tree, from Grove to Grove,
If he could speak, would say, *I am in love.*   260
But his heart sayes it, and his tongue doth say't
In language understood by his deer Mate:
And *Silvio*, hark how from that wildernesse
His dear Mate answers, *And I love no lesse.*
The Cowes low in the valley; and what's this   265
But an inviting unto amorous blisse?
The Lions roar in solitary Groves,
Not for their prey, but for their absent Loves.
All things that are, but *Silvio*, are in love,
The burthen's that: Here, round us, and above,   270
No soul but *Silvio* is a foe to joy.
Leave, leave the woods, leave following beasts, fond boy,
And follow Love.
    Sil.   Had I my tender yeers
Committed to the care of thy gray hairs,
That thou shouldst thus effeminate my heart   275
With love? Knowst thou who I am? who thou art?
    Lin. Thou art a man (or shouldst be one) and I
Another; what I teach Humanity.
And if thou scorn that name (which is my pride)
Take heed, in stead of being deifi'd,   280
Thou turn not beast.
    Sil.   That monster-taming King,
From whom my lofty pedegree I bring,
Had never grown so valiant, nor so fam'd,

258. plyes] 47/48; playes 64; plays 76/92.

If first the monster Love he had not tam'd.

    Lin. See foolish youth, how idly thou talkst now!   285
Had great *Alcides* been no Lover, how
Hadst thou been born? Rather, if he orecame
Monsters and men, to Love impute the same.
Knowst thou not yet, that to comply with fair
Omphales humour, he not onely ware   290
(In stead of the fierce Lions rugged skin)
Womens soft robes, but taught those hands to spin,
And hold a feeble distaffe, which did bear
The knotty Club? His interludes these were
Between his Acts; And when his ribs were beat   295
With dear-bought Counquests, he would then retreat
Into her lap (the bay of sweet delight)
As in Love's port to be new built for fight.
'His sighs from his past toils sweet breathings were,
'And spirits strengthning him new toils to bear.   300
'For as the iron, of it self too rough,
'And of a harsh unmalleable stuffe,
'Softned with fire, and gentler metall, strength
'From weaknesse gathers, and becomes at length
'Fit for the noblest use: so hearts untam'd,   305
'(Which their own stifnesse often breaks) enflam'd
'With generous Love, and with his sweets allay'd,
'Are cleerer, apter for great Actions made.
If th'art ambitious then to imitate
Great *Hercules*, and not degenerate   310
From thy high strain, since woods thou dost affect,
Follow the woods, but do not Love neglect:
I mean so lawfull and so worthy love
As that of *Amarillis.* I approve
(So far from blaming that as cruelty)   315
Thy shunning of *Dorinda*; For in thee
Who standst upon thy bloud, 'twere double shame
To scorch thy brest with an unlawfull flame,
For injuring thy Spouse.
    Sil.   What saist thou man?
Shee is not yet my Spouse.
    Lin.   Was there not than   320

290. *Omphales*] 47/48, 64; *Amphales* 76/92.

A promise solemnly receiv'd and giv'n?
Take heed proud Boy, how thou provokest Heav'n.

Sil. 'Man's freedom is Heav'ns gift, which doth not take
'Us at our word when forced vows we make.

Lin. I, but (unlesse our hopes and judgements fail)   325
Heav'n made this Match, and promis'd to entail
A thousand blessings on't.

Sil.   'Tis like that there
Is nothing else to do; a proper care
To vex the calm rest of the gods above!
Linco, I like nor this, nor t' other Love.   330
I was a Huntsman, not a Lover bred;
Thou who art all for love, go back to bed.

Lin. Thou sprung from Heav'n, harsh Boy? nor of divine
Can I suppose thee, nor of humane Line.
Alecto's poyson thy cold limbs did fashion;   335
Sweet *Venus* had no hand in thy creation.

SCENA SECUNDA.

Mirtillo, Ergasto.

Mir. O *Amarillis,* Authresse of my flame,
(Within my mouth how sweet now is thy name!
But in my heart how bitter!) *Amarillis,*
Fairer and whiter then the whitest Lillies,   340
But crueller then cruell Adders far,
Which having stung (least they should pitie) bar
Their ears, and flie: If then by speaking I
Offend thee, I will hold my peace and die.
I'll hold my peace, but what will that do good,   345
If hils and dales roar for me, and this wood
Which thy deer name can nere forget, from me
So often heard, and carv'd on every tree?
The windes shall sigh for me, the fountains shed
Abundant tears, grief mourn, and pitie plead.   350
Or couldst thou bribe whole Nature with a fee
To silence, lastly Death shall speak for me:

330. nor¹] 47/48; not 64, 76/92.

Hee'll thunder't out, and to the world proclaim,
I dy'd a Martyr in my true Loves flame.

    Erg. Mirtillo, 'Love is a great pain at best,   355
'But more, by how much more it is supprest.
'For as hot Steeds run faster at the check,
'Then if you laid the reins upon their neck:
'So love restrain'd augments, and fiercer growes
'In a close prison, then when loose he goes.   360
Why hidst thou thy flames cause so long from me,
When the effect could not concealed be?
Mirtillo burns: how often have I said?
But inward burns, and will not call for aid.

    Mir. Courteous *Ergasto*, out of my respect   365
To her (alas) I did my self neglect:
Nor would my festring passion yet unfold,
But that necessity hath made me bold.
I hear a buzzing rumour every-where
(Which to my heart findes passage through my ear)   370
That *Amarillis* shortly weds; nor dare
Ask more, lest so I should my love declare,
Or prove my fear too true. Full well I know
(Nor hath Love strook me blind) that in my low
And slender fortunes, it were simple pride   375
To hope a Nymph so shap't, so qualifi'd,
So rais'd in wealth, in spirit, and in blood,
Above all these, so gentle, and so good,
Can ere be mine: no, I have tane the height
Of my unhappy Star, my sullen fate   380
Made me for fuell onely, born to smother
In fires I cannot kindle in another.
Yet since Fate's pleas'd I should affect death more
Then life, at least I'ld have her know before,
That shee's beholding to me for my death,   385
And deigne when I sigh out my latest breath
To cast her fair eyes on me, and say, *Dye.*
This reasonable boon obtain would I,
That ere she go to make another blest
In having her, shee'ld hear me speak at least,   390
But once, my deer *Ergasto.* Now if love
Or pitie of me thy soft entrails move,

Procure me this, this physick onely lend,
To make the passage easie to my end.

   Erg. From one that loves, a just, from one that dies,   395
A small request: yet a hard enterprize.
Woe be to her, should her stern father hear
That to stoln pray'rs she ere had lent an ear!
Or if some baser pick-thank should disclose
It to the Priest her father-in-law! Who knows   400
But out of these respects she may eschew
Thy company, and yet affect thee too?
'For women are more prone to love then men;
'But to conceal't have more discretion then.
And if 'twere true that she did love thee, what   405
Could shee do lesse then shun thee for all that?
'She that wants power to help listens in vain,
'And flies with pity, when her stay breeds pain;
'And I have heard 'tis still the wisest course
'To quit that soon which one must quit perforce.   410

   Mir. O were this true, and could I think it so,
Sweet were my pain, and fortunate my woe!
But deer *Ergasto* (hide it not from me
So help thee *Pan*) who may this Bridegroom be
So lov'd of all the Starres?
   Erg.   Dost thou not know   415
(I'm sure thou dost) that famous *Silvio*,
Silvio the rich, the gallant and the fair,
The Priest *Montano*'s onely Son and Heir?
'Tis he.
   Mir.   O happy youth, whose joy appears
So ripe for harvest in his spring of yeers!   420
Pardon me gentle swain, I envie not
Thy happinesse, but mourn my own hard lot.

   Erg. Indeed there is no reason to envy,
Rather to pity him.
   Mir.   To pity? Why?
   Erg. Because he loves her not.
   Mir.   And hath he wit?   425
Hath he a heart? Is he not blind?—And yet
When I consider with what full aspect
Her starry eyes their influence direct

Into my brest, she cannot have a dart
Left in her quiver for another heart.   430
But why do they a gemme so precious throw
To one that knows it not, and scorns it so?
   Erg. Because the Heav'ns did through this Marriage
Unto Arcadia long ago presage
Deliverance. Hast not thou heard that here   435
Is paid to the great Goddesse ev'ry yeer
Of a Nymph's guiltlesse bloud a cruell and
Unconscionable tribute by this Land?
   Mir. 'Tis news to me; nor let that strange appear,
Since I my self am but a stranger here,   440
And since I came (by Fate's decree and Love's)
Almost a constant Burgesse of the Groves.
But what strange crime deserv'd so sharp a doom?
How could such monstrous cruelty finde room
In a Celestiall minde?
   Erg.   Of me then know   445
From the first head the torrent of our wo:
A Story that would tears of pitie wrest
From heart of oak, much more from humane brest.
Whilest yet the Priesthood was not ty'd to age,
A youthfull swain of noble Parentage,   450
Then *Dian*'s Priest (*Aminta* was his name)
The Nymph *Lucrina* did with love enflame.
All creatures of her sex exceeded shee
As much in beauty as unconstancie.
She long requited, or at least to sight   455
(If looks and eyes have tongues) she did requite
The pure affection of the Love-sick lad,
And fed his hopes whilst he no Rivall had.
But when a rustick swain her favour sought,
(See now a perfect woman!) in a thought,   460
She left the former, with one sigh was shook,
With the faint batt'ry of one amorous look:
Her hearts new guest now takes up all the room,
Dislodg'd *Aminta* ere he knew for whom.
Haplesse *Aminta*! who from that day forth   465
Was so abhorr'd, held of so little worth,

430. Left] 47/48; Let 64, 76/92.

By that ungrate whom he did still adore,
That she would neither hear nor see him more.
If this unkindnesse cut the wretch to th' heart,
If he sigh'd, wept, and rav'd, to thee who art   470
Acquainted with Love's pangs, I leave to ghesse.
    Mir. O, 'Twas a torment no man can expresse!
    Erg. When then his tears and prayers he had cast
After his heart, to *Dian* turn'd at last;
If ever with pure heart Goddesse (quoth he)   475
And guiltlesse hand I kindled flame to thee,
Revenge my faith, which a perfidious Maid
Under safe conduct of her smiles betraid.
The Goddesse (gentler then the Nymph was) hears
The faithfull Lover's and her servant's tears   480
And pray'rs: and pity kindling her just ire,
By opposition did augment the fire.
Her pow'rfull bow into her hand she took,
And in ARCADIA's wretched bosome stuck
Arrows of death and catching Pestilence   485
Invisible, and therefore without fence.
Without remorse they execute her rage
Without respect on every sex and age.
Nor Antidotes nor Med'cines here avail'd,
Nor flying now; weak Art her Master fail'd: 490
And oft, whilst he the remedy apply'd,
Before the Patient the Physitian dy'd.
The onely hope that's left is from the skie,
So to the neerest Oracle they flie,
Which soon return'd an answer cleer enough,   495
But above measure terrible and rough;
That Cinthia *was incenst, but that the Land*
Might be reliev'd, if by Aminta's *hand*
That faithlesse Nymph Lucrina, *or some one*
For her, of the Arcadian Nation   500
Were as an offring to Diana *slain.*
So she, when long sh' had prayd, long wept in vain,
And long expected her new Lovers ayd,
To th' holy Altars like a Bride array'd,
And with what pomp Religion could devise,   505

468. would] 47/48, 64; should 76/92.

Was led a miserable Sacrifice.
Where at those feet from which hers fled so fast,
(The feet of her Idolater) at last
Bending her trembling knees, she did attend
From the offended youth a cruell end.   510
The sacred knife he boldly did unsheathe,
Rage and revenge his nostrils seem'd to breathe,
His eyes to sparkle; turning then to her,
Said with a sigh (death's hollow messenger,)
Whom thou hast left *Lucrina*, and whom took,   515
Learn by this blow: And with that word he strook
Himself, and plung'd the knife in his own brest
To th' haft: In one both Sacrifice and Priest
Fell bleeding at her feet, whilst she (amaz'd
To see that dire unlookt for object) gaz'd   520
As one 'twixt life and death, nor yet did know
If grief had stab'd her, or the threatned blow.
But when she found her tongue again, and knew
Distinctly what was acted there, O true,
O brave *Aminta*, (bathing in a flood   525
Of tears) she said! O Lover, understood
Too late! who by thy death dost give to me
Both life and death. If in forsaking thee
I sinn'd; lo, I redeem that sin of mine,
Wedding my soul eternally to thine.   530
This said, that knife fresh reeking with the gore
Of the now lov'd in death, and purpled ore,
She drew from his pale brest, and in her own
Sheath'd it again; then willingly sunk down
Into *Aminta*'s arms, who yet had breath,   535
And felt perchance that lightning before death.
Such was this pair of Lovers tragick fall,
'Cause he kept too much faith, she none at all.
     Mir. O haplesse swain, yet happy in his Love,
Having so rich occasion to approve   540
His spotlesse faith, and dying to revive
That spark in her he could not being alive!
But what became then of the poor diseas'd?
Did the plague cease? was *Cinthia*'s wrath appeas'd?
     Erg. It did relent, but was not quite put out: 545

For the same month (the yeer being wheel'd about)
It burst out with more fury, and did make
A dire relapse: This forc'd us to betake
Our selves unto the Oracle agen;
Which utterd now a sadder doom; *That then*   550
And yeerly, we to Nights offended Queen
A Maid or Wife should offer, past fifteen
And short of twenty; by which means the rage
Which swallow'd thousands, one death should asswage.
Moreover a hard law, and weighing well   555
The nature of that sex, impossible
To keep; a law in bloudy letters writ
On wretched women was impos'd by it;
That whatsoever Maid or Wife should prove
In any sort a changeling in her love,   560
Unlesse some friend would pay the penalty
In stead of her, should without mercy die.
This dire, this nationall Calamitie
The good old man hath hope to remedie
By means of this desired Match; because   565
The Oracle after some little pawse
Being ask'd again, what end our woe should have,
To our demand this punctuall answer gave;
Your woe shall end when two of Race Divine
          Love shall combine: 570
And for a faithlesse Nymphs apostate state
A faithfull Shepherd supererogate.
Now there are are left in all Arcadia
Of heavenly Stock no other slips this day
But *Silvio* and *Amarillis*; She   575
From *Pan* descended, from *Alcides* He.
Nor had there ever (to our much regret)
Of those two Lines a Male and Female met,
As now there do: whence the believing Father
Great hopes of good not without cause doth gather.   580
For though the things foretold by th' Oracle
Be not fulfill'd yet in each particle,
This is the fundamentall point; the rest
Is still reserv'd in Fates own secret brest,
And of the Marriage one day shall ensue.   585

Mir. And all this do *Mirtillo* to undoe?
What a long swing is fetcht! what armies band
Against one heart half murtherd to their hand!
Is't not enough that cruell Love's my foe,
Unlesse Fate too conspire my overthrow?   590
  Erg. Alas, *Mirtillo*! grieving does no good,
'Tears quench not Love, but are his milk and food.
'T shall scape me hard, but ere the Sun descend
This cruell one shall hear thee, Courage friend:
'These sighs refresh not (as thou dost suppose)   595
'Thy burning heart; but rather are like those
'Impetuous winds, which in a Town on fire
'The bellows are to blow and fan it higher:
'Love's whirlwinds, bringing to poor Lovers ever
'Black clouds of grief, which showrs of tears deliver.   600

SCENA TERTIA.

Corisca.

Who ever saw, what heart did ever prove
So strange, fond, impotent a Passion? Love,
And cold Disdain (a miracle to me
Two contraries should in one subject be
Both in extremes!) I know not how, each other   605
Destroy, and generate; enflame, and smother.
When I behold *Mirtillo*'s every grace,
From his neat foot to his bewitching face,
His unaffected carriage, sweet aspect,
Words, actions, looks, and manners, they eject   610
Such flames of love, that every passion
Besides seems to be conquerd by this one.
But when I think how dotingly he prizes
Another woman, and for her despises
My almost peerlesse face (although I say't)   615
On which a thousand eyes for alms do wait,
Then do I scorn, abhor, and loath him more
Then ever I did value him before,
And scarce can think it possible that he
Had ever any interest in me.   620
O if my sweet *Mirtillo* were mine own,

So that I had him to my self alone!
(These are my thoughts sometimes) no mortall wight
More blisse could boast of then *Corisca* might!
And then I feel such kindly flames, so sweet   625
A vapour rise, that I could almost meet
His love half way; yea, follow him, adore
His very steps, and aid from him implore:
Nay, I do love him so, I could expire
His sacrifice in such a pleasing fire.   630
Then I'm my self again: And what (say I)
A proud disdainfull boy! one that doth fly
From me, and love another! that can look
Upon this face of mine, and not be strook!
But guard himself so well as not to dye   635
For love! Shall I, that should behold him lye
Trembling and weeping at these feet of mine
(As many better men have done) incline
Trembling and weeping at his feet? O no!
And with this thought into such rage I grow   640
Against my self, and him, that sounding straight
Unto my eyes and fancy a retreat,
Mirtillo's name worser then death I seem
To hate, and mine own self for loving him;
Whom I would see the miserablest swain,   645
The most despised thing that doth remain
Upon the earth; and if I had my will,
With mine own hands I could the villain kill.
Thus like two seas encountring, Hate and Love,
Desire and Scorn in me dire battell move: 650
And I (the flame of thousand hearts, the rack
Of thousand souls) languish, and burn, and lack
That pitie I deny'd to others. I
Who have in Cities oft been courted by
Gallants and wits, to whom great Lords have bent,   655
And yet withstood vollies of complement,
Squadrons of Lovers, jeer'd their idle fires,
And with false hopes deluded their desires;
And now enforc'd t' a rustick swain to yeild
In single fight t' a fellow that's unskill'd!   660

660. fight] ed.; sight 47/48.

O thou most wretched of all womankind
Corisca! Where couldst thou diversion find
Hadst thou no other Lover? how asswage,
Or by what means deceive thy amorous rage?
Learn women all from me this housewifery,   665
Make you conserve of Lovers to keep by.
Had I no Sweet-heart but this sullen Boy,
Were I not well provided of a joy?
'To extreme want how likely to be hurl'd
'Is that ill houswife, who in all the world   670
'But one Love onely, but one Servant hath?
Corisca will be no such fool. 'What's faith?
'What's constancy? Tales which the jealous feign
'To awe fond girls: names as absurd as vain.
'Faith in a woman (if at least there be   675
Faith in a woman unreveal'd to me)
'Is not a vertue, nor a heavenly grace,
'But the sad penance of a ruin'd face,
'That's pleas'd with one, cause it can please no more.
'A handsome woman sought unto by store   680
'Of gallant youths, if pleas'd with one alone
No woman is, or is a foolish one.
'What's beauty (tell me) if not view'd? or view'd,
'If not pursu'd? or if pursu'd, pursu'd
'By one alone? Where Lovers frequent are,   685
'It is a signe the partie lov'd is rare,
'Glorious and bright. A womans honour is
'T' have many Servants: Courtly Dames know this,
Who live in Towns, and those most practise it
Who have most wealth, most beauty, and most wit.   690
'Tis clownishnesse (say they) to reject any,
And folly too, since that's perform'd by many,
One cannot do: One Officer to wait,
A second to present, a third to prate,
A fourth for somewhat else; so it doth fall   695
Out oft, that favours being generall
No favours seem: or jealousie thus throwne
To whet them, all are easier kept then one.
This merry life is by great Ladies led
In Towns, and 'twas my fortune to be bred   700

With one of them; by whose example first,
Next by her rules, I in Loves art was nurst
Up from my childhood: she would often say,
'*Corisca*, thou must use another day
'Thy Lovers like thy garments, put on one,   705
'Have many, often shift, and wear out none.
'For daily conversation breeds distast,
'Distast contempt, and loathing at the last.
Then get the start, let not the servant say,
H' as turnd his Mistresse, not she him, away.   710
And I have kept her rules: I've choice, and strive
To please them all: to this my hand I give,
And wink on him; the handsom'st I admit
Into my bosome; but not one shall get
Into my heart: and yet I know not how   715
(Ay me!) *Mirtillo*'s crept too neer it now.
He made me sigh, not sigh as heretofore
To give false fire, but true flames to deplore;
Robbing my limbs of rest, my eyes of sleep,
Ev'n I can watch till the gray morning peep   720
(The discontented Lovers truce); ev'n I
(Strange change!) to melancholy walks can fly;
And through the gloomy horrors of this grove
Trace the sweet footsteps of my hated Love.
What wilt thou do, *Corisca*? sue? my hate   725
Permits not this, nor stands it with my State.
Wilt thou then fly him? That would shew more brains,
But Love sayes no to that: What then remains?
First I will try allurements, and discover
The love to him, but will conceal the Lover;   730
I'll use deceipts, if that avail me not;
And if those fail me too, my brain shall plot
A brave revenge: *Mirtillo* shall partake
Hate, if he spurn at Love; and I will make
His *Amarillis* rue, that she was ere   735
A Rivall unto me, to him so deer.
Last I will teach you both what 'tis to move
A woman to abhor where she did love.

701. With] 64, 76/92; with 47/48.

SCENA QUARTA.

Titiro, Montano, Dametas.

Tit. I speak *Montano* what I know is true,
And speak to one who knows more then I do.   740
'Your Oracles are still obscurer farre
'Then we imagine: and their answers are
'Like knives, which if they warily be caught
'By that safe part which for the hand was wrought,
'Are usefull; but if rashly they be tane   745
'By th' edge or point, one may be hurt or slain.
That *Amarillis* (as thou argu'st) should
By Heav'n be destin'd for the gen'rall good
And safety of Arcadia, who should rather
Desire and joy, then I who am her Father?   750
But when I mark the words of th' Oracle,
Me thinks with those the signes agree not well.
If Love must joyn them, and the one doth fly,
How can that be? How can the strings which tie
The true-Love's knot be hatred and disdain?   755
'That cannot be oppos'd which Heav'ns ordain:
Since then we see such opposition here,
That Heav'ns did not ordain it, is most cleer.
Had they been pleas'd that *Silvio* should have had
My *Amarillis*, they would him have made   760
A Lover, not a Huntsman.
    Mon.   Dost not see,
He's young, not yet seventeen? In time ev'n he
Will feel the dart of Love.
    Tit.   A dog hath got
His love: I know not why a Nymph should not.
    Mon. 'Youths are inclined more to recreation.   765
    Tit. 'And is not love a nat'rall inclination?
    Mon. 'Before the time 'tis an unnat'rall thing.
    Tit. 'Love is a blossome which adorns our spring.
    Mon. 'Your forward blossoms seldom come to good.
    Tit. 'They seldom fail where frosts nip not the bud.   770
But came I hither to dispute with thee,
Montano? I nor can, nor fits it me.

Yet I'm a Father too of a most deer
And onely child; and (if Love do not blear
My eyes) a worthy one; such (under favour)   775
That many woo'd me, and still do to have her.
    Mon. Were not this Marriage made in heav'n by Fate,
'Tis made in earth by Faith, to violate
Which (*Titiro*) were rashly to prophane
The godhead of great *Cynthia*, in whose Fane   780
The solemn oath was taken. Now how ready
She is to wrath, and how incens'd already
Against this Country, thou art not to learn.
But I professe, as far as I discern,
And a Priest's mind rapt up above the skie   785
Into th' eternall counsels there can prie,
This knot by th' hand of Destiny was knit,
And all those signes which should accompan' it
(Have thou but Faith) will fall out jump and right
In their due time. I'll tell thee more; this night   790
I in my dream a certain thing have view'd,
Which my old hopes hath more then ere renew'd.
    Tit. 'Dreams are but dreams: but well, what didst thou view?
    Mon. Thou dost remember, I presume (for who
Amongst us all is such a stupid wight   795
As to forget?) that lamentable night
When swelling Ladon (weary of his yoke)
The banks with his rebellious waters broke;
So that where birds were wont to build their nests,
Usurping fishes swam, and men, and beasts,   800
And flocks, and herds promiscuously tane
Th' impartiall deluge swept into the Main.
That very night (O bitter memory!)
I lost my heart, or rather that which I
More dearly priz'd, a child, a tender one   805
In swathing bands, and then my onely son.
Both then and since (though he be dead) as deer
To me, as if my onely son he were:
The cruel torrent ravish'd him away
Before the people of the house (who lay   810
In darknesse, fear and sleep buri'd alive)
With any timely succour could arrive:

We could not find the empty cradle neither,
But (as I ghesse) that and the child together
Were swallow'd by the flood.
   Tit.   What else can be   815
Suppos'd? I think I've heard (perchance from thee)
This losse of thine before, in very truth
A miserable one, and full of ruth;
And I may say, of thy two sons the Floods
Have swallow'd one, the other's lost i' th' Woods.   820
   Mon. Perhaps kind Heav'ns in the surviving brother
Will make me rich amends yet for the other:
"Tis alwayes good to hope. Now list me out:
'Twas at the dawning of the morn, about
That mungrell hour which gotten betwixt night   825
And day, is half an Ethiop and half white,
When having watcht out all the night almost,
With various fancies of this Marriage tost,
Quite overcome at length with wearinesse,
A gentle slumber did mine eyes oppresse,   830
Which with it such a lively vision brought,
That though I slept, I was awake. Me thought,
On fam'd Alfeo's bank I angling sate
Under a shady Beech, there came up straight
A grave old man, down to the middle bare,   835
His chin all dropping, and his grisled hair;
Who with both hands, and countenance beni'ne
Put a nak'd weeping infant into mine,
Saying, *Lo here thy Son, and take good heed*
Thou kill him not; then div'd into the reed.   840
With that, black clouds obscur'd the Heavens round,
And threatning me with a dire tempest, frown'd.
I to my bosome clapt the babe for fear,
And cry'd, Shall then one hour both give and bear
Away my joy? Straight all the welkin turn'd   845
Serene, and thunderbolts to ashes burn'd
Fell hissing in the River, with bows broken
And shafts by thousands, signes which did betoken
Extinguisht vengeance; then a shrill voice brake
From the riv'd Beech, which in his tongue thus spake,   850
Believe Montano, *and thy hope still nourish,*

Thy fair Arcadia once again shall flourish.
So ever since in my eyes, mind, and brest
The pleasing figure of this dream's imprest,
Standing before me still in every place;   855
But above all, the courteous meen and face
Of that old man (me thinks I see him yet)
Which made me coming now, when thee I met,
Directly to the Temple, there with pure
And holy Sacrifice my Dream t' insure.   860
    Tit. 'Truely *Montano*, Dreams are Histories
'Of what is past, rather then Prophecies
'Of what's to come: Meer fragments of some sight,
'Or thought of the past day, which prints at night
'A vain reflection of it self, like those   865
'Which in a cloud the Sunne opposed shows.
    Mon. 'Not alwayes with the senses sleeps the soul:
'Rather when she is free from all controll
'Of cousening forms, which do the senses blinde,
'Whilst they're asleep, more wakefull is the minde.   870
    Tit. In short: how Heav'ns have destin'd to dispose
Of our two children, neither of us knows.
But this is cleer to both of us, thine flyes,
And against *Nature*'s law, doth *Love*'s despise.
And mine (as't proves) is ty'd; her self yet hath   875
No benefit of her engaged faith.
Nor do I know whether she love or no:
That she makes others love, full well I know;
And can I think it probable that shee
Should others wound, and go her self still free?   880
Mee thinks of late she's alter'd in her cheer,
Who us'd all Mirth and Jollity t' appear.
'But to put Maids in mind of marrying,
'And then not marry them, is an ill thing.
'As in a curious garden a fair Rose,   885
'Which (cloystred up in leaves) did late repose
'Under the sable canopie of night
'Upon its mother-stalk, with the first light
'Raises its head, then opes its tender eye,
'Whence whispring Bees suck Nectar as they fly;   890

857. yet] ed.; wet 47/48. *Italian is 'che mi par di vederlo'.*

'Then to the Sun which on its form doth gaze,
'Its purple and perfumed brest displayes:
'But if it be not gathered then, and stay
'Till it be kist by the Meridian Ray,
'Before the Sun to th' other world be fled,   895
'Upon its mourning stalk it hangs the head;
'So pale, so shrunk, so without life it showes,
'That one can hardly say, This was a Rose.
'So a young Virgin, whilst her Mothers care
'Shuts and preserves her from the blasting air,   900
'Shuts her own bosom too against desire:
'But if she find some amorous youth to eye her,
'And hears him sigh, she opes him straight her heart,
'And in her tender brest receives Love's dart.
'Then if by fear, or else by maiden shame,   905
'She be withheld from shewing of her flame,
(Poor soul!) Concealment like a worm i' th' bud,
'Lies in her Damask cheek sucking the bloud:
'So all her beauty's gone, if that fire last,
'And all her Lovers when her Beauty's past.   910
    Mon. Take courage *Titiro*; do not embase
Thy soul with mortall fears, but nobly place
Thy hopes above; 'Heav'n favours a strong faith,
'And a faint pray'r nere clomb that arduous path.
'And if all men should pray to Heav'n at need,   915
'And pray with hope, much more should Heav'ns own seed.
Our childrens Pedigree it is Divine,
'And Heav'n that shines on all, will surely shine
'On its own Progenie. Come *Titiro*,
Together to the Temple let us go,   920
Together offer, thou a hee-goat there,
To PAN, and I to HERCULES a Steer.
'The Gods who blesse the herds, will blesse no lesse
'Them, who the Gods do with those blessings blesse.
Trusty *Dametas* go, and quickly cull   925
From my fair herd the best and gentlest Bull,
And bring him to me to the Temple straight;
Come by the hill, the neerest way is that.
    Tit. And good *Dametas*, from my herd bring one
Of the best Goats.

Dam.   Both shall with speed be done.   930
May the high Gods pleas'd in their goodnesse be
To blesse (*Montano*) this thy Dream to thee,
Ev'n to thy utmost wish: this memory
Of thy lost son is a good augury.

SCENA QUINTA.

Satyr.

'As frosts to Plants, to ripened Ears a storm,   935
'To Flowrs the mid-day sun, to Seed the worm,
'To Stags the toyls, to Birds the lime-twig; so
'Is Love to man an everlasting Foe.
And he that call'd it fire pierc'd well into
Its treach'rous nature; for if fire thou view,   940
How bright and beautifull it is? Approacht,
How warm and comfortable? But then toucht,
O how it burns! The monster-bearing earth
Did never teem such a prodigious birth:
It cuts like razors, like wild beasts devours,   945
And through a wood like winged lightning scowrs.
Where-ere it fixes its imperious foot,
Cottage and Pallace, all must yeeld unto't:
So Love, if thou behold it in a pair
Of starry eyes, in a bright tresse of hair,   950
How temptingly it looks! what kindly flames
It breathes! what peace, what pardons it proclaims!
But in thy bosome if thou do it keep,
So that it gather strength, and 'gin to creep,
No Tygresse in Hircanian mountains nurst,   955
No Lybian Lionesse is half so curst,
Nor frozen Snake fostred with humane breath.
His flames are hot as hell, bonds strong as death;
He is Wrath's hangman, Pitie's enemy,
And to conclude, Love void of love. But why   960
Accuse I him? Is he the Authour then
Of all those pranks which mortal wights, not when
They are in love, but out of their wits, do?
Women, perfidious women, 'tis to you
That I impute Love's rancour; all that's naught   965

In him from you is by infection caught.
He of himself is good, meek as the Dove
That draws the chariot of the Queen of Love:
But you have made him wild; for though ye joy
With your own hands to feed the winged Boy,   970
Yet do you shut each pore so of your brest,
That in your hearts He cannot build his nest.
And all your care, pride, pleasure ye do place
In the meer outside of a simpring face.
Nor is't your study how to pay true love,   975
And wager whether shall more constant prove;
To bind two souls in one, and of one heart
To make the other but the counter-part;
But how your silver hair with gold to hatch,
Then purse it up into a net, to catch   980
Poor souls withall, and like gold valence let
Some curles hang dangling ore your brows of jet.
How much against my stomack doth it go
To see you paint your cheeks, to cover so
The faults of Time and Nature! How ye make   985
Pale Feulemort a pure Vermilian take,
Fill up the wrincles, die black white, a spot
With a spot hide, where 'tis, make't where 'tis not.
You tie a thred acrosse, whereof one end
Held in your teeth, the other is sustein'd   990
By your left hand, whilst of the running knot
Your right hand makes a noose to ope and shut
Like shaving tongs: This instrument you fit
To your rough downy forheads, and with it
Shave all the down, and the wild hairs which shoot   995
Above their fellows, pull up by the root;
And all the while such torment you are in,
That 'tis at once a penance and a sin.
Nor is this all; your qualities are much
After your faces, and your faith is such   1000
As are your works. For what is there in you
That is not counterfeit and painted too?
Do your lips ope? before ye speak ye lye;
And if ye sigh, ye lye most damnably.
False lights your eyes are, and false weights your ears;   1005

Your hearts false measures, and false pearl your tears:
So talk, or look, or think, or laugh, or cry,
Seem or seem not, walk, stand, or sit, ye lye.
Nay, there's more yet, your cousening those
Most who on you do most repose;   1010
Your loving most those who do least love you,
And chusing to die rather then be true;
These are the arts, these are the wayes
That make Love hatefull in our dayes.
All his faults then we may most justly lay   1015
On you; or rather on our selves: for they
Sin that believe you. Then the fault's in me
(Perjur'd *Corisca*) who did credit thee;
Come hither onely for my bane (I think)
From Argos wicked streets, of vice the sink.   1020
Yet th' art so sly, and play'st so well the Scout,
To keep thy deeds and thoughts from tracing out,
That 'mongst the chastest Dames thou jettst it now,
With honesty stampt on thy haughty brow:
What scorns have I receiv'd, what discontent   1025
From this ungratefull woman! I repent,
Yea, blush I was so fond. Example take
By me, unskilfull Lovers, how ye make
'An Idol of a face, and take't for granted,
'There's no such divell as a woman sainted.   1030
'She thinks her wit and beauty without peer,
'And o're thy slavish soul doth domineer
'Like some great Goddesse, counting thou wert born
'(As a thing mortall) onely for her scorn;
'Takes all that praise as tribute of her merit   1035
'Which is the flattry of thy abject spirit.
Why so much serving? so much admirations?
Such sighs, such tears, such humble supplications?
These are the woman's arms: Let us expresse
Ev'n in our Loves valour and manlinesse.   1040
Time was when I (as lusty as I am)
Thought tears and sighs could womans heart enflame.
But now I find I err'd; for if she bears
A stony heart, in vain are sighs and tears.
We must strike fire out of her brest by dint   1045

Of steel: what fool us'd bellows to a flint?
Leave, leave thy tears and sighs, if thou wouldst make
A conquest of thy Dame; and if thou bake
Indeed with unextinguishable fire,
In thy hearts center smother thy desire   1050
The best thou canst, and watch thy time to doe
That which both Love and Nature prompt thee to,
'For Modestie's the charter of the woman,
'Who wil not have her priviledge made common;
'Nor though she uses it her self with men,   1055
'Would she have them to use't with her agen:
'Being a vertue for the admiration
'Of them that court her, not their imitation.
This is the plain and naturall way of Love,
Indeed the onely one that I approve.   1060
My coy *Corisca* shall not finde of me
A bashfull Lover (as I us'd to be)
But a bold Foe, and she shall feel I can
Assault her with the weapons of a man,
As well as with the womans arms. Twice now   1065
I've caught this Eel, and yet I know not how
She hath slipt through my hands; but if she come
A third time neer my boat, I'le strike so home
Through both her gils, that I shall marre her flight.
Here she comes forth to Rellief ev'ry night,   1070
And I like a good hound snuffe round about
To find her track: If I do sent her out,
Have at her coat; O how I mean to be
Reveng'd upon her! I will make her see
That Love sometimes (though he appear stark blind)   1075
Can from his eyes the hand-kerchief unbind:
And that no woman (though she may awhile)
Can glory long in perjury and guile.

CHORUS.

O Powerfull Law! which Heaven or Nature,
Writ in the Heart of every Creature.   1080
Whose amiable violence,
And pleasing rapture of the sense
Doth byas all things to that good

Which we desire not understood.
Nor the exteriour bark alone 1085
Subject to th' sense of every one,
Whose frail materials quickly must
Resolve again into their dust;
But the hid seeds and inward cause,
Whose substance is eternall, moves and draws. 1090

And if the ever-teeming world bring forth
So many things of admirable worth,
If whatsoever Heaven's great eyes
The Sun and Moon, or his small spies
The Starres behold, doth own a soul 1095
Whose active pow'r informs the whole;
If thence all humane seed have birth,
All plants and Animals; if th' earth
Be green, or on her wrinckled brow it snows,
From that immortall and pure Spring it flows. 1100

Nor this alone: On mortall Crown
What-ever restlesse Spheers rowl down;
Whence all our actions guided are
By a happy or unhappy Starre;
Whence our frail lives their Qu receive 1105
This Stage to enter, and to leave.
What-ever thwarts, what-ever stils
Our froward, and our childish wils
(Which seeming to be Fortune's Play
To give, and take our things away, 1110
The world ascribes to her) hath All
From that high vertue its originall.

Soul of the World: if it were thou didst say,
Arcadia *should have rest and peace one day,*
And like a snake renew her youth, 1115
What man dares question so divine a truth?
If what the famous Oracle
Of two whom Fate should couple did foretell,
It spake but as thy mouth, if fixt it be
In the eternall depth of thy Decree, 1120
And if the Tripods do not falshoods vent,
Ah! who retards thy wils accomplishment?
Behold, a scornfull boy, a foe

To Love and Beauty: Hee (although
Extract from Heav'n) with Heav'n contends! 1125
Behold another youth offends
In love as much, (in vain deserving
To be preferr'd for humbly serving)
And with his flame thwarts thy Decree!
And the lesse hope he hath to see 1130
His service and his true loves hire,
The cleerer burns his faith and fire;
And he now for that Beauty dyes,
Which t' other (whom 'tis kept for) doth despise.

 Is Jove divided then about his doom? 1135
Hath doubtfull Fate twins strugling in her womb?
Or doth man's mountain-hope, unleveld yet,
New impious Giants in rebellion set
On both sides to assault the Towr of Jove,
By loving, and by shunning Love? 1140
Have we such strength? and ore the Powrs above
Shall two blind Powrs triumph, Disdain, and Love?

 But thou high Mover of the Orb, that rid'st
The Starrs and Fate, and with thy Wisdom guid'st
Their course, look down upon our tott'ring State, 1145
And reconcile Disdain and Love with Fate.
That ice, this flame, thaw, quench with heavenly dew,
Make one not flye, another not pursue:
Ah! let not two mens obstinacy stand
Betwixt thy promis'd mercy and a Land. 1150

 And yet who knowes? what we imagine is
Our greatest crosse, may prove our greatest blisse.
'If on the Sunne no humane eye can gaze,
'Who then can pierce into Jove's hidden wayes?

ACTUS SECUNDUS.

SCENA PRIMA.

Ergasto, Mirtillo.

Erg. O What a walk have I had! At the Race, 1155
The Mead, Hill, River, Fountain, wrastling Place
I've been to seek thee: Heav'n be prais'd, at last
I've found thee here.

Mir.   What news requires such haste?
Bringst thou me life or death?
    Erg.   The last's a thing,
Which if I had for thee, I would not bring: 1160
The former, though I have not for thee yet,
I hope to bring. But why art thou ore-set
With thy own sighs? If thou wouldst overcome
Another, overcome thy self at home:
Breathe, and revy't again—. But to proceed   1165
To that which made me seek thee with such speed;
The matter's this: Knowst thou (who doth not know?)
Ormino's Sister? rather tall then low
She is of stature, cherry-cheekt, her hair
Inclin'd to red, and of a sprightly ayr.   1170
    Mir. What is her name?
    Erg.   *Corisca.*
    Mir.   Yes, I do
Know her, and have conversed with her too.
    Erg. Know then that she (see the good luck on't! What
Hath been the means to work it I know not,
Or on whose score it comes) is grown of late   1175
With *Amarillis* very intimate.
Which I perceiving, a relation made
Of thy affection unto her, and praid
Both her assistance and her secrecie
Therein, which she accorded readily.   1180
    Mir. O blest a thousand thousand times and more
Then all (*Mirtillo*) that ere lov'd before,
If this be true: But prethee, did she say
Nothing at all unto thee of the way?
    Erg. Nothing as yet, and I will tell thee why: 1185
Corisca said, shee could not certainly
Determine of the way till she might know
Some circumstances of thy love, that so
She might be better able to discern
The inclination of the Nymph, and learn   1190
How to addresse her selfe, with subtilty,
Or with intreaties; what 'twere best to try,
Or what to leave: This was the cause made mee

1174. Hath] 64, 76/92; hath 47/48.

To come so hastily in search of thee.
Therefore from first to last thou shalt doe well   1195
Thy Love's whole story unto me to tell.
   Mir. I'le do it. But know Friend, to stir again
The bitter memory of Love in vain,
Is like the tossing of a torch about
One's head i' th' air, thinking to shake it out,   1200
When agitation kindles it, and makes
The flame cling faster to the melting wax.
Or like the tugging of a deep-fixt dart,
By which the wound's made greater, and the smart.
Most true it is, I shall a tale relate   1205
Which will demonstrate the unsure estate
Of Lovers hopes, and that how-ere the root
Of Love be sweet, it bears a bitter fruit.
   In that fair season when Day's wheels out-run
The Night's ('twas just a twelvemonth since) this Sun   1210
Of Beauty, this fair Pilgrim came to bring
With her approach as 'twere a second Spring
To my then only rich and happy nest,
Elis and Pisa with her presence blest;
Brought by her Mother in those solemn dayes   1215
When Sacrifices and Olympick Playes
Through all the world so famous are kept there
In honour of the mighty Thunderer.
Shows worthy sure of those fair eyes; But those
Fair eyes themselves were farre the worthier shows.   1220
Whence I, who till that instant never knew
What flames of Love did mean, at the first view
Of those bright lamps, yeelded, and never fought
One stroke against her; for I felt (me thought)
Two fiery balls fly whizzing through my liver   1225
And Beauty (a bold thief) cry'd *Stand, Deliver*
Thy heart, *Mirtillo*.
   Erg.   O Love's piercing steel,
Which they alone can understand that feel!
   Mir. But now to see what cunning Love suggests
Ev'n to the youngest and the simplest brests!   1230
I made a deer young Sister of mine own
(Who was my cruell Nymph's companion

Whilst she in Elis and in Pisa staid)
Acquainted with my pain. This silly maid
Was all the councell Love allotted me   1235
For managing my amorous bus'nesse: she
With her own garments decks me in great order,
And imps my short hair with a borrow'd border,
Then braids it all with flowrs, hanging a bow
And Quiver by my side, and last doth show   1240
How I should frame my words and count'nance, where
No footsteps of a beard did then appear.
The hour approached, she conducted me
Where my Nymph us'd to play; and there found we
Some Noble Megarensian Maids, whom Blood   1245
And Love linkt to her, as I understood.
'Mongst them was she like Royall Rose 'mongst low-
Born Violets: And when as they had so
For a good space without more pastime staid,
A Megarensian Virgin rose, and said;   1250
What, at a time for Pastime so renown'd
Shall we without our sports be idle found!
And have not (Sisters) we our weapons then
To make mock-fights withall as well as men?
By my advice wee'll practice our arms now   1255
Against our selves in jest, as we must do
In earnest one day against men: Let's kisse,
And wage a kissing warre; and she that gi's
The best and sav'rest one, shall have for meed
This curious wreath. All laught, and cry'd *Agreed*.   1260
Forthwith, not staying for the word or signe,
These eager Amazons in battell joyn:
No ranks they kept, no colours knew, nor side,
But all confused, and each each defy'd.
The Megarensian this perceiving, straight   1265
To the disordered Troops sounds a retrait;
And after saith; Let her deservedly
The Judge of all our kisses be
Whose mouth is fairest. With one voice
Of peerlesse *Amarillis* they made choice.   1270
She sweetly bending her fair eyes,
Her cheeks in modest blushes dyes,

To shew through her transparent skin
That she is no lesse fair within
Then shee's without; or else her countenance   1275
Envying the honour done her mouth perchance,
Puts on her scarlet robes, as who
Should say, And am not I fair too?
   Erg. Blest man to be transform'd at such a time,
As if this accident thou couldst divine!   1280
   Mir. The fair Judge takes her seat, and now renews
The amorous fight, according to the use
Of war; by lots they march up one by one,
To try their mouthes by hers (the Paragon
Of sweetnesse) or (as I may term it well)   1285
Of orient pearls a perfum'd Indian shell,
And the two lips a two-leav'd Coral door
With honyed lock, to ope and shut with more
Facility upon the pearly treasure.
O my *Ergast'* that I could tell the pleasure   1290
Of those sweet kisses! But do thou hence ghesse it,
That mouth which tasted it, cannot expresse it.
Extract then all the sweetnesse which remains
In Hybla-combs, in Cyprian Sugar-canes,
It will be nothing to that world of blisses   1295
I suckt from thence.
   Erg.   O happy theft! sweet kisses!
   Mir. Sweet, but yet lame; the better half was missing,
The soul which gives perfection to kissing:
For though Love gave them, Love restor'd them not.
   Erg. But hadst thou not some fear when 'twas thy lot   1300
To kisse?
   Mir. My heart (*Ergasto*) to say true,
Was at my mouth, and my soul shrunk into
A narrow volume; 'twas one kisse, whence all
My limbs stood tott'ring like an ill propt wall.
And when I came under the battery,   1305
And within aim of her sure killing eye,
I fear'd the Majesty of that bright look,
Lest in the very act I should be took
Of theft and guile which I was then about.
But straight her count'nance clearing me that doubt   1310

By a serene and unsuspecting smile,
I ventur'd boldly on. Love stood the while
(*Ergasto*) like a Bee hid in the leaves
Of her lips Roses; and whilst she receives
The kisses of my mouth with hers unmov'd   1315
And passive, I the honey onely prov'd.
But when she active likewise growes,
And thrusts out this and t' other rose,
(Whether her gayety of heart it was,
Or my good luck, for 'twas not love alas)   1320
When our two mouthes snapt like a bone well set,
And like two tallies that are brothers met,
(O my deer sweet and num'rous treasure!
Do I outlive so great a pleasure?)
Then, then I felt the sharp sweet dart,   1325
The amorous sting piercing my heart.
Which was (it seems) restor'd me then,
That I might have it hurt agen.
I then, as soon as I had found
Her lips had giv'n me my deaths wound,   1330
Was ready, like some desperate gasping wight,
The weapon which had wounded me to bite:
When suddenly her sweet breath, like the blast
Of an inspiring Deity, did cast
An holy damp upon my sawcy blood,   1335
Which all immodest and wild heat withstood.
     Erg. O Modesty, the block and Remora
Which ever lies in the true Lovers way!
     Mir. Now all of them had had their turns, and come
With thoughts suspended to attend the doom,   1340
When *Amarillis* judging mine t' exceed
All th' others kisses, plac'd the Victors meed
(That curious wreath) with her own snowy hand
Upon my head. But O! no Lybian sand
Beneath the Syrian dog ere broyl'd so much,   1345
When he both barks and bites; his rage is such,
As my whole heart was then on fire
Betwixt fruition and desire.
And (being never conquerd half so much
As when I was a Conqu'ror) such   1350

My boldnesse was, that from my head
I reacht the wreath to her, and sed,
This is thy due, for thee 'tis meet,
Who with thy mouth hast made my kisses sweet.
And she most courteously accepting it, 1355
For her fair hair made it a Coronet,
And crown'd mine with another, which before
Upon her own divine temples she wore:
Which is the same I now do bear, and shall
(Heav'n willing) to my Funerall, 1360
Wither'd as 'tis, to keep in memory
That happy day; but most to signifie
My wither'd hopes.
 Erg. Thy case doth pity, and not envie claim,
Mirtillo: or hereafter let thy name 1365
'Be *Tantalus*, for he that jests with Love,
'Or playes with fire, shall pain in earnest prove.
Poor youth! thou took'st up transitory treasure
At too much use, and of thy theft the pleasure
And punishment together didst receive. 1370
But did she never the deceit perceive?
 Mir. I know not that, *Ergasto*; this I do,
Whilst shee thought Elis worthy of her view,
She was still bounteous to me of her eye,
And gracious smiles. But my hard destinie 1375
Snatching her thence, unwares to me almost,
I straight came flying hither, where thou knowst
My Father, though he sojourn'd long abroad,
Yet still retains his wonted poor aboad.
I came and saw (O sight!) my day begun 1380
In such a fair and smiling morn, now run
To its long West. When I appear'd in place
The lightning of disdain flash'd in her face;
Then did she bend her eyes, and turn'd away,
These Meteors boad my death, then did I say. 1385
Mean while, that I should so by stealth depart,
My tender Father took deeply to heart;
And with the grief on't an infirmity
So terrible, that he was like to die.
This forc'd me back, which prov'd (alas) in one 1390

Health to the Father, sicknesse to the Son.
For half a yeer of a Love-caused feaver
I languisht, and I think had languisht ever,
If my indulgent Father had not sought
In time the Tripods Counsell; whence he brought   1395
This Answer, *That th' Arcadian air alone*
Could make mee well again. I thereupon
Return'd (*Ergasto*) to revisite her
(O fallacy of that grand Sophister,
The Oracle!) who made my body whole   1400
To cause eternall sicknesse in my soule.

    Erg. Thou hast related a strange tale in truth,
Mirtillo, a case worthy of much ruth
Without all doubt. 'But oft a desperate state
'Hath prov'd the cause that cures as desperate   1405
'Have sav'd the sick. And now 'tis time I goe
To tell *Corisca* what from thee I know;
Expect me at the Fountain, there will I
Ere long be with thee.
    Mir.   Go on prosperously:
And Heav'n at need that pity shew to thee   1410
(Courteous *Ergasto*) which thou shewst to me.

SCENA SECUNDA.

Dorinda, Lupino, Silvio.

She bringing in Silvio'*s Dog.*

    Dor. Faithfull and fortunate, delight and care
Of my fair *Silvio*, and as proud as fair.
Thrice fortunate *Melampo*, that I were
Unto thy cruell Master half so deer!   1415
With that white hand with which he gripes my heart,
He stroaks and he feeds thee. He doth not part
From thee by night, nor part from thee by day;
Whilst I that so much love him, in vain pray,
And sigh in vain. And that which worse I bear   1420
Then all the rest, he gives to thee such deer
And lushious kisses, one of which would make
Me rich, and I too kisse thee for his sake

Happy *Melamp'*; O dog sent from above
To steer the erring footsteps of blind Love!   1425
Lead on, sure guide, whither Affection mee,
But Nature onely, and Instinct drawes thee.
But list a little, doth not a horn blow
In this neer thicket?
 Sil.   Sogh *Melampo*, Sogh!
 Dor. That is (if Love delude me not) the sound   1430
Of *Silvio*'s voice, who seems to call his hound
About these woods.
 Sil.   *Melampo*, Sogh, hogh, hogh.
 Dor. It is the very voice of *Silvio*.
Happy *Dorinda*, to whom Heav'n hath sent
The self same thing in search whereof I went!   1435
I'll hide the dog; with that he holds so deer
I may chance buy his love. *Lupino*!
 Lup.   Here.
 Dor. Go take this dog, and hide thee hereabout:
Conceiv'st thou me?
 Lup.   I do.
 Dor.   But come not out
Untill I call.
 Lup. I wo'n't.
 Dor.   Nay, quickly man.   1440
 Lup. And do thou quickly take some order than,
That if the dog should have a hungry fit,
He may not swallow me up at a bit.
 Dor. A Coward? Hence.
 Sil.   O whither shall I steer
My wretched steps to follow thee my deer   1445
Faithfull *Melampo*? over hill and plain
Till I am tir'd and foundred I in vain
Have hunted for thee. Cursed be the Doe
Thou follow'dst. But behold, a Nymph may know
Some news of him! O vile encounter! This   1450
Is she, who with her importunities
Torments me still: but there's no remedy
Save patience now. Fair Nymph, didst thou see my
Faithfull *Melampo*, whom I slipt while-ere
After a Doe?

Dor.   I (*Silvio*) fair? I fair?   1455
Why dost thou call me fair, if that I be
Not fair in thy eyes?
  Sil.   Fair or fowl, didst see
My dog? Answer me that: if not, I go.
  Dor. So harsh to her adores thee, *Silvio*?
Who would beleeve in that sweet shape could nest   1460
So sowr a soul? Thou follow'st a wild beast
That flyes thee, over rocks; and for a curre
Vexest thy body and thy minde: but her
That follows thee, and thy content doth prize
Above the world, thou fly'st and dost despise.   1465
Ah! do not follow a wild flying Doe,
Let not a tame one (caught already) goe.
Do not unbind her.
  Sil.   Nymph, I came in search
Of my *Melampo*, not to hear thee preach.
Adieu.
  Dor. O fly not, cruell *Silvio*:   1470
I'll tell thee news of thy *Melampo*.
  Sil.   Goe,
Thou mockst, *Dorinda*.
  Dor.   By that love I swear
That makes me *Silvio*'s servant, I know where
He is. Thou sayst he did a Doe pursue?
  Sil. He did: and straight I lost them both from view. 1475
  Dor. The Dog and Doe then at this present time
Are in my pow'r.
  Sil.   In thy pow'r?
  Dor.   Yes, in mine.
'Twas that I said: Dost thou think much that shee
Should love thy Dog (ungratefull) who loves thee?
  Sil. My deer *Dorinda*, give 'em to me straight.   1480
  Dor. Out Shittle-cock, I'm come to a fine state
When beasts endeer me to thee. But indeed
(My heart) thou gettst them not without some meed.
  Sil. And reason good, I'll give thee; Let me see—
(I'll cousen her).
  Dor.   What wilt thou give to me?   1485
  Sil. Two fair Queen-apples I will give to thee,

Which my own fairer Mother gave to me
The other day.
    Dor.   For apples, I want none:
I could give thee two fairer of my own,
And sweeter too, but that thou carest not   1490
For what I give.
    Sil.   Then wouldst thou have a goat?
Or Lambkin? (but my Father will not let
Me make so bold with what is his as yet.)
    Dor. Nor Goat, nor Lambkin do I care to have:
Thee onely, *Silvio*, and thy love I crave.   1495
    Sil. My love? No more?
    Dor.   No more.
    Sil.   I g' it thee: so,
Give me my Dog (deer Nymph) now, and my Doe.
    Dor. Ah, that thou knewst the worth of what thou art
So bounteous of, and spak'st now from thy heart!
    Sil. Nymph, mark my words: I finde thou talkst to me   1500
Still of a thing call'd Love; what this should be
I know not: thou wouldst have me love thee; and
I doe (as farre as I can understand)
With all my heart: thou call'st me cruell; I
Am ignorant of what is crueltie.   1505
How should I please thee?
    Dor.   In whom hop'st thou, poor
Dorinda? whence dost thou expect thy cure?
From such a Beauty as hath felt as yet
No spark of that which doth all Lovers set
On fire? Art thou my flame, and art not hot?   1510
Dost thou breath Love, and what it is knowst not?
That gentle Goddesse whom the Cyprians honour
Took a most beauteous humane shape upon her
To bring thee forth: Fire-brands thou hast and dart,
Witnesse my flaming and my bleeding heart.   1515
Add wings, another *Cupid* thou wilt prove,
At least want nothing to be Love, but love.
    Sil. What is this Love?
    Dor.   When I behold thy eyes,
It is the light of Paradise.
But mine own heart consider'd well,   1520

It is the very fire of hell.

    Sil. Nymph, what a prating is here with thee?
Give me my Dog and Doe, now prithee.

    Dor. Give me the love first that I bargain'd for.

    Sil. Have I not gi'n it thee? Fie, what a stir   1525
There is to please this woman! Take it: do
What thou wilt with it. Who forbids thee? who
Withholds it? On what trifles dost thou stand?

    Dor. Wretched *Dorinda*, thou dost sow the sand,
And fondly undertak'st labour in vain.   1530

    Sil. What dream'st thou of? why holdst thou me in pain?

    Dor. When thy desire's once granted, thou wilt go
And leave me straight, perfidious *Silvio*.

    Sil.   No
Indeed, fair Nymph.

    Dor.   Give mee a pawne then.

    Sil.   Name
The pawn.

    Dor.   Alas! I dare not.

    Sil.   Why?

    Dor.   For shame.   1535

    Sil. But how then can I give it thee?

    Dor.   I would
Fain without naming it be understood.

    Sil. If th' art asham'd to name it, thou maist be
Asham'd to take it.

    Dor.   Promise it to me,
And I will name it.

    Sil.   I do promise it: 1540
But thou must name it first.

    Dor.   Canst thou not hit
My thoughts then? I should have conceiv'd thee
If thou hadst said but half so much to me.

    Sil. Thou hast more wit then I, *Dorinda*.

    Dor.   I
Have more Love, *Silvio*, and lesse Cruelty.   1545

    Sil. Truth is, I am no witch: if thou'dst have me
To understand thee, speak.

    Dor.   O misery!

        1528. Withholds] 47/48; With-hold 64; With-holds 76/92.

That which I beg of thee is one of those
Things thy kind mother upon thee bestowes.
   Sil. A box o' th' ear?
   Dor.   To one that loves thee so?   1550
   Sil. Those things my mother doth on me bestow.
   Dor. Nay, that's not so: But doth not she give thee
A Kisse sometimes?
   Sil.   She neither kisses me,
Now would have others kisse me. Is't a Kisse
Thou dost desire of me? It is, it is: 1555
Thy blush betrayes thee. Come, I'le give it thee:
But first my Dog and Doe.
   Dor.   Dost promise me?
   Sil. I promise thee.
   Dor.   And with me wilt thou stay?
   Sil. Why dost thou vex me thus? Did I not say
I would?
   Dor.   Come forth *Lupino*, dost not hear?   1560
Lupino.
   Lup. Ogh! ogh! what a brawling 's there?
Who calls me? O I am come. It was not I
That slept, it was the Dog slept verily.
   Dor. Look *Silvio*, there's thy Dog, that might to thee
Have read a lecture of Humanitie.   1565
   Sil. How over-joy'd am I?
   Dor.   Upon this brest
Which thou despisest so he came to rest.
   Sil. (O my sweet true *Melampo*.)
   Dor.   Setting by
My sighs and kisses.
   Sil.   (I will certainly
Kisse thee a thousand times, poor Cur! But hast   1570
Thou got no harm at all, thou ran'st so fast?)
   Dor. Fortunate Dog, that I might change (alas!)
Estates with thee; I'm come to a fine passe
To envie a Dogs life. Bend thou thy gate
Homewards *Lupino*, I will follow straight.   1575
   Lup. Mistresse, I goe.

1550. one] 47/48 (*c*); ones 47/48 (*u*).

SCENA TERTIA.

Manent Silvio, Dorinda.

Sil. (In fine, th' ast got no harm.) Now let me see
Where is this Doe which thou hast promis'd me.
    Dor. Alive or dead woul'dst have her?
    Sil.   Strange demand!
Alive after the Dog hath kil'd her?
    Dor.   And   1580
If the Dog kild her not?
    Sil.   Alive is she?
    Dor. Alive.
                The deerer then the prey to me
And had my deer *Melampo* so much art
As not to hurt her?
    Dor.   Onely in the heart
She had a little prick.
    Sil.   Either th' art mad,   1585
Dorinda, or dost mock me. If shee had
A prick i' th' heart, how can she live?
    Sor.   The Doe
I speak of, I am, cruell *Silvio*:
Hurt by thee, without being hunted; Take me,
I am alive; but dead, if thou forsake me.   1590
    Sil. Is this that Doe? that prey?
    Dor.   Ev'n this: why now
Art thou so discontented? Dost not thou
Love a Nymph better then a beast?
    Sil.   My hate
Thou art, brute, lyar, vile, importunate.
    Dor. Is this the guerdon, cruell *Silvio*?   1595
Is this the meed thou dost on me bestow,
Ungratefull youth? Take thy *Melampo* free,
And me and all, so thou come back to me:
The rest I do remit. Let me be plac't
But in the sun-shine thy fair eyes do cast.   1600
Truer then thy *Melampo* I will trace
Thy steps, and when th' art wearied with the chase
I'le wipe thy sweating brow, and on this brest
(Which cannot rest for thee) thy head shall rest:

I'le bear thy arrowes, and thy quiver bear   1605
Through these rough woods; and if there want game there,
Shoot at *Dorinda*'s bosome. At this white
Set thy good bow, when ere it shoots not right.
For I'le be both the prey (if thou think fit)⎫
To keep in ure, and drudge to carry it;   ⎬   1610
Thy arrows, quiver, and their Butt to hit.   ⎭
But to whom do I talk? Alas! to thee
That hear'st me not, and fly'st away from me?
But wheresoe're thou fly (curs'd *Silvio*)
Dorinda will fly after thee: although   1615
To hell it self, if any hell there be
Worse then my Love is, and thy Crueltie.

SCENA QUARTA.
Corisca.

Fortune beyond my wish hath favoured me:
'And fit it is that they should favour'd be
'Who not with wishings onely seek her favour.   1620
'Pow'rfull she is; and men with reason have her
'In reputation of a Goddesse. But
'We must go meet her then, wait a foot
'To finde her humours; and must use our own
'Judgement in playing of our game: a drone   1625
'Seldome or never doth prove fortunate.
Had not my industry made me the Mate
Of her by whom under the name of friend
I have fit means and safe to work my end,
Where had I been? Some fool would now be shie,   1630
And view her Rivall with a jealous eye,
Bearing the open tokens of ill will
Writ in her forehead; and she would do ill:
'For open foes are easier to evade
'Then ambushes that are in friendship laid.   1635
'Wise Mariners by rocks hid in the sea
'Are oft deceiv'd: She knowes not how to be
'An enemy, that knows not how to seem
'A friend. *Corisca*'s skill shall now be seen
In both: Nor am I yet so simply dull   1640
To think she doth not love. Well may she gull

Others with this, not me; who am gone out
A Mistresse in the Art. A tender sprout
New peept out of the bark, within whose brest
There's built for Love already a soft nest,   1645
Long woo'd, and woo'd by so compleat a Lover,
And (which is worst) kist too over and over,
And yet hold tyte? Believe't (for me) that list.
But my good *Genius* doth me assist;
For look if *Amarillis* come not here   1650
As sent? I'le walk as if I did not see her.

SCENA QUINTA.
Amarillis, Corisca.

Am. Dear happy Groves, and you ye sollitary
And silent horrors where true peace doth tarry,
With how much joy do I review you? And
Had my stars pleas'd to give me the command   1655
Over my self, that I might chuse my lot,
And my own way of life, then would I not
For the Elisian groves, about which range
The happy shades, your happy shades exchange.
'For what we foolish mortals *Goods* do call   1660
'If rightly understood, are Evils all.
'He that hath most of them, in truth hath least,
'Nor is so much possessor, as possest;
'Not riches, no, but of our freedome snares.
'What boots it in the spring-time of one's yeers   1665
'To have the Attributes of Fair and Good,
'In mortall veins to lock celestiall blood,
'Graces of body and of mind, here fair
'And laughing fields of corn, rich meadows there,
'In fruitfull pasture-grounds more fruitfull flocks   1670
'If with all these the heart contentment lacks?
Happy that shepherdesse whom some course stuffe
Obscurely cloaths, yet clean and just enough!
Rich onely in her self, and bravely drest
With Nature's ornaments which are the best;   1675
Who in sweet poverty no want doth know,
Nor the distractions which from riches grow:
Yet whatsoever may suffice the mind,

In that estate abundantly doth finde:
Poor, but content! with Nature's gifts retrives   1680
The gifts of Nature, Milk with milk revives,
And with the sweet which from the Bee she gets,
Seasons the honey of her native sweets:
One fountain is her looking-glasse, her drink
Her bath; and if she's pleas'd, what others think   1685
It matters not; she heeds not blazing starres
That threaten mighty ones: warres or no warres,
It is all one to her; her battlement
And shield is that she's poor: *Poor, but content!*
One onely care ('tis a sweet care) doth keep   1690
Her heart awake; she feeds her Masters sheep
With pearled grasse, and with her lovely eyes
Some honest swain, that for her beauty dies:
Not such as men or Gods chuse to her hand,
But such as Love did to her choice commend;   1695
And in some favour'd shady Mirtle grove
Desires, and is desir'd: Nor feels of Love
One spark which unto him she doth not show,
Nor shows one spark with which he doth not glow.
Poor, but content! True life! which till the breath   1700
Forsakes the body, knowst not what is death.
Would Heaven had made me such a one!—But see,
Corisca! Sweet *Corisca*.
    Cor.   Who calls me?
My *Amarillis*? dearer then mine owne
Eyes, or life to me, whither so alone?   1705
    Am. No farther then thou seest; nor any where
Could I be better, since I meet thee here.
    Cor. Thou hast met her that never parts from thee,
Sweet *Amarillis*; and now, credit me,
Was thinking of thee, saying in my heart,   1710
If I'm her soul, how can she live apart
From me? When straight I saw thee here:—but go,
Thou car'st not for *Corisca* now.
    Am.   Why so?
    Cor. Why? Dost thou ask the question? thou dost wed
To day.

       1707. meet] ed.; weet 47/48. *Italian is 'poi che te trovo'.*

Am.   I wed?

Cor.   Yes: and thou keepst it hid   1715
From me.

Am.   How can I tell thee that which I
Am ignorant my self of?

Cor.   Do, deny,
And wear a mask to me.

Am.   Still jest with me
Corisca?

Cor.   I am jested with by thee.

Am. But speakst thou this for truth?

Cor.   I'le swear 'tis so.   1720
And knowst thou nothing of't indeed?

Am.   I know
I'm promis'd: but that I should be a wife
So soon, is news to me upon my life.
But from whom knowst it thou?

Cor.   From my own Brother
Ormino: and he sayes, there is no other   1725
Discourse abroad.—Thou seem'st perplext: is this
News to perplex one?

Am.   O *Corisca*! 'Tis
A hideous gulfe: I've heard my mother say,
W' are then new born.

Cor.   Most true: 'tis our birth day
T' a better life, therefore rejoyce. Dost fetch   1730
A sigh? leave sighing to that wretch.

Am.   What wretch?

Cor. Mirtillo: who was present casually
At what my brother told mee, and was nigh
Strook dead with grief; yea doubtlesse he had dy'd,
If a good cordiall I had not apply'd,   1735
By promising to break this Match. Which though
I said, onely to comfort him, I know
(If need were) how to do it.

Am.   Canst thou tell
How to break off this Match?

Cor.   Yes very well.

1719. Corisca?] 47/48 (*c*); Corisca. 47/48 (*u*).   1734. yea] 47/48 (*c*); and 47/48 (*u*).
1738. do it] 47/48 (*c*); do't 47/48 (*u*).   1739. off] 47/48 (*c*); *omitted* 47/48 (*u*).

Am. I prethee how?

Cor.   With ease, if thou wert but   1740
Consenting likewise, and assisting to't.

Am. Could I suppose this possible, and thou
Wouldst not reveal it, I would tell thee now
A secret that hath long burnt in my heart.

Cor. Who, I reveal it? Let the earth first part   1745
And swallow me alive miraculously.

Am. Know then *Corisca*, when I think that I
Must all my life be subject to a Boy
That hates and flyes me, and doth take no joy
But in the woods, preferring hunting farre   1750
Before the love of all the Nymphs that are,
It makes me male content, and desperate
Indeed almost, although I dare not say't,
Because my faith I have already given
Unto my Father, and (what's worse) to Heav'n,   1755
And break with them I neither will nor may.
But if thy industry can finde a way
(Always provided, that my Honestie,
My Faith, my Life, and my Religion be
Preserv'd) t' untie this knot that galls me so,   1760
To thee my life and safety I shall owe.

Cor. If this were it that caus'd thy sighing, thou
Hadst great cause for it *Amarillis*. How
Oft have I said? What pity 'tis to throw
So rich a thing to one that scorns it so!   1765
A pearl t' a swine! why speak'st not to thy Father?

Am. Shame stops my mouth.

Cor.   There's a disease! I'd rather
For my part have a Fistula, or Feaver.
'But 'twill be cur'd; Orecome it once, 'twill never
'Return again.

Am.   That cannot be orecome   1770
'That's naturall: For if I drive it from
'My heart, it flies into my face.

Cor.   Alas,
(My *Amarillis*) oft it comes to passe,
'She that through too much wisdom holds her tongue,

1764. throw] 64, 76/92; thtow 47/48.

'Roars out at last like mad, being throughly stung.   1775
Hadst thou before been willing to discover
Thy mind to me, this trouble had been over:
And now thou hast, *Corisca*'s power this day
In all its colours shall it self display.
Into more skilfull hands, more faithfull then   1780
Mine are, thou never couldst have faln. But when
From an ill Husband thou art freed by mee,
Shall not an honest Suitor welcom be?
    Am. Wee'l think of that at leasure.
    Cor.   That good youth
Mirtillo must not be forgot in sooth: 1785
For parts, for spotlesse faith, for shape thou knowst
Of all men living hee deserves thee most:
And canst thou let him dye? O cruelty!
Nor wilt so much as hear him say, *I dye?*
Hear him but once.
    Am.   'Twere better he would rest   1790
In peace, and root a love out of his brest
That's vain.
    Cor.   That comfort give him ere he dye.
    Am. 'Twould rather double his perplexity.
    Cor. If it do so, the seeking is his own.
    Am. And what must I expect, should it be known?   1795
    Cor. How cowardly thou art?
    Am.   And let me still
Be cowardly in any thing that's ill.
    Cor. If thou mayst fail me in this small request,
Then may I fail thee likewise in the rest
Most justly, *Amarillis*. So God bu'y.   1800
    Am. Nay, stay *Corisca*, hear.
    Cor.   Not a word I,
Unlesse thou promise me.
    Am.   I promise thee
To hear him speak, provided this may be
For all.
    Cor. It shall.
    Am.   And that he may not know
I was acquainted with't.
    Cor.   I'le make as though   1805

Ye met by accident.
   Am.   And that I may
At my own pleasure freely go away.
   Cor. Thou shalt, when thou hast heard him.
   Am.   And that hee
Shall briefly speak.
   Cor.   That too is granted thee.
   Am. Nor come within my darts length of me.
   Cor.   Fie,   1810
What a stir's here with thy simplicitie!
To make it sure, he shall not doe thee wrong,
I'le tie up all his limbs except his tongue.
Wouldst thou have more?
   Am.   'Tis well.
   Cor.   And when wilt thou
Do this?
   Am.   When ere thou wilt: Do but allow   1815
Me so much time, as to go home to hear
More certain news about this Marriage there.
   Cor. Go; but with caution, and before thou'rt gone,
Hear a contrivance I have thought upon
As thou wert speaking: In the afternoon   1820
I would have thee without thy Nymphs to come
Into this shady walk, where I will be
Before for this occasion, and with me
Nerina, Phillis, Celia, Aglaura,
Eliza, Daphne, Silvia, and *Laura*;   1825
All my no lesse discreet and witty, then
Faithfull and secret Mates. There thou with them
Shalt play (as thou art wont) at Blind-man-buffe,
So that *Mirtillo* will with ease enough
Be made believe, that for thy own passe-time   1830
Thou thither cam'st, and not to meet with him.
   Am. I like it wondrous well. But dost thou hear?
I would not any of those Nymphs were there
The while *Mirtillo* speaks.
   Cor.   I doe conceive:
'Twas thought upon with good discretion. Leave   1835
The getting them away to my endeavour.

        1834. conceive:] 47/48 (*c*); conceive 47/48 (*u*).

Go: and remember one thing,—to love ever
Thy faithfullest *Corisca*.
    Am.   In her hand
Since I have put my heart, she may command
As much love as she pleases.   [*Exit.*]   1840
    Cor. Is she not stiffe? We must assault this rock
With greater force; though she resist my shock,
Against *Mirtillo*'s she will finde no fence
I'm sure: I know by self-experience
The power of Lovers prayers when they invade   1845
The tender heart of an inclining maid.
If shee do yeeld, I'le make her smart so for't,
That shee shall finde her sport was not in sport.
Through her dark'st words her heart shall be to me
As visible as in a 'natomie.   1850
I'le ransack all her veins: that done, and I
Made Mistresse of her secret, easily
I'le winde her so, and lead her by the nose
To what I'de have, her self shall ne're suppose
(Much lesse shall others) that it was my skill   1855
That drew her to't, but her unbridled will.

SCENA SEXTA.
Corisca, Satyr.

    Cor. O I'm dead.
    Sat.   But I was *quick*.
There's a trick now for your trick.
    Cor. My *Amarillis*, I am caught.
O come back.
    Sat.   She hears thee not.   1860
'Twill now behove thee to be strong.
    Cor. O me, my hair!
    Sat.   I have so long
Stood angling for thee in my boat,
At last th' art strook. 'Tis not thy coat,
'Tis thy hair (Sister) this.
    Cor.   To mee   1865
This usage (*Satyr?*)
    Sat.   Yes, to thee

1840. *Exit*] ed.   1854. her self] 47/48 (*c*); that she 47/48 (*u*).

Corisca, or I am mistaken:
That Mistresse in the art of making
The fine-spun lyes, that sels so deer
False words, false hopes, and a false leer?   1870
Shee that so often hath betraid me;
Shee that so many fools hath made me
At every turn: the sorceresse,
The cheat *Corisca?*
  Cor.   I confesse,
I am *Corisca;* but not shee   1875
Now, that was once so lov'd by thee,
My gentile *Satyr.*
  Sat.   Pray since when
Am I *gentile?* I was not then
When me for *Coridon* thou didst change.
  Cor. Thee for another?
  Sat.   See how strange   1880
She makes it now! I warrant then
This is great news to thee; and when
Thou mad'st me *Silvia*'s Buskins steal,
The Bow of *Lilla*, *Cloris* Veile,
And *Daphne*'s Gown, that were to be   1885
The price of love, which promis'd me,
Thou gav'st another: and when that
Fair wreathe I on thy head did plat,
Thou upon *Niso* didst bestow;
And when thou mad'st me (cold as snow)   1890
Watch many a night out at the Fountain,
The Cave, Wood-side, and foot o' th' Mountain,
And for my pains didst laugh at me,
Did I then seem *gentile* to thee?
Ah thief! But now as I am here,   1895
I'le make thee pay thy whole arrear.
  Cor. O me! Thou dragg'st me like a beast.
  Sat. I drag thee like thy self then. Wrest
Thy neck out of the collar now;
Give me the slip if thou knowst how.   1900
Fox, though thy craft the time before
Did save thee, it shall do't no more.
For this I'm sure thou canst not scape,

Unlesse thou leave thy head i' th' trap.

    Cor. Yet give me so much time I pray,   1905
As for my self to answer.

    Sat.   Say.

    Cor. How can I if thou hold me so?

    Sat. 'Tis likely I should let thee go.

    Cor. I'le gage my faith not to go hence.

    Sat. What faith? Hast thou the impudence   1910
(Perfidious woman) to name faith
To me? I'le bear thee where there hath
No Sun, much lesse the feet of men
Approacht, unto the horrid'st den
Of all this Mountain: there—(but I   1915
Will act the rest) to mine own joy
And thy dishonour, I will kerve
Such vengeance as thy faults deserve.

    Cor. Canst thou then (cruell) to this hair (which has
Ty'd fast thy heart), unto this face (which was   1920
Once thy delight), to this *Corisca* (then
More dear to thee then thine own life was when
Thou swar'st by that, that thou couldst finde it sweet
On her behalf, ev'n death it self to meet),
Canst thou once think to offer injury,   1925
I say, to her? O Heav'ns! O Destinie!
Whom have I hop't in? whom can I believe
Again?

    Sat. Ah Syren! thinkst thou to deceive
Me still? still rock me with thy flatt'ring charms?

    Cor. My sweet deer *Satyr*, do no harm   1930
To her that loves thee. Thou art not a beast,
Nor hast a marble or a flinty brest:
Behold me at thy feet! O pardon me
If ever I (by chance) offended thee,
My Idol. By those sinewy and more   1935
Then humane knees, which clasping I adore;
By that rough manly visage; by that dear
Affection which thou once to me didst bear;
By the sweet influence of those eyes which thou
Wert wont to call two stars (two fountains now;)   1940
By these salt tears which trickle down so fast,

Pitie me now, and let me go.
   Sat.   Thou hast
Mov'd me (I must confesse) and I were gone,
If I should hearken to affection.
But to be short, I doe not credit thee;   1945
Thou art too full of wiles and tricks for me,
And he that takes thy word, believes his snares:
Beneath this humble shew, beneath these pray'rs
There's hid *Corisca*: *Thou* canst never be
Another. Struggling still?
   Cor.   My head, O me!   1950
Ah cruell! stay a little longer yet,
And grant me but one favour.
   Sat.   What is it?
   Cor. Hear me a little more.
   Sat.   Thou hopest now
With flatt'ries and squeez'd tears to make me bow.
   Cor. Ah courteous Satyr! wilt thou kerve in me   1955
Such cruell vengeance?
   Sat.   Come, and thou shalt see.
   Cor. And take no Pity of me?
   Sat.   None at all.
   Cor. But art thou firm in this?
   Sat.   As a brasse-wall.
Is this charm ended?
   Cor.   O thou base, and not
To be exampled Rogue; half man, half goat,   1960
And all a beast; thou carrion that doth stink,
By-blow and blush of nature; If thou think
Corisca loves thee not, thou thinkst the truth.
What should she love in such a comely youth?
That fair Stags head? that chimney-sweepers broom?   1965
Goats ears? that grave of rottennesse and rheume
Which once had bones in't?
   Sat.   This to me,
Thou wicked varlet?
   Cor.   Ev'n to thee.
   Sat. To me, thou scold?
   Cor.   To thee, thou Goat.

      1950. struggling] 64, 76/92; sruggling 47/48.

Sat. And with these pincers pull I not   1970
Thy barking tongue out?
      Cor.   Would thou durst
Come neer't, there's that will scour their rust.
      Sat. A paltry woman, and in such
Condition (being in my clutch)
To injure me! and dare mee too!   1975
I will—
      Cor.   Base slave, what wilt thou do?
      Sat. Eat thee alive I will.
      Cor.   Where be
The teeth to do't?
      Sat.   Heav'n, dost thou see
And suffer this! But if I doe not
Chastise thee—Come along.
      Cor.   I wo' not.   1980
      Sat. Wo' not, my Mistresse Malapert?
      Cor. Wo' not in spight of thy foul heart.
      Sat. That shall be seen; Come, or I swear,
This arm I'le from thy shoulder tear.
      Cor. Tear my head off, I wo' not go   1985
One foot.
      Sat. Art thou resolved so?
Let's ne're dispute then any longer,
But put to tryall whether's stronger
And faster on, thy neck-piece, or
My arm.—Thy hands to help too? Nor   1990
Are these (perverse one) enough guard.
      Cor. That shall be try'd.
      Sat.   It shall.
      Cor.   Pull hard.—
Satyr adieu, Get thy neck set.   [*Exit*]
      Sat.   O me!
How I am shatter'd! O my head! my knee!
O my back-bone! my thigh! what a vile fall   1995
Was here! to get upon my legs is all
I have the pow'r to do. But can it be
That she should fly, and leave her head with me?
O marvellous! ye Nymphs and Shepherds run,

1993. *Exit*] ed.

Flock hither to behold a wonder; one   2000
That runs away without her head, by skill
In Magick. Hah! how light it is! how ill
Peopled with brains! How comes it that I see
None of the blood spirt forth? But stay; let me
Peruse it better. O thou stock! thou stone!   2005
Thou hast no head, if thou think she hath none.
Was ever any man so fool'd? See now
If she had not a trick to scape, when thou
Thoughtst her most sure! Thou all made up of wiles,
Was't not enough thy heart, thy face, thy smiles,   2010
Thy looks and speeches falsified were,
But thou must likewise falsifie thy hair?
The glowing Amber, and the flowing Gold,
Which you (mad Poets) so extoll, behold!
Blush, blush now at your errour, and recant   2015
Your thred-bare theam; in stead whereof, go paint
The arts of a deform'd and impious Witch
Breaking up Sepulchres by night, from which
She steals the hair that upon Death's head growes,
To imp her own, which she so neatly does,   2020
That she hath made you praise what ye should more
Then dire *Megara*'s snakie locks abhor.
These (*Lovers*) are your gyves (I take it) too!
Look on 'em Idiots: and if (as you
Protest) your hearts are fastned to these hairs,   2025
Now every one may without sighs or tears
Come by his owne. But why do I forbear
To publish her disgrace? Surely that hair,
Which stuck with starres adorns the azure skye,— ⎫
Never so famous was as this; and shee   ⎬   2030
Much more that wore it by my tongue shall be ⎫
Made infamous to all posterity.——   ⎭

Chorus.

Ah! 'Twas a grievous fault in her (the Cause
Of all our sorrows) who, the sacred Lawes
Of Love offending, by her breach of troth,   2035
Kindled against this Land the mortall wrath
Of the immortall Gods, which not a Flood

Of generall tears, nor so much guiltlesse blood
'Can quench yet or abate; so high a price
'Unspotted Faith (Expeller of all vice,   2040
'And most undoubted Argument to prove
'A mind descended nobly) bears above.
'And such a care to plant love in his creature
'(By which we deïfie our humane Nature)
'Hath the eternall Lover. O those blind   2045
Mistaken mortals, who addict their mind
To wealth, (for which affection's basely sold)
Watching the carcasse of their coffin'd gold,
Like a pale ghost that walks about his grave!
Or why should beauty our free hearts enslave?   2050
'These are dead loves; the living and divine
'Is where two souls by vertue do combine.
'No outward object can with reason move
'The heart to love it, 'cause it cannot love:
'Onely the soul, 'cause that can love again,   2055
'Deserves a Love, deserves a Lovers pain.
     Well may that kisse be sweet that's giv'n t' a sleek
And fragrant rose of a vermilion cheek;
And understanding tasters (as are true
And happy Lovers) will commend that too.   2060
'Tis a dead kisse, say I, and must be poor,
Which the place kist hath no means to restore.
But the sweet ecchoing, and the Dove-like billing
Of two encountring Mouthes, when both are willing;
And when at once both Loves advance their bows,   2065
Their shafts drawn home, at once sound at the loose,
(How sweet is such Revenge!) This is true kissing,
Where there is one for t' other without missing
A minute of the time, or taking more
Then that which in the taking they restore.   2070
Where by an interchange of amorous blisses
At the same time they sow and gather kisses.
Kisse a red swelling lip, then kisse a wrist,
A brest, a forehead, or what else thou list,
No part of a fair Nymph so just will be,   2075
Except the lip, to pay this kisse to thee.

2066. shafts] 47/48, 76/92; shaf 64.

Thither your souls come sallying forth, and they
Kisse too, and by the wandring pow'rs convey
Life into smacking Rubies, and transfuse
Into the live and sprightly kisse their use   2080
Of reason; so that yee discourse together
In kisses, which with little noyse deliver
Much matter; and sweet secrets, which hee spels,
Who is a Lover; Gibbrish to all else.

  Like life, like mutuall joy they feel, where Love   2085
With equall flames as with two wings doth move.
'And as where lips kisse lips is the best Kisse:
'So where one's lov'd, to love, best loving is.

ACTUS TERTIUS.

SCENA PRIMA.

Mirtillo.

Spring, the yeers youth, fair Mother of new flowrs,
New leaves, new loves, drawn by the winged hours,   2090
Thou art return'd; but the felicity
Thou brought'st me last is not return'd with thee.
Thou art return'd, but nought returns with thee
Save my lost joyes regretfull memory.
Thou art the self same thing thou wert before,   2095
As fair and jocund: but I am no more
The thing I was, so gracious in her sight
Who is Heav'ns master-piece, and Earth's delight,
'O bitter-sweets of Love! Far worse it is
'To lose, then never to have tasted blisse.   2100
'But O how sweet were Love, if it could not
'Be lost, or being lost could be forgot!
Though if my hopes (as mine are wont to be)
Are not of glasse, or my love make me see
Them through a multiplying glasse; If I   2105
Be not deceiv'd both by my self, and by
Another: Here I shall that Sun behold
Which I adore, impart her beams of gold

2080. *live and sprightly*] 47/48; *love and sprightly* 64; *love sprightly* 76/92.
2100. *lose*] 64, 76/92; *love* 47/48. *Correction is made in errata list in 47/48.*

To my blest sight, behold her flying feet
Stop at my sad notes; here upon the sweet 2110
Food of that lovely face I shall suffice
After a tedious fast my greedy eyes.
Here, here behold that proud one on me turn
Her sparkling lamps, if not to light, to burn.
And if not fraught with amorous delight, 2115
So kindly cruell as to kill outright.
Yet were't but just, that after so much pain
As I have hitherto endur'd in vain,
Thou Love at length shouldst make the Sun appear
To this benighted earth serene and cleer. 2120
Hither *Ergasto* did direct me, where
Corisca and my *Amarillis* were
To play at Blindman-buffe: but I can finde
In this place nothing but my love that's blind,
And so deceiv'd, mis-led by a false guide 2125
To seek that light which is to me deny'd.
Pray Heav'n my hard and envious fate beneath
This sugred Pill now have not hid my death.
This tedious stay afflicts me: 'For to those
'That go to meet their Loves, each moment shows 2130
'An age. Perchance I have arriv'd too late,
And made for me too long *Corisca* wait:
Yet I made haste. Now woe is me! If I
Have done this fault, I will lie down and dye.

SCENA SECUNDA.

Amarillis, Mirtillo, *Chorus of
Nymphs*, Corisca.

Am. Behold *the Buff*!
Mir.   O sight!
Am.   Come on.
Mir.   O voice! 2135
That makes my heart both tremble and rejoyce.
    Am. What do you do? *Lisetta*, where art thou
That wert so eager of this sport but now?
And thou *Corisca*, whither gone?
    Mir.   I finde
Now it is true indeed, that Love is blinde. 2140

Am. You there that are appointed for my guides
To hand and to support mee on both sides,
Before the rest of our Companions come,
Out of these trees conduct me to field-room:
Then leaving me alone amidst the plain,   2145
Amongst our other fellows herd again:
So joyning all together, make a ring
About me round, and let the sport begin.
    Mir. But what shall I do? Yet I cannot see
Of what advantage this should be to me   2150
In my desires; nor see I my north-starre
Corisca: Succour me blest Heav'n!
    Am.   O are
Yee come at last? yee wantons, did you mean
Only to bind my eyes? Begin now then.
    Cho. Love, thou art not blind, I know,   2155
'But dost onely appear so
'To blinde us: if thy sight 's small,
'Thou hast, I'm sure no faith at all.
Blinde or not, thou try'st in vain
Mee into thy net to train.   2160
And to keep out of thy pound,
Off I get, and traverse ground.
Blind as thou art, thou couldst see more
Then Argus *hundred eyes of yore.*
Thou couldst see (blind as thou art)   2165
Well enough to hit my heart.
But I were a fool indeed,
Should I trust thee now I'm freed.
Sport with thee henceforth that will;
'Tis a sport with thee to kill.   2170
    Am. I, but with too much warinesse you play:
Yee should strike first, and after get away.
Approach me, touch me, and ye shall not fly
Me then.
    Mir. O ye high Gods! In heav'n am I?
Or earth? O heav'ns! do your eternall rounds   2175
Move in such order, warble such sweet sounds?
    Cho. Well, blind Archer, since thou still

2154. bind] 47/48; blind 64, 76/92.

Urgest me to play, I will.
Now I clap thy shoulder hard:
Now I fly unto my guard: 2180
Strike, and run, and strike again,
And thou wheel'st about in vain.
Now I pinch thee, now remove:
And have at thee now blind Love.
Yet thou canst not light on me;   2185
Why? because my heart is free.

     Am. In faith *Licoris*, I had surely thought
T' ave caught thee there, and 'twas a tree I caught.
I, dost thou laugh?
     Mir.   Would I had been that tree.
But do I not *Corisca* hidden see   2190
Amongst those brakes? and she makes signes as who
Should say, that something she would have me do.
     Cho. '*A free heart makes a nimble heel.*
Ah traitour! dost thou tempt me still
With thy flattering false delight?   2195
Thus then I renew the fight.
Slash, and fly, and turn, and shove;
And about again blind Love:
Yet thou canst not light on me;
Why? because my heart is free.   2200
     Am. Would thou wert puld up by the root, base tree:
That I should ever thus be catching thee!
Deceived by the dancing of a bough,
I did suppose I'd had *Eliza* now.
     Mir. Corisca still is making signes to me,   2205
And looks as shee were angry: perhaps she
Would have me mix with those Nymphs.
     Am.   Must I play
With nothing but with trees then all this day?
     Cor. I must come forth and speak, or hee'l not stir—.
To her (white liver) and lay hold on her.   2210
Why dost thou gape? to have her run into
Thy mouth? At least, if that thou dar'st not do,
Let her lay hold of thee. Come, give me here
This dart, and go to meet her fool.
     Mir.   How neer

To impotence is strong desire! O Love!   2215
That thou shouldst make a man a coward prove!
    Am. Play but once more, for now I weary grow.
Troth, y' are too blame for making me run so.
    Cho. That triumphant God survey,
To whom amorous mortals pay   2220
Impious tribute! See him snaffeld!
See him laught at! See him baffeld!
As a hooded Hawke or Owle
With light blinded, when the fowle
With their Armies flock about her,   2225
Some to beat, and some to flout her;
She in vain doth rowze and peck
This and that way with her beak:
So we baffle and deride
Thee (blind Love) on ev'ry side.   2230
One doth pinch thy elbow black;
T'other has thee by the back;
And thy baiting does no good,
Nor thy pecking through thy hood,
Nor thy stretching out thy clawes.   2235
'But sweet meats have sowr sawce.
'Birds are caught by playing thus:
'So do Nymphs grow amorous.

SCENA TERTIA.

Amarillis, Corisca, Mirtillo.

    Am. I' Faith, *Aglaura*, art thou caught at last?
Thou'dst fain be gone, but I will hold thee fast.   2240
    Cor. Surely, unlesse at unawares by main
Strength I had thrust him on her, I in vain
Had tyr'd my self to make him thither go.
    Am. Thou wilt not speak now: Art thou she or no?
    Cor. I lay his Dart here by him, and unto   2245
My bush return, t' observe what will ensue.
    Am. Thou art *Corisca*, now it is most cleer;
I know thee by thy tallnesse and short hair.
'Twas thee I wish'd to catch; that I might use thee
Just as I list, and thus, and thus abuse thee;   2250
And thus, and thus. Not yet? But since 'twas thou

That boundst me, do thou too unbinde me now:
Quickly (my heart) and thou shalt have of me
The sweetest kisse that ere was given thee.
What dost thou stick at? thy hand trembles: what,   2255
Art thou so weary? If thy nails will not,
Let thy teeth do't: come fumbler, let mee see;
I can my self untangle without thee.
Fye, how with knots on knots it is perplext?
The best on't is, thou must be blinded next.   2260
So, now 'tis loos'd: Hah! whom have we here?
Traitor avaunt. I am unspirited.
    Mir.   Dear
Soul, do not strive to goe away.
    Am.   Unhand
(Forcer of Nymphs) unhand me, I command.
Ay me! *Aglaura* and *Eliza* tarry,   2265
Betrayers of my innocence, where are ye?—
Unhand me villain.
    Mir.   I obey.
    Am.   This plot
Corisca laid: Now tell her what th' ast got.
    Mir. O whither fly'st thou Cruell? ere thou go
Banquet thy eyes yet with my death: for lo,   2270
I pierce my bosome with this dart.
    Am.   Ay me!
What wilt thou do?
    Mir.   That which it troubles thee
Perchance (dire Nymph) that any should be sed
T' have done, but thou.
    Am.   (Ay me! I'm almost dead.)
    Mir. And if this action to thy hand be due,   2275
Behold the weapon and the brest!
    Am.   'Tis true,
Thou hast deserv'd it of me. What could move
Thy heart to such a high presumption?
    Mir.   Love.
    Am. 'Love never causes rudenes.
    Mir.   Then conclude,
'I was in love, because I was not rude: 2280
For if within thy arms thou caughtst me first,

I cannot well with rudenesse be asperst,
Since with so fair an opportunity
To be audacious, and to use with thee
The Lawes of Love, I had such power yet over   2285
My self, I ev'n forgot I was a Lover.
 Am. Upbraid me not with what I blind did doe.
 Mir. I being in Love was blinder of the two.
 Am. 'Pray'r and sweet language discreet Lovers use
'To winne their Loves; not theft and cheats, t' abuse.   2290
 Mir. As a wild beast enrag'd with want of food
Rushes on travellers out of the wood:
So I, that onely live on thy fair eyes,
Since that lov'd food thy crueltie denyes,
Or else my Fate, if like a ravenous Lover   2295
Rushing to day upon thee from this Cover,
Where I had long been famish't, I did prove
One stratagem to save my life (which Love
Prompted me to) then blame not, cruell Maid,
Me but thy self; for if (as thou hast said)   2300
Pray'r and sweet language onely should be us'd
By discret Lovers, which thou hast refus'd
To hear from me; thou by thy crueltie,
Thou by thy flight mad'st me I could not be
A discreet Lover.
 Am.   If th' adst gi'n her over   2305
That fled from thee, th' adst been a discreet Lover.
But know, thou persecutest me in vain;
What wouldst thou have of me?
 Mir.   I'd have thee daign
Once ere I die to hear me.
 Am.   See! as soon
As thou hast askt, thou hast receiv'd the boon.   2310
Now then be gone.
 Mir. Ah Nymph! I've scarcely yet
Powr'd one small drop out to thee of the great
Sea of my tears. If not for Pitie's sake,
Yet for the Pleasure thou therein wilt take,
List' to a dying man's last accents.
 Am.   Well,   2315
To shun more trouble, and thy hopes to quell,

To hear thee I'm content. But this before;
Say little, quickly, part, and come no more.
  Mir. Thou dost command me, cruell'st Nymph, to bind
In volume too too small that unconfin'd   2320
Desire, which scarcely humane thought (though it
Be as the soul that holds it, infinit)
Hath line to fathom.
That I do love thee more then I do love
My life (if thou doubt'st, Cruel) ask this Grove,   2325
And that will tell thee; and with it each beast,
Each stupid stock there can the same attest;
Each stone of these high mountains, which so oft
I with the voice of my complaints made soft.
But what need I call any witnesse else   2330
To prove my love, where so much beauty dwels?
Behold these flow'rs which make low earth so proud!
Those Stars which nail Heav'ns pavement! all these crowd
Into one ring: A beautie like that same
Is the high cause and forcer of my flame.   2335
For as by nature Water doth descend,
The Fire unto the higher Regions tend
The Air obliquely spread it self, the Ground
Lie still, and heav'n about all these turn round.
So naturally do I incline to thee,   2340
As to my chiefest good; so naturally
To those lov'd beauties (as unto her sole)
With all her wing'd affections flyes my soul.
And he that should imagine he had force
Her from her dearest object to divorce,   2345
Might with as much facility command
The Air, the Fire, the Water and the Land,
The Heavens too from their accustom'd track,
And make the Pillars of the world to crack.
But since thou bidst me say but little, I   2350
Shall say but little, saying that *I dye*:
And shall doe lesse in dying, since I see
How much my death is coveted by thee.
Yet I shall doe (alas) all that is left
For me to do, of hopes in love bereft.   2355
But (cruell soul) when I am in my grave,

Some pitie then upon my suffrings have.
Ah! fair and lov'd, and that wert once the sweet
Cause of my life (whilst Heaven thought it meet)
Turn those bright lamps upon me, as beni'ne 2360
And pitifull as ere I saw them shine,
Once ere I dye, that I may dye in peace.
Let those fair amiable eyes release
My life, now bitter, which once sweetned it;
And those bright Starres, which my loves torches li't, 2365
Light too my Funerall tapers, and forerun,
As once my rising, now my setting Sun.
But thou more hard then ere thou wert before,
Feel'st yet no spark of pity; but art more
Stiffe with my pray'rs. Must I then talk alone? 2370
Wretch that I am, discourse I to a stone?
Say *Dye*, at least, if nothing else thou'lt say;
And thou shalt see me dye. O Love! what way
Canst thou not plague me? when this Nymph that's nurst
In cruelty, and for my blood did thirst, 2375
Finding my death would now a favour be,
Ev'n that sad favour doth deny to me?
Nor will reply a syllable, or daign
One stabbing word to put me out of pain?
    Am. To answer thee if I had promised, 2380
As well as hear thee, this were justly sed.
Thou call'st me cruell, hoping, that to shun
That vice, into the contrary I'le run.
But know, my ears are not so tickeled
With that (by me so little merited 2385
And lesse desired) praise thou giv'st to me
Of beauty, as to hear my self by thee
'Stil'd Cruell; which to be to any other
'I grant were vice; 'tis vertue to a Lover:
'And what thou harshnesse call'st and crueltie, 2390
'Is in a woman perfect honestie.
But say, that ev'n t' a Lover 'twere a sin;
Yet tell me, when hath *Amarillis* bin
Cruell to thee? was't then when justice bad
To use no pitie; yet on thee I had 2395
So much, that I from death deliver'd thee?

I mean, when 'mongst a noble companie
Of modest Virgins mingled, thou didst cover
With a Maid's habit a libidinous Lover:
And, our chast sports polluting, didst intrude   2400
'Mongst kisses feign'd and innocent thy lewd
And wanton kisses (such an act, as yet
I blush as oft as I but think on it).
But at that time I knew thee not (Heav'n knows)
And when I did, my indignation rose.   2405
Thy wantonnesse I from my mind did keep,
And suffred not the amorous plague to creep
To my chast heart: on my lips outer skin
The poyson stuck, but none of it got in.
        'A mouth that's kiss'd perforce,   2410
'If it spit out the kisse, is ne're the worse.
But what wouldst thou by that bold theft have got,
If I had to those Nymphs discover'd what
Thou wert? the *Thracian* women never tore
And murther'd *Orpheus* so on Hebrus shore,   2415
As they had thee, unlesse her clemencie
Whom thou call'st cruell now had rescu'd thee.
But she is not so cruell as she ought
To be: for if when she is cruell thought
Thy boldnesse is so great, what would it be   2420
If she were judged pitifull by thee?
That honest pitie which I could, I gave;
Other it is in vain for thee to crave,
Or hope: 'for amorous pitie she can ill
'Bestow, who gave it all to one that will   2425
'Give her none back. If thou my Lover be,
Love my good name, my life, my honestie.
Thou seek'st impossibles; I am a ward
To Heav'n, Earth watches me, and my reward
If I transgresse, is death: but most of all,   2430
Vertue defends me with a brasen wall.
'For she that is protected by her honour,
'Scorns there should be a safer guard upon her.
Look to thy safety then, and do not give
Battell to me, *Mirtillo*: fly, and live,   2435

2409. stuck] 47/48; suck 64, 76/92.

If thou be wise. 'For out of sense of smart
'T' abandon life, argues but a faint heart.
'And 'tis the part of vertue to abstain
'From what we love, if it will prove our bane.
   Mir. 'He that no longer can resist must yeeld.   2440
   Am. 'Where vertue is, all passions quit the field.
   Mir. 'Love triumphs over vertue.
   Am.   Let that man
'That cannot what he will, will what he can.
   Mir. 'Necessitie of loving hath no law.
   Am. 'Love's wounds will heal, which salves of absence draw.   2445
   Mir. 'We fly in vain what we about us carry.
   Am. 'Love drives out love like following billows: Marry.
   Mir. Strange levitie in me thou dost presume.
   Am. 'If all wayes fail, time will thy love consume.
   Mir. But first my love will have consumed me.   2450
   Am. Is there no cure then for thy malady?
   Mir. No cure at all but that which death affords.
   Am. Death? let me speak then; and be sure these words
Be as a charm unto thee: though I know
'When Lovers talk of dying, it doth show   2455
'An amorous custome rather of the tongue,
'Then a resolve of minde (continuing long)
'To do't indeed: yet if thou ere shouldst take
So strange a frenzie; know, when thou dost make
Away thy self, thou murtherst my fame too: 2460
Live then (if thou dost love me) and adieu:
I shall esteem thee henceforth most discreet,
If thou take care we two may never meet.
   Mir. Sad doom! without my life how can I live?
Or without death end to my torments give?   2465
   Am. Mirtillo, 'Tis high time thou wentst away,
Thou hast already made too long a stay:
Be gone; and take this cordiall along,
'Of hopelesse Lovers there's a numerous throng,
'There is no wound but carries with it pain,   2470
And there are others may of love complain.
   Mir. I know I'm not the only man hath lost
His Love; but onely wretched I am tost
'Twixt life and death; of whom it may be sed,

That I am neither living, nor yet dead. 2475
   Am. Be gone, be gone.
   Mir.   O wofull parting! O
End of my dayes! from thee how can I go,
And yet not dye? The pangs of death I'm sure
I feel, and all that parting souls endure.
For mine, 'tis past into my griefs: Hence I 2480
Have ceas'd to live, those live immortally.

SCENA QUARTA.

Amarillis.

Mirtillo, O *Mirtillo!* couldst thou see
That heart which thou condemn'st of cruelty,
(Soul of my soul) thou unto it wouldst show
That pity which thou begg'st from it I know. 2485
O ill starr'd Lovers! what avails it me
To have thy love? T' have mine, what boots it thee?
Whom Love hath joyn'd why dost thou separate,
Malitious Fate! And two divorc'd by Fate
Why joyn'st thou perverse Love? How blest are you 2490
Wild beasts, that are in loving ty'd unto
No lawes but those of Love! whilst humane lawes
Inhumanely condemn us for that cause.
'O why, if this be such a naturall
'And powerfull passion, was it capitall! 2495
'Nature too frail, that do'st with Law contend!
'Law too severe, that Nature do'st offend!
'But what? they love but little who death fear.
Ah, my *Mirtillo!* would to heav'n that were
'The onely penaltie. Vertue, which art 2500
'The bindingst Law to an ingenuous heart,
This inclination which in me I feel,
Lanc'd with the sharp point of thy holy steel,
To thee I sacrifice; and pardon (deer
Mirtillo) her, that's onely cruell, where 2505
She must not pitie. Pardon thy fierce foe
In looks and words: but in her heart not so.
Or if addicted to revenge thou be,

2475. nor] 47/48; noe 64, 76/92.

What greater vengeance canst thou take on me
Then thine own grief? for if thou be my heart   2510
(As in despight of Heaven and Earth thou art)
Thy sighs my vitall spirits are, the flood
Of tears which follows is my vitall blood,
And all these pangs, and all these groans of thine
Are not thy pangs, are not thy groans, but mine.   2515

SCENA QUINTA.
Corisca, Amarillis.

Cor. Sister, no more dissembling.
Am.   Woe is me!
I am discovered.
Cor.   I heard all: now see,
Was I a Witch? I did believe (my Heart)
Thou wert in love; now I am sure thou art.
And would'st thou keep't from me? thy closet? tush,   2520
This is a common evill, never blush.
   Am. Corisca, I am conquer'd (I confess't).
   Cor. No, now I know't, deny it thou wert best.
   Am. 'Alas! I knew a womans heart would prove
'Too small a vessell for o're-flowing love.   2525
   Cor. Cruell to thy *Mirtillo*! but unto
Thy self much more!
Am.   'Tis cruelty that grew
From pitie.
   Cor.   'Poyson ne're was known to grow
'From wholsom root: What diff'rence canst thou show
'Twixt such a crueltie as doth offend,   2530
And such a pitie as no help will lend?
   Am. Ay mee, *Corisca*!
   Cor.   'Tis a vanitie
(Sister) to sigh, an imbecillitie
Of mind, and tastes too much of woman.
Am.   Wer't
Not crueller to nourish in his heart   2535
A hopeless love? To fly him is a signe
I have compassion of his case and mine.
   Cor. But why a hopeless love?

  Am.   Do'st thou not know
I am contracted unto *Silvio*?
Do'st thou not know besides what the Law saith,   2540
'Tis death in any woman that breaks faith?
  Cor. O fool! and is this all stands in thy way?
Whether is ancienter with us (I pray)
'The Law of *Dian*, or of Love? this last
'Is born with us, and it growes up as fast   2545
'As we do, *Amarillis*; 'tis not writ,
'Nor taught by Masters, Nature printed it
'In humane hearts with her own powerfull hand:
'Both Gods and men are under Loves command.
  Am. But if that Law my life away should take,   2550
Can this of Love a restitution make?
  Cor. Thou art too nice; if women all were such
And on these scruples should insist so much,
Good dayes adieu. I hold them simple souls
Will live obnoxious to such poor comptrolls.   2555
'Lawes are not for the wise: if to be kind
Should merit death, *Jove* help the cruell mind!
But if fools fall into those snares, 'tis fit
They be forbid to steal, who have not wit
'To hide their theft. For honestie is but   2560
'An art, an honest glosse on vice to put.
Think others as they list; thus I conceive.
  Am. These rotten grounds, *Corisca*, will deceive.
'What I can't hold 'tis wisdome soon to quit.
  Cor. 'And who forbids thee fool? our life doth flit   2565
'Too fast away to lose one jot of it;
'And men so squemish and so curious grown,
'That two of our new Lovers make not one
'O' th' old. We are no longer for their tooth
'(Believ't) then while w' are new. Bate us our youth,   2570
'Bate us our beauty, and like hollow trees
'Which had been stuff'd with honey by the bees,
'If that by licourish hands away be ta'ne,
'Dry and despised trunks we shall remain.
Therefore let them have leave to babble what   2575
They please, as those who know nor reckon not

What the poor woman *Amarillis* bears,
Our case alas is differing much from theirs.
'Men in perfection as in age increase,
'Wisdome supplies the losse of handsomnesse: 2580
'But when our Youth and Beauty (which alone
'Conquers the strength and wit of men) are gone,
'All 's gone with us; nor canst thou possibly
'Say a worse thing, or to be pardon'd thee
'More hardly, then *Old woman*. Then before   2585
Thou split on that unevitable shore,
Know thine own worth, and do not be so mad,
As when thou mayst live merry, to live sad.
What would the lion's strength boot him, or wit
Avail a man, unlesse he used it?   2590
Our beauty is to us that which to men
Wit is, or strength unto the lion. Then
'*Let us use it whilst wee may;*
'*Snatch those joyes that haste away.*
'*Earth her winter-coat may cast,*   2595
'*And renew her beauty past;*
'*But, our winter come, in vain*
'*We sollicite spring again:*
'*And when our furrows snow shall cover,*
'*Love may return, but never Lover.*   2600
    Am. Thou say'st all this only to try me sure,
Not that thy thoughts are such. But rest secure,
Unlesse the way thou unto me shalt show
Be a plain way, and warrantable too
To break this Match; I am resolv'd to die   2605
A thousand deaths, ere stain my honestie.
    Cor. More wilfull woman I did never know.
But since thou art so resolved, be it so.
Tell me good *Amarillis*, seriously,
Do'st thou suppose thy *Silvio* sets by   2610
His faith as much as thou thy honestie?
    Am. Thou mak'st me laugh at this: wherein should he
Expresse a faith, who is to love a foe?
    Cor. Love's foe? O fool! thou knowst not *Silvio*.
He is the still sow, hee. O these coy souls!   2615

2615. these] 47/48, 64; those 76/92.

Believe them not: the deep stream silent rowls.
'No theft in Love so subtil, so secure,
'As to hide sin by seeming to be pure.
In short, thy *Silvio* loves: but 'tis not thee
(Sister) he loves.
  Am.   What Goddesse may she be? 2620
For certainly she is no mortall Dame
That could the heart of *Silvio* inflame.
  Cor. Nor Goddesse, nor yet Nymph.
  Am.   What hast thou said?
  Cor. Do'st thou know my *Lisetta*?
  Am.   Who? the Maid
That tends thy Flocks?
  Cor.   The same.
  Am.   It cannot be 2625
She, I am sure, *Corisca*?
  Cor.   Very she,
I can assure thee, she is all his joy.
  Am. A proper choice for one that was so coy.
  Cor. But wilt thou know how he doth pine away
And languish for this Jewell? Every day 2630
He feigns to go a hunting.
  Am.   Every morn
Soon as it dawns I hear his cursed horn.
  Cor. And just at noon, when others are i' th' heat
Of all the sport, he doth by stealth retreat
From his Companions, and comes all alone 2635
Unto my garden by a way unknown:
Where underneath a haw-thorn hedges shade
(Which doth the garden fence about) the Maid
Hears his hot sighs, and amorous pray'rs, which she
Comes laughing afterwards and tels to me. 2640
Now hear what I to serve thee've thought upon;
Or rather, what I have already done.
I think thou knowst, that *the same Law which hath*
Enjoyn'd the woman to observe her faith
To her betrothed, likewise doth enact, 2645
That if the woman catch him in the fact
Of falshood, spight of friends she may deny
To have him, and without disloyalty

Marry another.
    Am.   This I know full well;
And thereof some examples too could tell,   2650
Of my own knowledge; *Egle* having found
Licotas false, remain'd her self unbound.
Armilla did from false *Turingo* so,
And *Phillida* from *Ligurino* go.
    Cor. Now list' to me: My Maid (by me set on)   2655
Hath bid her credulous Lover meet anon
In yonder cave with her; whence he remains
The most contented of all living swains,
And waits but th' hour: there thou shalt catch him; where
I too will be witnesse of all to bear: 2660
(For without this our plot would be in vain.)
So without any hazard, or least stain
To thine, or to thy fathers honour, thou
Shalt free thy self from this distastefull vow.
    Am. I like it rarely: but the way, the way,   2665
Corisca?
    Cor.   Marry thus (observe me pray)
I' th' middle of the cave (which narrow is
And very long) upon the right hand lies
Another lesser Grot (I know not whether
By nature, or by art, or both together   2670
Made) in the hollow stone, whose slimie wall
Is hid with clinging Ivie, and a small
Hole in the roof lets light in from above,
(Fit receptacle for the thefts of Love,
Yet cheerfull too enough) there thou shalt hide   2675
Thy self, and hidden in that place abide
Till the two Lovers come; I mean to send
Lisetta first, and after her, her friend,
Following his steps my self aloof: And when
I shall perceive him stept into the den,   2680
Rush after him will I. But lest he should
Escape from me: when I have laid fast hold
Upon him, I will use *Lisetta*'s aid,
And joyning both (for so the plot is laid
Between us two) together we will make   2685

2674. receptacle] ed.; receptacles 47/48. *Italian is* '*ricetto*'.

A Cry, at which thou too shalt come, and take
The penalty o' th' law 'gainst *Silvio*.
Then my *Lisetta* and we two will go
Before the Priest; and so thou shalt unty
The Nuptiall knot.
    Am.   Before his Father?
    Cor.   Why?   2690
What matters that? Think'st thou *Montano*'s blood
Will stand in balance with his Countries good?
Or that his sacred function hee'l neglect
For any carnall or profane respect?
    Am. Go to then (setting all disputes aside)   2695
I wink, and follow thee my faithfull guide.
    Cor. Then linger not (my Heart) enter into
The Cave.
    Am.   Unto the Temple first I'le go
'T' adore the gods: For unlesse Heaven give
'Successe, no mortall enterprise can thrive.   2700
    Cor. 'To devout hearts all places Temples are:
It will lose too much time.
    Am.   'In using pray'r
'To them that made time, time cannot be lost. [*Exit.*]
    Cor. Go and return then quickly—. So almost
I'm past the bad way; onely this delay   2705
Gives me some cause of trouble; yet this may
Be of use too. Something there would be done
T' abuse my honest Lover *Coridon*.
I'le say, I'le meet him in the Cave, and so
Will make him after *Amarillis* go.   2710
This done, by a back way I'le thither send
The Priest of *Dian* her to apprehend:
Guilty she will be found, and sentenced
To death without all doubt. My Rivall dead,
Mirtillo is mine own: His cruelty   2715
To me being caus'd by's love to her. But see
The man! I'le sound him till she comes. Now rise,
Rise all my love into my tongue and eyes.

2703. *Exit*] ed.

SCENA SEXTA.
Mirtillo, Corsica.

Mir. Hear ye damn'd spirits that in hell lament,
Hear a new sort of pain and punishment.   2720
See in a Turtles look a Tigers minde!
She, crueller then death, 'cause she did find
One death would not suffice her bloody will,
And that to live was to be dying still,
Enjoyns me, not to make my self away,   2725
That I might die a thousand times a day.
    Cor. (I'le make as though I saw him not) I hear
A dolefull voice pierce my relenting ear,
Who should it be? *Mirtillo*, is it thou?
    Mir. I would it were my ghost.
    Cor.   Well, well: but how   2730
(And tell me true) thy self now dost thou find,
Since to thy dearest Nymph thou brak'st thy mind?
    Mir. As one who in a feaver cast,
Forbidden liquor long'd to taste,
If gotten, sets it to his mouth,   2735
And quenches life, but cannot drouth:
So I, with amorous feaver long
Consumed, from her eyes and tongue
Sweet poyson suck'd, which leaves me more
Enflamed then I was before.   2740
    Cor. 'Love upon us no power can have
'But what our selves (*Mirtillo*) gave.
'As a Bear doth with her tongue
'Polish her mishapen young
'Which had else in vain been born: 2745
'So an Am'rist giving form
'To a rude and faint desire
'That would otherwise expire,
'Hatches Love; which is at first
'Weak and raw, but when 'tis nurst,   2750
'Fierce and cruell. Take't upon
'My word, an old affection
'Tyrannizes in a brest,
'And grows a Master from a guest.

'For when the soul shall once be brought   2755
'To be fettred to one thought,
'And that, not have the pow'r to move
'A minute from its object, Love
'(Made for delight) will turn to sadness;
'And which is worse, to death or madness.   2760
'Therefore my advice shall be,
'To part thy love to two or three.
   Mir. Let death or madness me betide,
Rather then my Flame divide.
Amarillis (though she be   2765
Cruell and unkind to me)
Is my Life and Reason too,
And to her I will be true.
   Cor. Foolish Swain! that canst not tell
How to make a bargain well.   2770
What? change love for hatred? I
Rather now then do't would dye.
   Mir. 'Cruelty doth faith refine,
'As the fire the golden mine:
'Where were the loyaltie of Love,   2775
'If women should not tyrants prove?
In my many suffrings this
All my joy and comfort is,
Sorrows, tortures, exile, gall,
Here's a cause will sweeten all.   2780
Let me languish, let me burn,
Let me any thing but turn.
   Cor. O brave Lover! valiant brest!
More impetuous then a beast!
And yet tamer then a rock   2785
Which endures the Ocean's shock!
'In Lovers hearts there cannot be
'A worse disease then Constancie.
'O most unhappy those in whom
'This foolish Idol finds a room!   2790
'Which shackles us, when we might prove
'The sweet variety of Love.
With this dull vertue Constancie,
Tell me (simple Lover) why

Amarillis? For her face?   2795
Whom another must embrace?
Or do'st thou affect her mind,
Which to thee is not inclin'd?
All then thou canst doat upon
Is thine own destruction.   2800
And wilt thou be still so mad
To covet that cannot be had?
Up *Mirtillo*, know thy parts:
Canst thou want a thousand hearts?
Others I dare swear there be,   2805
That would sue as much to thee.
    Mir. To be *Amarillis* thrall
Is more then to command them all.
And if she my suit deny,
All that's pleasure I defie.   2810
I to make another choice?
In another I rejoyce?
Neither could I if I would,
Neither would I if I could:
But if possible to me   2815
Such a will or power be,
Heav'n and Love before that hour
Strip me of all will and pow'r.
    Cor. Thou art enchanted: otherwise
Couldst thou too thy self despise?   2820
    Mir. I must, when I'm despis'd by her
(*Corisca*).
    Cor. Come *Mirtillo*, ne're
Deceive thy self: perhaps thou dost suppose
Shee loves thee in her heart, although shee showes
An outward scorn. If thou but knewst what shee   2825
Talks oftentimes to me concerning thee.
    Mir. All these are trophies of my constant love,
With which I'le triumph o're the Pow'rs above,
And men below, my torments, and her hate,
O're Fortune and the world, o're Death and Fate.   2830
    Cor. (Wonder of Constancy! if this man knew
How much hee's lov'd by her, what would hee do?)
Mirtillo, how it pities me to hear

These frantick speeches! Tell me, wert thou e're
In love before?
   Mir.   Fair *Amarillis* was   2835
My first, and shall be my last Love.
   Cor.   Alas!
It should seem then that thou didst never prove
Any but cruell, but disdainful Love.
O that't had been thy chance but once to be
In love with one that's gentle, courteous, free!   2840
Try that a little: try it, and thou'lt finde
How sweet it is to meet with one that's kinde,
That loves and honours thee as much as thou
Thy sowre and cruell *Amarillis*; how
Delightful 'tis to have a joy as great   2845
As is thy love, a happinesse compleat
As thy own wish: to have thy Mistresse twine
About thy neck, and her sighs eccho thine:
And after say, My Joy, all that I have,
All that I am, and thy desires can crave,   2850
As thy devotion is: If I am fair,
For thee I'm fair; for thee I deck this hair,
This face, this bosome; from this brest of mine
I turn'd out my own heart to harbour thine.—
But this is a small river to that vast   2855
Sweet sea of pleasure which love makes us taste,
And they alone that taste can well relate.
   Mir. A thousand thousand times most fortunate
Is he that's born under so blest a star!
   Cor. Hear me *Mirtillo*: (ere I was aware   2860
I'd almost call'd him mine) a Nymph as fair
As the proud'st she that curls or spreads to th' air
Her golden tresses, worthy of thy love
As thou of hers, the honour of this Grove,
Love of all hearts; by every worthier swain   2865
In vain sollicited, ador'd in vain,
Doth love thee onely, and thee onely prize
More then her life, and more then her own eyes.
Mirtillo, scorn her not, if wise thou be;
For as the shadow doth the body, she   2870
Will follow thee through all the world: she will

At thy least word and beck be ready still
As thy obedient hand-maid: night and day
With thee shee'll passe the tedious hours away.
Ah! do not wave (*Mirtillo*) do not wave   2875
So rare a blisse; the perfect'st joyes we have
Are those which neither sighs nor tears do cost,
Nor danger, and on which least time is lost.
Here thou hast passe-time at thy door, a feast
Upon the table alwayes ready drest   2880
To please thy taste. Ay me! canst thou receive
A greater gift then this? *Mirtillo*, Leave,
Leave this cold hunting after flying feet,
And her that runs to thy embraces, meet.
Nor do I feed thee with vain hopes; command   2885
Her come, and she that loves thee is at hand,
Now, if thou say the word.
   Mir.   I prethee rest
Content, my pallat is not for a feast.
   Cor. Try but what joy is made of once, and then
Return unto thy wonted grief agen,   2890
That thou maist say, thou hadst a taste of both.
   Mir. 'Distemper'd palats all sweet things do loath.
   Cor. Yet do't in pitie unto her that dyes,
Unless sh' enjoy the sun of thy fair eyes.
Uncharitable youth, art not thou poor?   2895
And canst thou beat a beggar from thy door?
Ah! what thou wouldst another should extend
To thee, do thou now to another lend.
   Mir. What alms can beggers give? In short, I swore
Allegeance to that Nymph whom I adore,   2900
Whether she tyrant prov'd, or mercifull.
   Cor. O truly blind, and most unhappy, dull
Mirtillo! who is't thou art constant to?
I am unwilling to add woe to woe;
But thou art too much wrong'd i' faith, and I   2905
That love thee am not able to stand by
And see thee so betraid. If thou suppose
This crueltie of *Amarillis* growes
From zeal to vertue or Religion,
Th' art gull'd: another doth possesse the throne,   2910

And thou (poor wretch!) whilst he doth laugh, must cry.
What, stricken dumb?
    Mir.   I'm in an ecstasie,
'Twixt life and death suspended, till I know
Whether I should believe thee now or no.
    Cor. Do'st not believe me then?
    Mir.   If I did, I   2915
Had not surviv'd it sure: and I will dye
Yet, if it be a truth.
    Cor.   Live (Caitiffe) live
To be reveng'd.
    Mir.   But I cannot believe
It is a truth.
    Cor.   Wilt thou not yet believe,
But force me to tell that which it will grieve   2920
Thy soul to hear? Do'st thou see yonder cave?
That is thy Mistresse Faith's and Honour's grave:
There laughs sh' at thee, there makes of thy anoy
A poynant sawce to thy tir'd Rivals joy.
In short; there oft a base-born shepherd warms   2925
Thy vertuous *Amarillis* in his arms.
Now go and sigh, and whine, and constant prove
Unto a Nymph that thus rewards thy love.
    Mir. Ay me *Corisca*! do'st thou tell me true?
And is it fit I should believe thee too?   2930
    Cor. The more thou searchest, 'twill the worser be.
    Mir. But didst thou see't *Corisca*? wo is me!
    Cor. Truth is, I did not see it, but thou mayst,
And presently, for she her word hath past
To meet him there this very hour: But hide   2935
Thy self beneath that shady hedges side,
And thou thy self shalt see her straight descend
Into the cave, and after her, her friend.
    Mir. So quickly must I dye?
    Cor.   See! I have spi'd
Her coming down already by the side   2940
O' th' Temple: mark! how guiltily she moves!
Her stealing pace betraying their stoln loves.
To mark the sequell, do thou here remain,
And afterwards we two will meet again.

Mir. Since the discovery of the truth's so neer,   2945
With my belief I will my death defer.

SCENA SEPTIMA.

Amarillis.

'No mortall work successfully is done
'Which with th' immortall gods is not begun.
Full of distractions, and with heavie heart
I did from hence unto the Temple part: 2950
Whence (Heaven be prais'd) I come as light as air,
And strangely comforted: for at my pray'r
Pure and devout, I felt from thence, (me thought)
Another soul into my body shot,
Which whisper'd, Fear not *Amarillis*, go   2955
Securely on. I, and I will do so,
Heav'n guiding.—Fair Mother of Love, befriend
Her that on thee for succour doth depend:
Thou that as Queen in the third Orb do'st shine,
If e're thou felt'st thy Son's flames, pitie mine.   2960
Bring (courteous Goddesse) by a secret path
Quickly that youth to whom I've pawn'd my faith.
And thou deer cave, till I have done my work,
Suffer this slave of Love in thee to lurk.
But *Amarillis*, all the coast is cleer,   2965
None nigh to see thee, and none nigh to hear;
Securely enter. O *Mirtillo*, O
Mirtillo, if thou dream'dst wherefore I go!—

SCENA OCTAVA.

Mirtillo.

I wake, and see, what I could wish t' have been
Born without eyes, that I might not have seen: 2970
Or rather not to have been born. Curst Fate!
Why hast thou thus prolonged my lifes date,
To bring me to this killing spectacle?
Mirtillo, more tormented then in hell
The blackest soul is, not to doubt thy grief?   2975
Not to be able to suspend beleif?

Thou, thou hast heard and seen't: thy Mistresse is
Another man's. And (which is worse) not his
Whose by the world's Lawes she was bound to be,
But by Love's Lawes snatcht both from him and thee.   2980
O cruell *Amarillis*! to undo
This wretched man, and then to mock him too
With that unconstant mouth which once did meet,
And once did call *Mirtillo*'s kisses sweet:
But now his loathed name (which haply rose   2985
Like bitter drink that 'gainst the stomack goes)
Because it should not bitternesse impart
To thy delight, hath spu'd out of thy heart?
Since therefore she who gave thee life, hath ta'ne
That life away, and given it again   2990
T' another: why do'st thou thy life survive,
Wretched *Mirtillo*? Why art thou alive?
   Dye, dye *Mirtillo* unto grief and smart,
As unto joy already dead thou art.
Dye, dead *Mirtillo*; since thy life is so,   2995
Let thy pangs likewise be concluded. Go
Out of the anguish of this death, which still
Keeps thee alive, that it may longer kill.
But shall I dye then unrevenged? Sure
I'le slay him first that did my death procure.   3000
I will dispense with my dire love of death
Till I have justly ta'ne away his breath
Who slew my heart unjustly. Yeeld stout grief
To anger, death to life, till in my life
I have aveng'd my death.   3005
Let not this steel be drunken with the flood
Of its own Master's unrevenged blood:
Nor this right hand be Pitie's, till it hath
First made it self the Minister of wrath.
Thou that enjoy'st my spoyls (what ere thou be)   3010
Since I must fall, I'le pull thee after me.
In the same brake I'le plant my self agen;
And when I spie him coming to the den,
Will rush upon him with this piercing dart
At unawares, and strike him through the heart.   3015

3013. spie] 47/48, 64; see 76/92.

But is't not base to strike him out of sight?
It is: defie him then to single fight,
Where valour may my justice prove. But no:
This place is unto all so known, and so
Frequented, that some swains may interpose: 3020
Or (which is worse) enquire of me whence grows
Our quarrell; which if I deny, 'tis naught
They'l think; if feign a cause, I may be caught
Then in a lie; if tell't, her name will be
Blasted with everlasting infamie: 3025
In whom, although I never can approve
That which I see, yet I must ever love
That which I fanci'd, and did hope t' have seen,
And that which ought (I'm sure) in her t' have been.
Dye basely then the base Adulterer,   3030
Who hath slain me, and hath dishonour'd her.
I, but the blood may (if I kill him here)
The murther show, and that the Murtherer?
What do I care? I, but the murth'rer known,
Bewrays the cause for which the murther 's done.   3035
So this ungratefull woman runs the same
Hazard this way of shipwrak in her fame.
Enter the cave then, and assault him there.
Good, good; tread softly, softly, lest she hear:
That she's at th' other end her words imply'd.   3040
Now (hid with branches) in the Rock's left side
There is a hollow at the steep stairs foot,
There without any noyse, I'le wait to put
In execution my designe. My foe
Dispatch'd, his bleeding carcasse I will throw   3045
To my she-foe, to be reveng'd on two
At once. The self-same steel I'le then imbrue
In mine own blood: so three shall die in brief,
Two by my weapon, and the third of grief.
A sad and miserable tragedie   3050
Of both her lovers shall this Tigresse see,
Of him she loves, and him she scorns. And this
Cave which was meant the chamber of their blisse,
To her and to her minion shall become
And (which I more desire) t' her shame, a tombe.   3055

But you dear footsteps (which I long have trac'd
In vain) unerring path, lead me at last
To where my Love is hid; To you I bow,
Your print I follow. O *Corisca*! now
I doe beleeve thee: now th' hast told me true.   3060

SCENA NONA.

Satyr.

Does he believe *Corisca*? and pursue
Her steps to *Erycina*'s Cave? a beast
Hath wit enough to apprehend the rest.
But if thou dost believe her, thou hadst need
Have from her good security indeed,   3065
And hold her by a stronger tie then I
Had lately of her hair. But stronger tie
On her there cannot be then gifts. This bold
Strumpet her self to this young swain hath sold.
And here, by the false light now of this vaut   3070
Delivers the bad ware which he hath bought.
Or rather, 'tis Heav'ns justice which hath sent
Her hither to receive her punishment
From my revenging hands. His words did seem
T' imply she made some promise unto him,   3075
Which he believ'd: and by his spying here
Her print, that she is in the cave, 'tis cleer.
Do a brave thing then: stop the mouth o' th' cave
With that great hanging stone, that they may have
No means of scaping; to the Priest then go,   3080
And bring by the back-way (which few do know)
His ministers to apprehend, and by
The Law deservedly to make her dye.
For 'tis not unto me long since unknown,
That she contracted is to *Coridon*,   3085
How-ever he (because he stands in fear
Of me) to lay his claim to her forbear.
But now I'le give him leave at once to be
Reveng'd on her both for him self and me.
But I lose time in talk. From this young Grove   3090
I'le pull a tree up by the root, to move

The stone withall. So, this I think will do.
How heavie 'tis! The stone hath a root too.
What if I min'd it with this trunk? and so,
As with a leaver heav'd it from below? 3095
Good, good; now to the other side as much.
How fast it sticks? I did not think it such
A difficult attempt as it hath prov'd;
The Center of the earth were easier mov'd.
Nor strength, nor skill will do this work, I see: 3100
Or do's that vigour which was once in me
Now fail me at my need? What do ye do
My perverse Stars? I will, (in spight of you)
I will remove it yet. The Divell haule
Corisca, (I had almost said) and all 3105
The sex of them. O *Pan Liceus*, hear,
And to move this, be moved by my pray'r!
Pan, thou that all things canst, and all things art,
Thou once thy self didst woe a stubborn heart,
Revenge on false *Corisca* now, thine own, 3110
And my despised Love. I move the stone
Thus by the vertue of thy sacred name;
Thus rowls it by the vertue of the same.
So, now the Fox is trapt, and finely shut
Where she had earth'd her self. I'le now go put 3115
Fire to the hole; where I could wish to find
The rest of women, to destroy *the kind*.

CHORUS.

O Love! how potent and how great thou art!
Wonder of nature and the world! What heart
So dull, as not to feel thy pow'r? What wit 3120
So deep and piercing, as to fathom it?
Who knows thy hot lascivious fires; will say,
Infernall spirit, thou dost live and sway
In the corporeall part. But who so knowes
How thou dost men to vertuous things dispose, 3125
And how the dying flame of loose desires
Looks pale, and trembles at thy chaster fires;
Will say, Immortall God, i' th' soul alone

3100. work, I] ed.; work I, 47/48.

Thou hast established thy sacred Throne.
'Rare Monster! wonderfully got betwixt   3130
'Desire and Reason; an affection mixt
'Of sense and intellect: With knowing wilde:
'With seeing blinde: A God, and yet a childe:
And (such) thou sway'st the Earth and Heaven too;
On which thou tread'st as we on t' other do.   3135
Yet (by thy leave) a greater miracle,
A mightier thing then thou art I can tell.
For all thou do'st (that may our wonder claim)
Thou dost by vertue of a womans name.
Woman! the gift of heav'n; or of Him rather   3140
Who made thee fairer, being of both the Father,
Wherein is Heav'n so beautifull as thou?
That rowls one goggle eye in its vast brow
(Like a grim Cyclop) *not a lamp of light,*
But cause of blindnesse and Cymerian night   3145
To the bold gazer: if that speak, it is
A thundring voice; and if it sigh, the hisse
Of earth-engendred windes. Thou, with the fair
Angel-like prospect of two Suns, which are
Serene and visible, doest still the windes   3150
And calm the Billows of tempestuous mindes;
And Sound, Light, Motion, Beauty, Majesty,
Make in thy face so sweet a harmony,
That heav'n (I mean this outward heav'n) must needs
Confesse thy form the form of that exceeds: 3155
Since beauty that is dead lesse noble is
Then that which lives, and is a place of blisse.
With reason therefore man (that gallant creature,
That lords it over all the works of Nature)
To thee as Lady Paramount payes duty,   3160
Acknowledging in thine, thy Makers beauty.
And if hee Triumphs gain, and Thrones inherit,
It is not because thou hast lesse of merit;
But for thy glory: since a greater thing
It is to conquer, then to be a King.   3165
But that thy conqu'ring beauty doth subdue

3140. *Him*] ed.; *him* 47/48, 64, 76/92.   3148. *Of*] 47/48 (c); *of* 47/48 (u).
3161. *Acknowledging*] 64, 76/92; *Acknowleding* 47/48.

Not onely man, but ev'n his Reason too,
If any doubt, hee in Mirtillo *hath*
A miracle that may constrain his faith:
This wanted (Woman) to thy pow'r before   3170
To make us love *when we can* hope *no more.*

ACTUS QUARTUS.

SCENA PRIMA.

Corisca.

My heart and thoughts till now were so much set
To train that foolish Nymph into my net,
That my dear Hair (which by that Rogue was ta'ne
From me) and how to get it back again   3175
I quite forgot: O how it troubled me
To pay that ransome for my liberty!
But't had been worse t' have been a prisoner
To such a beast: Who though he doth not bear
A mouses heart, might have mouz'd me: For I   3180
Have (to say truth) fool'd him sufficiently:
And like a Horse-leech did him suck and drein
As long as he had blood in any vein.
And now hee's mov'd I love him not; and mov'd
He well might be, if him I e're had lov'd.   3185
How can one love a creature that doth want
All that is lovely? As a stinking plant
Which the Physitian gather'd for the use
He had of it; when he hath strain'd the juice
And vertue out, is on the dunghill thrown;   3190
So having squeez'd him, I with him have done.
Now will I see if *Coridon* into
The cave's descended. Hah! what do I view?
Wake I? or sleep I? or am drunk? but now
This cave's mouth open was I'm sure; then how   3195
Comes it now shut? and with a ponderous
And massie stone rowl'd down upon it thus?
Earth-quake I'm sure t' unhenge it there was none.
Would I knew certainly that *Coridon*

And *Amarillis* were within; and then   3200
I car'd not how it came. Hee's in the den,
If (as *Lisetta* said) he parted were
From home so long ago. Both may be there,
And by *Mirtillo* shut together. 'Love,
'Prickt with disdain, hath strength enough to move   3205
'The world, much more a stone. Should it be true,
Mirtillo could not have deviz'd to doe
Ought more according to my heart then this,
Though he *Corisca* had enthron'd in his
In stead of *Amarillis*. I will goe   3210
The back way in, that I the truth may know.

SCENA SECUNDA.

Dorinda, Linco.

Dor. But *Linco*, didst not thou know me indeed?
Lin. Who could have known thee in this savage weed
For meek *Dorinda*? But if I had been
A ravenous hound (as I am *Linco*) then   3215
I to thy cost had known thee for a beast.
What do I see? What do I see?
    Dor.   Thou seest
A sad effect of Love; a sad and strange
Effect of loving (*Linco.*)
    Lin.   Wondrous change!
Thou a young Maid, so soft, so delicate,   3220
That wert (me thinks) an infant but of late,
Whom in mine arms I bore (as I may say)
A very little childe but yesterday,
And steering thy weak steps, taught thee to name
(When I thy Father serv'd) Daddy and Mam,   3225
Who like a tim'rous Doe (before thy heart
Was made a prey t' insulting Love) didst start
At every thing that on the sudden stirr'd,
At every winde, at every little bird
That shook a bough, each Lizard that but ran   3230
Out of a bush, made thee look pale and wan;
Now all alone o're hils, through woods do'st passe
Fearlesse of hounds or savage beasts.

Dor.   Alas!
'She whom Love wounds no other wound doth fear.
   Lin. Indeed fair Nymph, Love shew'd his godhead here,   3235
From woman to a man transforming thee,
Or rather to a wolf.
   Dor.   If thou couldst see
Into my brest (O *Linco*!) then thou'dst say,
A living wolf upon my heart doth prey
As on a harmlesse lamb.
   Lin.   Is *Silvio*   3240
That wolf?
   Dor.   Alas, who else can be't?
   Lin.   And so
'Cause he's a wolf, thou a shee-wolf wouldst be,
To try, since on thy humane visage he
Was not enamour'd, if he would at least
Affect thee in the likenesse of a beast,   3245
As being of his kind. But prethee where
Gotst thou these robes?
   Dor.   I'le tell thee: I did hear
Silvio would chase to day the noble Bore
At Erimanthus foot; and there before
The morning peept, was I from wood to wood   3250
Hunting the Hunter; by a crystall flood
From which our flocks did climb the hils, I found
Melampo the most beauteous *Silvio*'s hound,
Who having quench'd his thirst there as I ghesse,
Lay to repose him on the neighb'ring grasse.   3255
I, who love any thing that's *Silvio*'s,
Even the very ground on which he goes,
And shadow which his beauteous limbs do cast;
Much more the dog on which his love is plac't,
Stooping, laid sudden hold on him, who came   3260
Along with me as gentle as a lamb.
And whilst 'twas in my thoughts to lead him back
Unto his Lord and mine, hoping to make
A friend of him with what he held so deer,
He came himself to seek him, and stopt here.   3265
Deer *Linco*, I'le not lose thee so much time,

3261. gentle] 47/48 (*c*), gently 47/48 (*u*).

As to tell all that's past 'twixt me and him;
This onely, to be brief, After a long
Preface of oathes on one another strung,
And treach'rous promises, this cruell swain   3270
Flung from me full of Anger and disdain,
Both with his own *Melampo* (to his Lord
So true) and with my deer and sweet reward.
    Lin. O cruell *Silvio*! ruthlesse swain! But what
Didst thou do then (*Dorinda*?) didst thou not   3275
Hate him for this?
    Dor.   Rather (as if the fire
Of his disdain Loves fire had been) his ire
Increast my former flame. His steps I trace,
And thus pursuing him towards the chace,
I met (hard by) with my *Lupino*, whom   3280
Before a little I had parted from.
When straight it came into my head, that I
In his attire, and in the company
Of Shepherds might be thought a shepherd too,
And undiscover'd my fair *Silvio* view.   3285
    Lin. In a wolves likenesse amongst hounds? and none
Bite thee? 'Tis much (*Dorinda*) thou hast done.
    Dor. This (*Linco*) was no miracle: for they
Durst not touch her who was their Masters prey.
There I, out of the tents, amidst the crue   3290
Of neighb'ring shepherds that were met to view
The famous passe-time, stood admiring more
To see the Huntsman, then the hunted Bore:
At every motion of the furious beast,
My cold heart shiv'red in my brest: 3295
At every action of the brave young man
My soul with all her touch'd affections ran
In to his aid. But my extreme delight
Again was poyson'd with the horrid sight
Of the fierce Bore, whose strength and vast   3300
Proportion, all proportion past.
As an impetuous whirlwind in a great
And sudden storm, which all that it doth meet

3274. ruthlesse] 47/48; ruthful 64, 76/92.   3290. the crue] 47/48; a crue 64,
76/92.

(Houses, and trees, and stones) before it bears,
All it can get within its circle tears   3305
To pieces in an instant: so the Bore
Wheeling about (his tusks all foam and gore)
Pil'd in one heap dogs slain, spears knapt, men wounded.
How oft did I desire to have compounded
For *Silvio*'s life, with the inraged Swine!   3310
And for his blood, t' have giv'n the Monster mine!
How oft was I about to run between,
And with my body his fair body screen!
Spare cruell Bore, (how often did I cry!)
Spare my fair *Silvio*'s brest of Ivory;   3315
Thus to my self I spake, and sigh'd, and pray'd;
When his fierce dog (arm'd with a brest-plate made
Of hard and scaly barks of trees) he slipt
After the beast, now prouder, being dipt
Throughly in blood, and lifted from the ground   3320
On slaughter'd trunks. The valour of that hound
(*Linco*) exceeds beliefe: and *Silvio*
Not without reason surely loves him so.
As a chaft Lion, which now meets, now turns
From an untamed Buls well brandish'd horns,   3325
If once he come with his strong paw to seize
Upon his shoulder, masters him with ease:
So bold *Melampo* shunning with fine slights
The Bores short turns, and rapid motion, lights
At length upon his ear; which having bit   3330
Quite through, and lugg'd him twice or thrice by it,
He with his teeth so naild him to the ground,
That at his vast bulk now a mortall wound
Might levell'd be with greater certainty,
(Before but slightly hurt) then suddenly   3335
My lovely *Silvio* (calling on the name
Of *Dian*) Goddesse do thou give me aim
(Quoth he) the horrid head is thine. This sed,
His golden Quiver's swiftest shaft to th' head
He drew; which flying to that very point   3340
Where the left shoulder knits with the neck joint,
There wounded the fierce Bore, so down he fell.
Then I took breath, seeing my *Silvio* well,

And out of danger. Happy beast! to die
So sweet a death, as by that hand, which I   3345
Would beg my end from.
    Lin.   But what then became
Of the slain beast?
    Dor.   I know not; for I came
Away, for fear of being known; but, I
Suppose, the head to th' Temple solemnly
They'l bear, according to my *Silvio*'s vow.   3350
    Lin. But wilt thou not get out of these weeds now?
    Dor. Yes: but my garments with my other geer
Lupino has, who promis'd to stay here
With them, but fails. Dear *Linco*, if thou love
Me, seek him for me up and down this grove: 3355
Far off he cannot be; mean while I'le take
A little rest (dost see there?) in that Brake;
There I'le expect thee; for I am ore-come
With wearinesse and sleep, and will not home
Accoutred thus.
    Lin.   I go: but stir not then   3360
Out of that place till I return agen.

SCENA TERTIA.
Chorus, Ergasto.

    Cho. Have ye heard Shepherds that our Demy-God
(*Montano*'s and *Alcides* worthy blood)
This day hath freed us from that dreadfull beast
Which all Arcadia lately did infest?   3365
And that he is preparing himself now
I' th' Temple for it to perform his vow?
If for so great a benefit wee'd show
Our gratitude, to meet him let us go,
And joyn our tongues and hearts together there,   3370
To honour him as our Deliverer.
'Which honour, though it be reward too small
'For such a fair and valiant soul; 'tis all
'Vertue can have on earth.
    Erg.   O sad disaster!
O bitter chance! O wound that hath no plaister!   3375

O day to be for ever steep'd in tears!
  Cho. What dolefull voice is this that strikes our ears?
  Erg. Starres, that are enemies to man alwayes,
Why do you mock our faith? why do you raise
Our hope on high, that when it falls again   3380
The precipice may be with greater pain?
  Cho. Ergasto by his voice; and it is hee.
  Erg. But why do I accuse Heav'n wrongfully?
Accuse thy self *Ergasto*: Thou alone,
Thou, thou against the steel didst knock the stone;   3385
Thou layd'st the match unto the tinder; whence
A flame unquenchable is kindled since.
But Heav'n doth know, I for the best did do it,
And pitie onely did induce me to it.
O ill starr'd Lovers! wretched *Titiro*!   3390
Poor *Amarillis*! childlesse Father! O
Mourning *Montano*! O Arcadia gone
In a consumption far! and we undone!
In short, most sad, all I have seen! or see!
Or speak! or hear! or think!
  Cho.   What may this be   3395
(Alas!) that in one accident alone
Includes a generall desolation?
This way hee bends his course, let us go meet
Him (swains).
  Erg.   Eternall Gods! is it not yet
Time to abate your wrath?
  Cho.   Unfold to us   3400
(Courteous *Ergasto*) what afflicts thee thus.
What dost thou moane?
  Erg.   Your ruine and mine own:
The ruine of Arcadia I moane.
  Cho. Alas! why so?
  Erg.   The very staffe, the stay
Of all our hope is broke, is pull'd away.   3405
  Cho. Speak plainer.
  Erg.   *Titiro*'s daughter, that sole prop
Of her old House, and Father, the sole hope
Of our deliverance, promis'd here below,

3387. kindled] 47/48, 76/92; kindlest 64.

Above decreed to marry *Silvio*,
As th' onely means that should Arcadia save;   3410
That Heav'nly Maid, so sober, and so grave,
That President of honour (crown'd with Lillies
Of chastitie) that peerlesse *Amarillis*;
Shee, she (alas! I have no heart, no breath
To tell it you).
    Cho.   Is dead?
    Erg.   Is neer her death.   3415
    Cho. Alas! what have we heard?
    Erg.   Nothing as yet:
She dies a malefactresse: That, That's it.
    Cho. A malefactresse *Amarillis*? how
Ergasto?
    Erg. Caught with an Adult'rer now.
And, if ye stay a little longer here,   3420
Led pinion'd to the Temple ye shall see her.
    Cho. 'O female structures, glorious and most fair,
'But weak withall! O chastitie, how rare
Art thou! and shall it then be truly taxt,
No woman's chast but shee that ne're was akst?   3425
    Erg. Indeed, when she that's vertue's self doth fall,
We well may doubt the vertue of them all.
    Cho. Pray, if it will not too much trouble be,
Tell the whole story to these swains and me.
    Erg. I will: The Priest early today (ye know)   3430
Did with this wretched Nymph's sad Father go
Unto the sacred Temple; with one care
Both moved, to facilitate with pray'r
Their childrens desired marriage. For this end
At once their incense did to heav'n ascend,   3435
At once their offrings bled, their sacrifice
At once was done with due solemnities,
And such glad auspice, that no entrails e're
Were fairer seen, no flame was more sincere,
And lesse ecclips'd with smoke: mov'd with such signes,   3440
Thus the blind prophet speaks, and thus divines;
This day (Montano) *shall thy* Silvio *love:*
Thy Daughter (Titiro) *a wife shall prove:*
Go and prepare the Marriage. O absurd,

And vain depending on an Augur's word!   3445
And thou as blind in soul, as in thy eyes!
If thou hadst said, *Prepare her Obsequies,*
Then a true Prophet thou hadst prov'd indeed.
Yet all the standers by were comforted,
And the old Fathers wept for joy apace,   3450
And *Titiro* was parted from the place.
When in the Temple suddenly were heard
Sinister omens, and dire signes appear'd
Boading Heav'ns wrath. At which (alas!) if each
Stood there astonisht and bereft of speech   3455
After so fair beginnings, Friends, judge you.
Mean while the Priests themselves alone withdrew
Into an inner room: and whilst they there
And we without intent in praying were,
Devout and weeping; puffing through the presse   3460
The cursed *Satyr* (loe!) demands accesse
Unto the Priests. I (Porter of that place)
Admit him: Hee then (O he has a face
To bring ill news!) cry'd; Fathers, if your Pray'r
Find not the Gods, your vows and incense are   3465
Not acceptable, and your sacrifice;
If from your altars an impure flame rise,
Think it not strange, that likewise is impure
Which is committing now hard by your door,
In *Ericina*'s cave: a false Nymph there   3470
Is breaking with a base adulterer
Your lawes, and her own faith. Send with me now
Your Ministers, and I will shew them how
I' th' act to take 'em. Then (O humane mind,
When thy Fate's neer, how dull thou art! how blind!)   3475
The good Priests breath'd: supposing 'twas no more
But remove them, and Heaven would as before
Look on their sacrifice beni'nely. There-
Upon they order their chief Minister
Nicandro presently to take that guide,   3480
And bring both Lovers to the Temple ty'd:
With all his under-ministers he goes,
Pursuing that vile *Satyr* through a close

3461. cursed] ed.; curled 47/48. *Italian is 'malvagio'.*

And crooked way into the cave. The Maid,
Strook with their torches sudden light, assay'd 3485
From where she was to run out of the door,
Which that base dog had stopt (it seems) before.
　Cho. And what did he the while?
　Erg.　　　　　　　　　He went his waies
When he had led *Nicandro* to the place.
But (friends) I cannot tell the generall 3490
Astonishment that fell upon us all,
When it the Daughter prov'd of *Titiro*:
Who taken, in a trice (I do not know
Out of what place) forth bold *Mirtillo* flew,
And a sharp dart which he was arm'd with threw 3495
Like lightning at *Nicandro*: which, if it
The place that it was aimed at had hit,
Had sent him to the shades: But (whether I
May call it Fortune, or agility)
At the same instant the one aim'd his blow, 3500
The other stept a little backward; so
The mortall steel past by, leaving his brest
Untoucht, and in his coat of skins did rest,
Into the which (I know not how) 'twas wove
So intricately, that *Mirtillo* strove 3505
In vain to pull it out; and so he too
Was taken.
　Cho.　　And with him what did they do?
　Erg. He to the Temple by himself was brought.
　Cho. For what?
　Erg.　　　　　　To try if he'd discover ought
Touching the fact in question. Perhaps too 3510
Th' affront he in their Minister did do
Unto the priestly majesty might some
Penance deserve. Would yet I might have come
To comfort my poor friend!
　Cho.　　　　　　　What hindred thee?
　Erg. The waiters at the altar may not be 3515
Admitted to delinquents: therefore I
Sequesterd from the other company,
Go by my self unto the Temple; where
With many a prayer and devouter tear

I'le beg of Heaven that it would chase away   3520
This sullen storm that overclouds our day.
Deer Shepherds rest in peace, and joyn with ours
Your pray'rs, to batter the celestiall towers.
   Cho. We will, when we have paid to *Silvio*
That duty first we to his goodnesse owe.   3525
O ye great Gods! now, now, if ever, prove
Your *anger* lesse eternall then your *love.*

SCENA QUARTA.
Corisca.

Empale ye triumph-decking Lawrell boughs,
Empale my glorious and victorious brows.
Into Love's lists (hedg'd round about with flame)   3530
This day *I came, I saw, I overcame*:
This day hath Heav'n and Earth, Nature and Art,
Fortune and Fate, Friend and Foe ta'ne my part.
Ev'n that base *Satyr* who abhorres me so
Hath helpt me too, as if he too did go   3535
Some share with me. How much more happily
Did fortune bring *Mirtillo* in, then I
Contriv'd to have brought *Coridon*? to make
Her crime more show of likelihood to take?
And though *Mirtillo*'s apprehended too,   3540
That matters not; they soon will let him go:
Th' Adultresse onely payes the penaltie.
O famous triumph! Solemn victorie!
If lying may deserve a trophie, I
Deserve a trophie for my amorous lye;   3545
Which from this tongue and bosome hath done more
For me then Love with all his charms before.
But this is not a time to talk: Withdraw
Thy self *Corisca*, till the doom of Law
Fall on thy Rivals head, for fear that she   3550
T' excuse her self, should lay the blame on thee.
Or that the Priest himself should wish to know
What thou canst say, before he give the blow.
'When a mine springs, 'tis good to stand aloof;
'A lying tongue requires a flying hoof.   3555
I'le hide me in those woods, and there will make

Some stay, till it be time to come and take
Possession of my joyes. O! it hath hit
Beyond all thought. Successe hath crown'd my wit.

SCENA QUINTA.

Nicandro, Amarillis.

Nic. A Heart of flint, or rather none had he   3560
Nor human sense, that could not pitie thee,
Unhappy Nymph! and for thy sorrow grieve
The more, by how much lesse they can believe
This should befall thee, who have known thee best.
For were it but to see a Maid distrest   3565
Of venerable count'nance, and that show'd
So vertuous and so excellently good;
One that for heav'nly beauty merited
Temples and Sacrifices, to be led
Unto the Temple as a Sacrifice,   3570
Who could behold it without melting eyes?
But he that should consider further, how,
And for what purpose thou wert born; That thou
Art Daughter unto *Titiro*, and shoud
Have married been unto *Montano*'s bloud,   3575
(Two the most lov'd and honour'd shall I say
Shepherds, or Fathers of Arcadia?)
And that being such, so great, so famous, and
So beautifull a Nymph, and that did stand
By nature so remote from thy death's brink,   3580
Thou shouldst be now condemn'd. He that doth think
On this and weeps not, wails not thy mishap,
Is not a man, but wolf in humane shape.
    Am. If my mishap had come through mine own fault,
And the effect had been of an ill thought   3585
As of a deed that seems ill, it had been
Lesse grievous to mee to have death pay sinne;
And very just it were I should have spilt
My bloud to wash my impure soul from guilt,
To quench Heav'ns wrath; and since man too had wrong,   3590
Pay what to human justice did belong:
So might I still a crying conscience,

And mortifi'd with a due inward sense
Of deserv'd death, render my self more fit
To die, and through that purgatory get   3595
Perchance to Paradise. But now in all
My pride of youth and fortune thus to fall,
Thus innocent, is a sad case, a sad—
Nicandro.
 Nic. Nymph, would to Heav'n men had
Sinn'd against thee, rather then thou 'gainst Heav'n.   3600
For satisfaction might be easier giv'n
To thee for thy wrong'd Fame, then unto it
For its wrong'd Deities. Nor know I yet
Who wrong'd thee but thy self. Wert thou not caught
Alone with the adult'rer in a vault?   3605
To *Silvio* precontracted wert not thou?
And so thy nuptiall faith hast broken? How
Then innocent?
 Am. For all this have not I
Transgrest the Law: and innocently dye.
 Nic. Not Natures law perchance, *Love where thou wilt.*   3610
But that of Men and Heav'n, *Love without guilt.*
 Am. Both men and Heav'n (if all our fortune be
Deriv'd from thence) transgrest have against me.
For what but an ill destiny could bid
That I should die for what another did?   3615
 Nic. What was that Nymph? bridle thy tongue (with high-
Flown grief transported ev'n to blasphemie).
'The ils we suffer our own sins pull down:
'Heav'n pardons many wrongs, but it doth none.
 Am. I blame in Heaven onely my own starre: 3620
But one that hath deceiv'd me, more by farre.
 Nic. Then blame thy self, thy self thou didst deceive.
 Am. I did when I a coz'ner did believe.
 Nic. 'They who desire to be deceiv'd, are not.
 Am. Dost think me naught?
 Nic.   Nay ask thy actions that.   3625
 Am. 'Actions are oft false comments on our hearts.
 Nic. 'Yet those we see, and not the inward parts.
 Am. 'The heart may be seen too with th' eys o' th' mind.
 Nic. 'Without the senses help those eyes are blind.

Am. 'The senses must submit to reasons sway.   3630
Nic. 'Reason in point of fact must sense obay.
Am. Well; I am sure an honest heart I have.
Nic. Prethee who brought thee then into the cave?
Am. My folly and too much credulity.
Nic. Thou trustedst with a friend thy honesty?   3635
Am. I trusted a friends honestie.
Nic.   Thy blood?
Was that the friend thou wouldst have understood?
Am. Ormino's Sister, who betraid me thither.
Nic. "Tis sweet when Lovers are betraid together.
Am. Mirtillo enterd without my consent.   3640
Nic. How enter'dst thou then? and for what intent?
Am. Let this suffice, 'twas not for him I came.
Nic. It cannot, if no other cause thou name.
Am. Examine him about my innocence.
Nic. Him? who hath been the cause of thy offence?   3645
Am. Call her to witnesse who betraid me hath.
Nic. Why should we hear a witnesse without faith?
Am. By chast *Diana*'s dreadfull name I swear.
Nic. Thou by thy deeds art perjur'd unto her.
Nymph, I am plain, I cannot flatter thee   3650
Into a hope which in extremitie
Will leave thee more confounded; these are dreams:
'A troubled fountain cannot yeeld pure streams,
'Nor a bad heart good words. And where the deed
'Is evident, Defence offence doth breed.   3655
What dost thou talk? thou shouldst have guarded more
Then thy life now, thy chastitie before.
Why do'st thou cheat thy self?
Am.   O miserie!
Must I then dye, *Nicandro*? must I dye?
None left to hear? none to defend me left?   3660
Of all abandon'd? of all hope bereft?
Onely of such a mocking pity made
The wretched object as affords no aid?
Nic. Be patient Nymph, and give me cause to tell,
Though thou didst ill, yet that thou suffredst well.   3665
Look up to heav'n, since thence thou drawst thy birth;
'All good or ill we meet with upon earth

'From thence as from a fountain doth distill.
'And as no good is here unmix'd with ill,
'So punishment, that's ill to flesh and blood,   3670
'As to th' accompt we must make there is good.
And if my words have cut thee, 'tis but like
A faithfull Surgeon, who a vein doth strike,
Or thrusts his instrument into the wound
Where it is mortallest and most profound   3675
(In being cruell, mercifull). Then be
Content with what is writ in Heav'n for thee.
   Am. O 'tis a cruell sentence, whether it
In heaven for me, or in earth be writ:
Yet writ in heav'n I'm certain it is not: 3680
For there my innocence is known. But what
Doth that avail me, if that dye I must?
That's the straight narrow passage! to be dust,
Nicandro, that's the bitter cup! But oh!
By that compassion thou to me dost show,   3685
Lead me not to the Temple yet: stay, stay.
   Nic. 'Who fears to dye, dyes ev'ry hour o' th' day.
Why hang'st thou back? and draw'st a painfull breath?
'Death hath no ill in't, but the fear of death.
'And he that dies when he hath heard his doom,   3690
'Flyes from his death.
   Am.   Perchance some help may come.
Father, dear father, dost thou leave me too?
An onely daughters father, wilt thou do
Nothing to save me? Yet before I die
A parting kisse to me do not deny.   3695
Two bosoms shall be pierced with one blow:
And from thy daughter's wound thy blood must flow.
O father! (once so sweet and deer a name,
Which I was never wont t' invoke in vain)
Thy belov'd Daughter's *Wedding* callst thou this?   3700
To day a bride; to day a Sacrifice.
   Nic. Good Nymph no more: why dost thou bootlesly
Stay thus tormenting both thy self and mee?
The time calls on: I must convey thee hence,
Nor with my duty longer may dispense.   3705
   Am. Deer woods adieu then, my deer woods adieu:

Receive these sighs (my last ones) into you,
Till my cold shade, forc'd from her seat by dire
And unjust steel, to your lov'd shades retire.
(For sink to hell it can't, being innocent;   3710
Nor soar to heav'n, laden with discontent.)
Mirtillo, (O *Mirtillo*!) most accurst
The day I saw, the day I pleas'd thee first!
Since I, whom thou above thy life didst love,
Became thy life, that thou my death mightst prove.   3715
She dies condemn'd for kindnesse now to thee,
Whom thou hast still condemn'd of cruelty,
I might have broke my faith as cheap: Ay me!
Now without fault, or fruit I dye, or Thee
My deer *Mirtill*—
      Nic.   Alas! she dies indeed.   3720
(Poor wretch!) Come hither shepherds with all speed,
Help me to hold her up. (O piteous case!)
She finish'd in *Mirtillo*'s name her Race.
(Unhappy maid!)—she breathes yet, and I feel
Some signes of life pant in her bosome still.   3725
To the next fountain let us carry her;
Perchance cold water may recover there
Her fleeting spirits.—Stay, will not relief
Be cruelty to *her* who dies of grief,
To prevent dying by the Axe? How-e're,   3730
Yet let not us our charitie forbear.
'Men ought to lend their aid in present woe:
'What is to come, none but the Gods foreknow.

SCENA SEXTA.

Chorus of $\begin{Bmatrix} Huntsmen, \\ Shepherds, \end{Bmatrix}$ with Silvio.

Cho. Hunts. O Glorious youth! true child of Hercules;
That kilst so soon such monstrous beasts as these!   3735
      Cho. Shep. O glorious youth! by whom lies slain and queld
This Erimanthian Monster, (living) held
Invincible! Behold the horrid head,
Which seems to breath death when it self is dead!
This is the famous Trophie, noble Toile   3740

Of him whom we our Demy-god do stile.
Extoll his great name (Shepherds) and this day
Keep ever solemn, ever holyday.
    Cho. Hunts. O glorious youth &c.
    Cho. Shep. O glorious youth! that do'st despise thine own   3745
For other safeties. 'Vertue climbes her Throne
'By these steep stairs: and the high Gods have set
'Before her Palace gates labour and sweat.
'He that would land at joy must wade through woes:
'Nor by unprofitable base repose   3750
'Abhorring labour, but from gallant deeds
'And vertuous labour true repose proceeds.
    Cho. Hunts. O glorious youth, &c.
    Cho. Shep. O glorious youth! by whom these Plains depriv'd
Of tillage, and of tillers long, retriv'd   3755
Their fruitfull honours have. The plough-man now
Securely goes after the lazie plough,
Sowes his plump seed, and from earth's pregnant womb
Expects the wish'd fruits when the season's come.
No more shall churlish tusk, or churlish foot   3760
Trample them down, or tear them up by th' root.
Nor shall they prosper so as to sustain
A beast, to be their own, and others bane.
    Cho. Hunts. O glorious youth! &c.
    Cho. Shep. O glorious youth! as if presaging thine,   3765
The Heav'n to day doth in full glory shine.
Such peradventure was that famous Boar
Alcides slew, yet so thy act is more;
It being (*Silvio*) thy first labour, as
Of thy great Ancestor the third it was.   3770
But with wilde Beasts thy infant valour playes,
To kill worse monsters in thy riper dayes.
    Cho. Hunts. O glorious youth! &c.
    Cho. Shep. O glorious youth! how well are joyn'd in thee
Valour and pietie! See *Cynthia*, see   3775
Thy devout *Silvio*'s vow! behold with white
And crooked tusk, (as if in thy despight)

3756. honours] 47/48, 64; humours 76/92.   3766. Heav'n] 47/48 (*c*); Have'n
47/48 (*u*).   3772. worse] 64, 76/92; more 47/48. *Correction is made in errata list
in 47/48.*

The proud head arm'd on this side and on that,
Seeming thy silver horns to emulate!
If then (O powerfull Goddesse) thou didst guide 3780
The young mans shaft, he is in justice tyde
To dedicate the Trophie unto thee
By whom he did obtain the victorie.
   Cho. Hunts. O glorious youth, true child of Hercules,
That kill'st so soon such monstrous beasts as these! 3785

SCENA SEPTIMA.

Coridon.

I have forborn till now to credit what
The *Satyr* told me of *Corisca* late,
Fearing it might be some malicious lye
Devis'd by him to shake my constancie.
For most improbable it seem'd, that she 3790
In the same place where she expected me
(Unlesse the message which *Lisetta* brought
To me from her were false) should straight be caught
With an adulterer. And yet (the truth
To say) here's a shrewd token, and it doth 3795
Perplex me much, to see the mouth o' th' den
Just in that manner he related then
Shut and damm'd up with such a massie stone.
Ah false *Corisca*! too well by mine own
Experience of thy ungracious deeds 3800
I know thee now: stumbling so oft, thou needs
Must fall at last. So many frauds, so many
Lyes, and vow-breaches might have warned any
(Whom folly or affection did not blear)
That some such fearfull tumbling cast was neer: 3805
'Twas well for me I tarried by the way;
A happy chance my father made me stay:
Though then I did suppose him foolishly
T' have been a tedious Remora. Had I
Come at *Lisetta*'s hour, I might have seen 3810
Something which poyson to my eyes had been.
But what shall I do now? arm'd with disdain,
Shall I revenge and mischief entertain?

No: I have lov'd her, and this act doth crave
My pity, not my anger. Shall I have   3815
Pity on one deceiv'd me? Mee! she hath
Deceiv'd her self, leaving a man of faith,
To give her self a prey into the hand
Of an ignoble Swain, a stranger and
A vagabond, that will to morrow be   3820
More wavering, more without faith then she.
Shall I take pains then to revenge a wrong
That carryes with it the revenge along?
And quenches all my indignation so,
'Tis turn'd to pitie? She hath *scorn'd* me though: 3825
Sh' has *honour'd* me: for she who *thus* could chuse,
Highly commends the man she doth refuse.
She scorn'd me, who the way did never know,
How she should love receive, or how bestow.
Who lik'd at random still, or had this curse,   3830
If two were offerd her, to take the worse.
But tell me *Coridon*, how can it be,
If scorn of being scorned move not thee
To take revenge; but that to have been crost
By such a losse should do't? I have not lost   3835
Her whom I never had: My self I have
Regain'd, whom I unto another gave.
Nor can't a losse be termed to remain
Without a woman so unsure and vain.
In fine, What have I lost? Beautie without   3840
Vertue: A head with all the brains pickt out:
A brest that hath no heart: A heart that hath
No soul in it: A soul that hath no faith.
A shade, a ghost, a carcasse of affection,
Which will to morrow turn to putrefaction.   3845
Is this a losse? I will be bold to say't,
'Tis a great purchase and a fortunate.
Is there no woman in the world but she?
Can *Coridon* want Nymphs as fair as she,
And far more true? But she may well want one   3850
Will love her with such faith as *Coridon*,
Whom she deserv'd not. Now if I should do
That which the *Satyr* did advise me to,

Accusing her of *vow-breach*, in my breath
I know it lies to have her put to death.   3855
But I have not an heart so Aspine, I,
That with the wind of womans levitie
It should be mov'd. Too great a happinesse
And honour 'twere to their perfidiousnesse,
If with the trouble of a manly brest,   3860
And breaking of the happy peace and rest
Of an ingenuous soul, I were to be
Reveng'd upon *Corisca* now. For me
Then let her live: or (to expresse it better)
By me not die, Live for my Rivall let her.   3865
Her life's revenge for me sufficient:
Live let her to dishonour; to repent:
I know not how to envie him, or loath
Her; but with all my heart do pity both.

SCENA OCTAVA.

Silvio, Eccho *within*.

O Goddesse of the slothfull, blind, and vain,   3870
Who with foul hearts, Rites foolish and profane,
Altars and Temples hallow to thy name!

Temples? or Sanctuaries vile said I?
To protect Lewdnesse and impietie,
Under the robe of thy Divinity?   3875

And thou base Goddesse: that thy wickednesse,
When others do as bad, may seem the lesse,
Giv'st them the reins to all lasciviousnesse.

Rotter of soul and body, enemie
Of reason, plotter of sweet theevery,   3880
The little and great World's calamitie.

Reputed worthily the Ocean's daughter:
That treacherous monster, which with even water
First soothes, but ruffles into storms soon after.

Such windes of sighs, such Cataracts of tears,   3885
Such breaking waves of hopes, such gulfs of fears,
Thou mak'st in men, such rocks of cold despairs.

Tydes of desire so head-strong, as would move
The world to change thy name, when thou shalt prove
Mother of Rage and Tempests, not of Love.   3890

Behold what sorrow now and discontent
On a poor pair of Lovers thou hast sent!
Go thou, that vaunt'st thy self Omnipotent,

Go faithlesse Goddesse, save that Nymph whom thou
Hast poyson'd with thy sweets (if thou knowst how)   3895
From her swift deaths pursuing footsteps now.

O what a happy day was that for me,
When my chaste soul I did devote to thee
Cynthia, my great and onely Deitie!

True Goddesse! unto whose particular shrine   3900
The fairest souls in all the Earth incline,
As thou in Heav'n do'st all the Starrs out-shine.

How much more laudable and free from pain
The sports are which thy servants entertain,
Then those of faithlesse *Ericina*'s train!   3905

Wilde Boars are killed by thy Worshippers:
By wilde Boars miserably kild are hers.
O Bow, my strength and joy! My conquerers

My Arrows! Let that bug-bear Love come trie
And match with you his soft Artillerie.   3910
They whom you wound do in good earnest die.

But too much honour hence to thee would come,
Vile and unwarlike Boy, to chastise whom
(I speak't aloud) a rod's enough.
   [*Eccho*]   *Enough.*

[*Sil.*] What art thou that reply'st? Eccho? or Love?   3915
That so doth imitate the same?
[*Eccho*]   *The same.*
[*Sil.*] Most wish'd! but tell me true; Art thou hee?
[*Eccho*]   *Hee.*
[*Sil.*] The son of her that for *Adonis* once
So miserably pin'd away?
[*Eccho*]   *Away.*
[*Sil.*] Well: of that Goddesse who was found in bed   3920
With *Mars*, when the stars shot to see her shame,
And the chast Moon blush'd at her folly?
[*Eccho*]   *O ly!*
[*Sil.*] What madnesse 'tis to whistle to the winde!
Come (if thou darest) to the wide air,
[*Eccho*]   *I dare.*
[*Sil.*] And I defie thee. But art thou her son   3925
Legitimate, or else a by-blow?
[*Eccho*]   *I glow.*
[*Sil.*] O! the Smith's son that's call'd a God.
[*Eccho*]   *A God.*
[*Sil.*] Of what? the follies of the world?
[*Eccho*]   *The world.*
[*Sil.*] The Bawd thou art. Art thou that terrible Boy
That tak'st such sharp revenge upon those wights   3930
Who thy absurd commands digest not?
[*Eccho*]   *Jest not.*
[*Sil.*] What punishments dost thou inflict on those
Who in rebellion persevere?
[*Eccho*]   *Severe.*
[*Sil.*] And how shall I be punish'd, whose hard heart
Hath alwayes been at odds with Love?
[*Eccho*]   *With Love.*   3935
[*Sil.*] When (Sot), if my chaste brest be to those flames
More opposite then night to day?
[*Eccho*]   *To day.*
[*Sil.*] So quickly shall I be in that streight?
[*Eccho*]   *Streight.*
[*Sil.*] What's she can bring me to adoring?
[*Eccho*]   *Dorin.*
[*Sil.*] *Dorinda*, is it not, my little childe,   3940

Thou wouldst say in thy lithping gibberish?
[*Eccho*]   *Ish.*
[*Sil.*] Shee whom I hate more then the Lamb the Wolf?
And who to this shall force my will?
[*Eccho*]   *I will.*
[*Sil.*] And how? and with what Arms? and with what bow?
Shall it be happily with thine?
[*Eccho*]   *With thine.*   3945
[*Sil.*] Thou mean'st perchance, when by thy wantonnesse
It is unbent, and the nerve broken?
[*Eccho*]   *Broken.*
[*Sil.*] Shall my own bow, after 'tis broken too,
Make war on me? and who shall break't? thou?
[*Eccho*]   *Thou.*
[*Sil.*] 'Tis plain now thou art drunk: go sleep. But say,   3950
Where shall these miracles be wrought? here?
[*Eccho*]   *Here.*
[*Sil.*] O fool! and I am going now from hence.
See if thou hast not prov'd thy self to day
A prophet with the wine inspir'd.
[*Eccho*]   *Inspir'd.*
[*Sil.*] But stay, I see (unlesse I much mistake)   3955
A greyish thing at couch in yonder Brake:
'Tis like a Wolf, and certainly 'tis one.
O what a huge one 'tis! how over-grown!
O day of prey to me! What favours are
These, courteous goddesse? in one day a pair   3960
Of such wilde beasts to triumph ore? But why
Do I delay this work, my Deity?
The swiftest and the keenest shaft that is
In all my Quiver (let me see,—'tis this)
I do select: to thee I recommend it   3965
(O Archeresse eternall) do thou send it
By Fortunes hand, and by thy pow'r divine
Guide it into the beast. His skin is thine.
And in thy name I shoot. O lucky hit!
Just where the eye and hand designed it.   3970
Would now I had my javelin here, to make
An end of him at once, before he take
The wood for shelter: but the place shall yeeld

Me weapons. Not a stone in all the field?
But why do I seek weapons, having these? 3975
This second arrow layes him at his ease.
Alas! what do I see? what hast thou done,
Unhappy *Silvio*? what hast thou run
Thy self into? Thou hast a shepherd slain
In a wolfe's skin. O action to remain 3980
For ever overwhelm'd with grief! to lie
Under salt water everlastingly!
The wretch too I should know, and he that so
Doth lead and prop him up is *Linco*. O
Vile *arrow*! viler *vow*! but vilest *Thou* 3985
That didst direct that arrow, hear that vow!
I guilty of anothers blood? I kill
Another? I that was so free to spill
My blood for others, and my life to give?
Throw down thy weapons, and inglorious live, 3990
Shooter of men, hunter of men. But lo
The wretched Swain! then thee lesse wretched though.

SCENA NONA.

Linco, Silvio, Dorinda.

Lin. Lean, daughter, on my arm with all thy weight,
(Wretched *Dorinda*) do.
    Sil.   *Dorinda*'s that?
I'm a dead man.
    Dor.   O *Linco, Linco*! O 3995
My second Father!
    Sil.   'Tis *Dorinda*: woe,
Woe on thee *Silvio*!
    Dor.   *Linco*, thou wert sure
Ordein'd by Fate to be a stay to poor
Dorinda. Thou receivedst my first cry
When I was born: Thou wilt, now I'm to dye, 4000
My latest groan: and these thy arms which were
My cradle then, shall now become my biere.
    Lin. Ah daughter! (or more deer then if thou wert
My daughter) speak now to thee for my heart

3976. arrow] 47/48, 64; arrows 76/92.

I can't, grief melts each word into a tear.				4005
 Dor. Not so fast *Linco*, if thou lov'st me: deer
Linco, nor go, nor weep so fast; one rakes
My wound too bad, t' other a new wound makes.
 Sil. (Poor Nymph! how ill have I repaid thy love!)
 Lin. Be of good comfort daughter, this will prove			4010
No mortall wound.
 Dor.   It may be so; but I
That am a Mortall, of this wound shall die.
Would I knew yet who hurt me!
 Lin.   Get thee sound,
And let that passe: 'Revenge ne're cur'd a wound.
 Sil. (Why dost thou stay? what mak'st thou in this place?		4015
Wouldst thou be seen by her? Hast thou the face?
Hast thou the heart t' indure it? *Silvio*, flee
From the sharp dart of her revenging eye:
Fly from her tongues just sword. I cannot go
From hence: and what it is I do not know,				4020
But something holds me, and would make me run
To her whom I of all the world did shun.)
 Dor. Must I then die and not my Murtherer know?
 Lin. 'Twas *Silvio*.
 Dor.   How dost know 'twas *Silvio*?
 Lin. I know his shaft.
 Dor. Then welcom death, if I			4025
Shall owe thee to so sweet an enemy!
 Lin. Look where he stands! we need demand no further,
His posture and his face confesse the murther
Alone. Now Heav'n be praised *Silvio*,
Thy all-destroying Arrowes and thy Bow				4030
Th' hast pli'd so well about these woods, that now
Th' art gone out thy Arts-master. Tell me, thou
That *dost like* Silvio, *not like* Linco, who
Made this brave shoot, *Linco* or *Silvio*?
This 'tis for boyes to be so overwise:				4035
Would thou hadst taken this old fools advice!
Answer, thou wretch: What lingring miserie,
What horrour shalt thou live in if she die?
I know thou't say, thou err'dst, and thought'st to strike

4019. Fly] 47/48; Flie 64; Flee 76/92.

A Wolfe: as if 'twere nothing (school-boy like)   4040
To shoot at all adventures, and not see,
Nor care, whether a man or beast it be.
What Goat-herd, or what plough-man doth not go
Clad in such skins? O *Silvio*, *Silvio*!
'Soon ripe, soon rotten. If thou think (fond childe)   4045
This *chance* by chance befell thee, th' art beguild.
'These monstrous things without Divine decree
'Hap not to men. Dost thou not plainly see
How this thy unsupportable disdain
Of Love, the world, and all that is humane   4050
Displeases Heav'n? 'High Gods cannot abide
'A Rivall upon earth: and hate such pride,
'Although in vertue. Now th' art mute, that wert
Before this hap unsufferably pert.
      Dor. *Silvio*, give *Linco* leave to talk: for hee   4055
Knows not what pow'r Love gave thee over me
Of life and death. If thou hadst strook my heart,
Th' hadst strook what's thine (mark proper for thy dart.)
Those hands to wound mee thy fair eyes have taught.
See *Silvio* her thou hat'st so! see her brought   4060
To that extremity where thou wouldst see her!
Thou sought'st to wound her, see her wounded here!
To prey upon her, loe she is thy prey!
Thou sought'st her death, and loe she's dying! Say,
Wouldst thou ought else of her? What further joy   4065
Can poor *Dorinda* yeeld thee? Cruell Boy!
And void of Bowels! thou wouldst ne're believe
That wound which from thy eyes I did receive:
This which thy hands have giv'n canst thou deny?
Those crystall showrs which issued from my eye,   4070
Thou couldst not be perswaded were my blood:
What dost thou think now of this crimson flood
Which my side weeps? But (if orewhelm'd with scorn
That bravery be not wherewith thou wert born)
Deny me not (though cruell soul, yet brave)   4075
Deny me not ('tis all the boon I crave)
When I shall sigh into thee my last breath,
One sigh of thine. O happy, happy death!
If thou vouchsafe to sweeten it with these

Kind words and pious; *Soul depart in peace.*   4080
  Sil. Dorinda, my *Dorinda,* shall I say
(Alas!) when I must lose thee the same day
Th' art mine? now mine, when death to thee I give,
That wert not mine when I could make thee live?
Yes mine I'le call thee: and thou mine shalt be   4085
In spight of my opposing destinie.
For if thy death our meeting souls disjoyn,
My death shall reunite us. All that's mine
Haste to revenge her: I have murder'd thee
With these curs'd arrows; with them murder me.   4090
I have been cruell unto thee; and I
Desire from thee nothing but crueltie.
I scorn'd thee in my pride; look! with my knee
(Low louting to the earth) I worship thee,
And pardon of thee, but not life demand.   4095
Take Shafts and Bow: But do not strike my hand
Or eye (bad ministers, 'tis true, yet still)
But ministers of an unguilty will:
Strike me this brest, this monster hence remove,
Sworn enemy of Pity, and of Love.   4100
Strike me this heart, to thee so cruell. Loe,
My bared brest!
    Dor.   I strike it, *Silvio?*
I strike that brest? sure if thou didst not mock,
Thou wouldst not shew't mee naked. O white rock!
Already by the windes and briny main   4105
Of my rough sighs and tears oft strook in vain!
But dost thou breath? nor art to pity barr'd?
Art thou a tender brest, or marble hard?
I would not idolize fair Alablaster,
(Led by the humane likenesse) as thy Master   4110
And mine, when on the outside he did look,
A harmlesse woman for a beast mistook.
I strike thee? strike thee Love. Nor can I wish
For my revenge a greater plague then this.
Yet must I blesse the day that I took fire,   4115
My tears and martyrdome. All I desire
Is that thou praise my faith, my zeale, but no
Revenging me. But courteous *Silvio,*

(That to thy servant kneel'st) why this to me?
Or if *Dorinda* must thy Mistresse be,   4120
Obey her then; the first command I give,
Is that thou rise; the second, that thou live.
Heav'ns Will be done with me: I shall survive
In thee, and cannot dye, whilest thou'rt alive.
But if thou thinkst unjust I should be found   4125
Without all satisfaction for my wound,
Be that, which did it, punish'd. 'Twas that Bow:
Let that be broke; I'm well revenged so.
 Lin. (A very heavie doom).
 Sil.   Come then thou mad,
Thou bloody actor of a deed so sad: 4130
That thou maist ne're break thred of life again,
Thus do I break thee and thy thred in twain,
And send thee a uselesse trunk back to the wood.
Nor you (ill sanguin'd with an innocents blood!)
Which my deer Mistresse side so rudely rent,   4135
(Brothers in ill) shall scape your punishment.
Not shafts, nor flights, but sticks, since yee shall want
Those wings and heads which garnisht you: Avant
Plum'd and disarmed Arms. How well, O Love,
Didst thou foretell me this from yonder grove   4140
In a prophetick Eccho! O thou high
Conqu'rour of Gods and men, once enemy,
Now lord of all my thoughts! if 'tis thy glory
To tame a heart that's proud and refractory,
Divert Death's impious shaft, which with one blow   4145
Slaying *Dorinda*, will slay *Silvio*
(Now thine): so cruell death, if it remove
Her hence, will triumph o're triumphant Love.
 Lin. Now both are wounded: but the one in vain,
Unlesse the other's wound be heal'd again.   4150
About it then.
 Dor.   Ah *Linco*! do not (pray)
Carry me home disguis'd in this array.
 Sil. Why should *Dorinda* go to any house
But *Silvio*'s? surely she shall be my Spouse
'Ere it be night, either alive, or dead.   4155
And *Silvio* in life or death will wed

Dorinda.

Lin. Now she may become thy Wife,
Since *Amarillis* is to *marriage*, *life*,
And *vertue* lost. Blest pair! Ye Gods (that doe
Wonders) with one cure now give life to two.   4160
  Dor. O *Silvio*! I shall faint, my wounded thigh
Feebly supporting me.
  Sil.   Good remedy
For that! take heart: th'art mine and *Linco*'s care,
And I and *Linco* thy two crutches are.
Linco, thy hand.
  Lin.   There 'tis.
  Sil.   Hold fast: a chair   4165
Let's make for her of our two arms. Rest here
Dorinda, suffring thy right hand t' imbrace
The neck of *Linco*, thy left mine: Now place
Thy body tenderly, that the hurt part
May not be strain'd.
  Dor.   O cruell pricking dart!   4170
  Sil. Sit at more ease, my Love.
  Dor.   It is well now.
  Sil. Deer *Linco* do not stagger.
  Lin.   Nor do thou
Swag with thine arme, but steddy go and wary;
It will concern thee. Ah! we do not carry
A Boars head now in triumph.
  Sil.   Say, my Deer,   4175
How is it now?
  Dor.   In pain; but leaning here
(My Heart) to be in pain, is pleas'd to be;
To languish, health; to die, eternity.

CHORUS.

Fair golden Age! when milk was th' onely food,
And cradle of the infant-world the wood   4180
(Rock'd by the windes); and th' untoucht flocks did bear
Their deer young for themselves! None yet did fear
The sword or poyson: no black thoughts begun
T' eclipse the light of the eternall Sun:

4175. now] 47/48; *omitted* 64, 76/92.

Nor wandring Pines unto a forreign shore   4185
Or War, or Riches, (a worse mischief) bore.
That pompous sound, Idoll of vanity,
Made up of Title, Pride, and Flattery,
Which they call Honour whom Ambition blindes,
Was not as yet the Tyrant of our mindes,   4190
But to buy reall goods with honest toil
Amongst the woods and flocks, to use no guile,
Was honour to those sober souls that knew
No happinesse but what from vertue grew.
Then sports and carols amongst Brooks and Plains   4195
Kindled a lawfull flame in Nymphs and Swains.
Their hearts and Tongues concurr'd, the kisse and joy
Which were most sweet, and yet which least did cloy
Hymen bestow'd on them. To one alone
The lively Roses of delight were blown;   4200
The theevish Lover found them shut on triall,
And fenc'd with prickles of a sharp denyall.
Were it in Cave or Wood, or purling Spring,
Husband and Lover signifi'd one thing.
    Base present age, which dost with thy impure   4205
Delights the beauty of the soul obscure:
Teaching to nurse a Dropsie in the veins:
Bridling the look, but giv'st desire the reins.
Thus, like a net that spread and cover'd lies
With leaves and tempting flowrs, thou dost disguise   4210
With coy and holy arts a wanton heart;
'Mak'st life a Stage-play, *vertue but a* part:
'Nor thinkst it any fault Love's sweets to steal,
'So from the world thou canst the theft conceal.
    But thou that art the King of Kings, create   4215
In us true honour: Vertue's all the state
Great souls should keep. Unto these cels return
Which were thy Court, but now thy absence mourn:
From their dead sleep with thy sharp goad awake
Them who, to follow their base wils, forsake   4220
Thee, and the glory of the ancient world.
'Let's hope: our ills have truce till we are hurld
'From that: Let's hope; the sun that's set may rise,
'And with new light salute our longing eyes.

ACTUS QUINTUS.

SCENA PRIMA.

Uranio, Carino.

Ura. 'All places are our Country where w' are well:　　4225
'Which to the wise is wheresoe're they dwel.
Car. It is most true *Uranio*: and no man
By proof can say it better then I can:
Who leaving long ago my Fathers house,
(Being very young, and then ambitious　　4230
Of something more then holding of the plough,
Or keeping sheep) travell'd abroad: and now
To the same point where I began, return,
When my gilt locks are to the silver worn.
'Yet a sweet thing (it needs must be confest)　　4235
'To any that hath sense, is his first nest.
'For Nature gave to all men at their birth
'Something of secret love unto that Earth
'Where they were born, which never old doth grow
'In us, but follows wheresoe're we go.　　4240
'The Loadstone which the wary Mariner
'Doth as Directer of his travels bear
'Now to the rising Sun, now to his set,
'Doth never lose that hidden vertue yet,
'Which makes it to the North retort its look:　　4245
'So he that hath his native soil forsook,
'Though he may wander far, much compasse take,
'I, and his nest in forraign Countries make;
'Yet that same naturall love doth still retain
'Which makes him wish his native soil again.　　4250
O fair Arcadia! the sweetest part
Of all the world (at least to me thou art)
Which my feet trod on, but my thoughts adore!
Had I been landed blindfold on thy shore,
Yet then I should have known thee, such a floud　　4255
Of sudden joy runs races with my bloud:
Such a Magnetick powerfull sympathie,
And unaccustom'd tendernesse feel I.
Thou then, that my companion hast been

In travels and in sorrowes, shalt be in   4260
At my joyes too: 'tis reason thou shouldst go
My half in happinesse, as well as woe.
   Ura. Companion of thy travels I have been,
Not of the fruit thereof; for thou art in
Thy native soil, where thou repose maist find   4265
For thy tir'd body, and more tired mind:
But I that am a stranger, and am come
So many leagues from my poor house, and from
My poorer and distressed Family,
Trailing my wearied lims along with thee,   4270
For my afflicted body well may find
Repose, but not for my afflicted mind:
Thinking what pledges do behinde remain,
And how much rugged way I must again
Tread over e're I rest. Nor do I know   4275
Who else could have prevail'd with me to go
From *Elis* in my gray unweildy age
(Not knowing why) so long a pilgrimage.
   Car. Thou knowst, my sweet *Mirtillo* (who was giv'n
As a son to me by propitious Heav'n)   4280
Some two months since came hither to be well
(By my advice, or of the Oracle,
To speak more true, which said, *Th' Arcadian air
Was th' only means that could his health repair.*)
Now I, that find it an exceeding pain   4285
Without so deer a pledge long to remain,
Consulting the same Oracle, enquir'd
When he'ld return whom I so much desir'd.
The Answer was the same I tell thee now;
Unto thy ancient Country return thou: 4290
Where with thy sweet Mirtillo *thou shalt be*
Happy; for in that place (by Heaven) hee
Is mark'd out for great things: But till thou come
Into Arcadia, touching this be dumb.
Thou then, my faithfullest Companion,   4295
My lov'd *Uranio*, who hast ever gone
A share in all my fortunes hitherto,
Repose thy body, and thou shalt have too

4293. *things*] 47/48, 76/92; *thinge* 64.   4296. gone] 47/48 (*c*); gone. 47/48 (*u*).

Cause to repose thy minde: 'twixt me and thee
(If Heav'n perform what it hath promis'd me)   4300
All shall be common: no successe can glad
Carino, if he see *Uranio* sad.
   Ura. My deer *Carino*, what I do for thee,
Rewards it self, if it accepted be.
But what at first could make thee to forgo   4305
Thy native Country, if thou lov'st it so?
   Car. A love to Poetry, and to the lowd
Musick of Fame resounding in a crowd.
For I my self (greedy of forraigne praise)
Disdain'd Arcadia onely should my Layes   4310
Hear and applaud: as if my native Soile
Were narrow limits to my growing Style.
I went to *Elis*, and to *Pisa* then,
(Famous themselves, and giving fame to men)
There saw I that lov'd *Egon*, first with Bayes,   4315
With Purple then, with Vertue deckt alwayes:
That he on earth *Apollo*'s self did seem:
Therefore my heart and Harp I unto him
Did consecrate, devoted to his name.
And in his house (which was the house of Fame)   4320
I should have set up my perpetuall rest,
There to admire and imitate the best,
If as Heav'n made me happy here below,
So it had gi'n me too the grace to know
And keep my happinesse. How I forsook   4325
Elis and *Pisa* after, and betook
My selfe to *Argos* and *Micene*, where
An earthly god I worshipt, with what there
I sufferd in that hard captivity,
Would be too long for thee to hear, for me   4330
Too sad to utter. Onely thus much know,
I lost my labour, and in sand did sow:
I writ, wept, sung, hot and cold fits I had,
I rid, I stood, I bore, now sad, now glad,
Now high, now low, now in esteem, now scorn'd;   4335
And as the Delphick iron, which is turnd
Now to Heroick, now Mechanick use,
I fear'd no danger, did no pains refuse,

Was all things, and was nothing; chang'd my hair,
Condition, custome, thoughts, and life, but ne're   4340
Could change my fortune. Then I knew at last
And panted after my sweet freedome past.
So flying smoaky *Argos*, and the great
Storms that attend on greatnesse, my retreat
I made to *Pisa* (my thoughts quiet port)   4345
Where (praise be giv'n to the Eternall for 't)
Upon my deer *Mirtillo* I did light,
Which all past sorrowes fully did requite.
      Ura. 'A thousand thousand times that man is blest
'Can clip the wings of his aspiring brest!   4350
'Nor for the shadow of great happinesse
'Doth throw away the substance of the lesse!
      Car. But who'd have dreamt midst plenty to grow poor?
Or to be lesse by toiling to be more?
I thought by how much more in Princes Courts   4355
Men did excell in Titles and Supports,
So much the more obliging they would be
(The best enamell of Nobility).
But now the contrary by proof I've seen:
Courtiers in name, and *Courteous* in their meen   4360
They are; but in their actions I could spie
Not the least spark or drachm of *Courtesie*.
People in shew smooth as the calmed waves:
Yet cruell as the Ocean when it raves.
Men in appearance onely I did finde,   4365
Love in the face, but malice in the minde:
With a streight look a squinting heart; and least
Fidelity where greatest was profest.
That which elsewhere is vertue, is vice there:
Plain troth, square dealing, love unfeign'd, sincere   4370
Compassion, faith inviolable, and
An innocence both of the heart and hand,
They count the folly of a soul that's vile
And poor, a vanity worthy their smile.
To cheat, to lie, deceit and theft to use,   4375
And under shew of pity to abuse,
To rise upon the ruines of their Brothers,
And seek their own by robbing praise from others,

The vertues are of that perfidious race.
No worth, no valour, no respect of place,   4380
Of Age, or Law, bridle of Modestie,
No tie of love, or blood, nor memorie
Of good receiv'd; no thing's so venerable,
Sacred or just, that is inviolable
By that vast thirst of Riches, and desire   4385
Unquenchable of still ascending higher.
Now I (not fearing, since I meant not ill,
And in Court-craft not having any skill,
Wearing my thoughts caracterd in my brow,
And a glasse-window in my brest) judge thou   4390
How open and how fair a mark my heart
Lay to their Envie's unsuspected dart.
    Ura. 'Who now can boast of earth's felicity,
'When Envie treads on vertues heels?
    Car.   O my
Uranio, If since my Muse and I   4395
From *Elis* past to *Argos,* I had found
Such cause to sing, as I had ample ground
To weep, perchance in such a lofty key
I'd sung my *Master*'s glorious Arms, that hee
Should have no cause, for the felicity   4400
Of his Meonian trumpet to envie
Achilles: and my Country (which doth bring
Such haplesse Poets forth as Swan-like sing
Their own sad fates) should by my means have now
A second Lawrell to impale her brow.   4405
But in this age (inhumane age the while!)
The art of Poetry is made too vile.
'Swans must have pleasant nests, high feeding, fair
'Weather to sing: and with a load of care
'Men cannot climb Parnassus cliffe: for he   4410
'Who is still wrangling with his Destinie
'And his malignant fortune, becomes hoarse,
'And loses both his singing and discourse.
—But now 'tis time to seek *Mirtillo* out:
Although I find the places hereabout   4415
So chang'd and alter'd from their ancient wont,
I for Arcadia in Arcadia hunt.

But come *Uranio* gladly for all this;
A traveller with language cannot misse
His way: Or, since th' art weary, thou wert best   4420
To stay at the next Inne to take some rest.

SCENA SECUNDA.

Titiro, *Messenger.*

Tit. Which first, my Daughter, shall I mourn in thee,
Thy losse of Life, or of thy Chastitie?
I'le mourn thy Chastitie: for thou wert born
Of mortall parents, but not bad. I'le mourn   4425
Not thy life lost; but mine preserv'd, to see
Thy losse of Life, and of thy Chastitie.
Thou with thy Oracles mysterious cloud
(Wrongly conceiv'd *Montano,*) and thy proud
Despiser both of love, and of my Daughter,   4430
Unto this miserable end hast brought her.
Ay me! how much more certain at this time
My Oracles have shew'd themselves then thine!
'For honesty in a young heart doth prove
'But a weak sconce against assaulting love.   4435
'And 'tis most true, a woman that's alone,
'Hath a most dangerous companion.
     Mess. Were he not under ground, or flown through th' air,
I should have found him sure. But soft, he's there
(I think) where least I thought. Th' art met by me   4440
Too late, old Father, but too soon for thee:
I've news.
     Tit.   What bringst thou in thy mouth? the knife
That hath bereft my Daughter of her life?
     Mess. Not that; yet little lesse. But how I pray
Got'st thou this news so soon another way?   4445
     Tit. Doth she then live?
     Mess.   She lives, and in her choice
It is to Live or Die.
     Tit.   Blest be that voice!
Why is she then not safe, if she may give
Her *no* to death?
     Mess.   Because she will not live.

Tit. Will not? what madnesse makes her *life* despise?   4450
Mess. Another's death. And (if that thy advice
Remove her not) she is thereon so bent
That all the world cannot her death prevent.
Tit. Why stand we talking here then? Let us go.
Mess. Stay: yet the Temple's shut. Dost thou not know   4455
That none but holy feet on holy earth
May tread, till from the vestry they bring forth
The destin'd Sacrifice in all its trim?
Tit. But before that—
Mess.   She's watch't.
Tit.   I' th' interim
Relate then all that's past, and to me show   4460
The truth unveil'd.
Mess.   Thy wretched Daughter (Oh
Sad spectacle!) being brought before the Priest,
Did not alone from the beholders wrest
Salt tears; but (trust me) made the marble melt,
And the hard flint the dint of pity felt.   4465
Shee was accus'd, convict, and sentence past
All in a trice.
Tit.   (Poor girl!) and why such haste?
Mess. Because the evidence was cleer as day:
Besides, a certain Nymph (who she did say
Could witnesse she was guiltlesse) was not there,   4470
Nor could by any search be brought t' appear.
Then the dire Omens of some threatned ill
And horrid visions which the Temple fill
Brook no delay, to us more frightfull farre,
By how much more unusuall they are,   4475
Nor ever seen, since the vext Pow'rs above
Reveng'd the wrong of scorn'd *Aminta*'s Love.
(Who was their Priest whence all our woes had birth)
The Goddesse sweats cold drops of blood, the Earth
Is Palsey-shook; the sacred Cavern howls   4480
With such unwonted sounds as tortur'd souls
Send out of graves, and belches up a smell
From its fowl jawes, scarce to be match'd in hell.
His sad Procession now the Priest began
To lead t' a bloody death thy Daughter, whan   4485

Mirtillo seeing her, (behold a strange
Proof of Affection!) profferd to exchange
His life for hers; crying aloud, Her hands
Untie (Ah how unworthy of such bands!)
And in her stead (who is design'd to be   4490
A Sacrifice to *Dian*) offer me
A sacrifice to *Amarillis*.
    Tit.   There
Spake a true Lover, and above base fear!
    Mess. The wonder follows: she that was afraid
Before of dying, on the sudden made   4495
Now valiant by *Mirtillo*'s words, reply'd,
Thus, with a heart at death unterrifi'd,
But dost thou think (*Mirtillo*) then to give
Life by thy death to her, who in thee doth live?
It cannot, must not be: Come Priests, away   4500
With me to th' Altar now without delay.
Ah! (cry'd the Swain) such love I did not lack:
Back cruell *Amarillis*, O come back:
Now thou art more unkind then e're thou wert:
'Tis I should die. Quoth she, thou act'st my part.   4505
And here between them grew so fierce a strife,
As if that life were death, and death were life.
O noble souls! O Pair eternally
To be renown'd, whether ye live or die!
O glorious Lovers! if I had tongues more   4510
Then Heaven hath eyes, or sands are on the shore,
Their voices would be drowned in the main-
Sea of your endlesse Praises. Glorious Dame,
Daughter of *Jove* (eternall as thy Father)
That Mortals deeds immortallizest, gather   4515
Thou the fair story, and in diamond pages
With golden letters write to after ages
The bravery of both Lovers.
    Tit.   But who wan
The conquest in that strife of death?
    Mess.   The Man.
Strange warre! which to the victor death did give,   4520
And where the vanquish't was condemn'd to live.
For thus unto thy daughter spake the Priest;

Nymph, let's alone, and set thy heart at rest;
Chang'd for another none can be again,
Who for another in exchange was ta'ne.   4525
This is our Law. Then a strict charge he gave,
Upon the Maid such carefull watch to have,
As that she might not lay a violent hand
Upon her self through sorrow. Thus did stand
The state of matters, when in search of thee   4530
Montano sent me.
    Tit.   'Tis most true I see,
'Well-water'd Meads may be without sweet flowers
'In Spring; without their verdant honour Bowers;
'And without chirping birds a pleasant Grove;
' 'Ere a fair maid and young without her Love.   4535
But if we loiter here, how shall we know
The hour when to the Temple we should go?
    Mess. Here better then elsewhere: For here it is
The honest Swain must be a sacrifice.
    Tit. And why not in the Temple?
    Mess.   Because in   4540
The place 'twas done our law doth punish sin.
    Tit. Then why not in the cave? The sin was there.
    Mess. Because it must be in the open air.
    Tit. By whom hast thou these mysteries been told?
    Mess. By the chief Minister, and hee by old   4545
Tirenio; who the false *Lucrina* knew
So sacrificed, and *Aminta* true.
But now 'tis time to go indeed; for see,
The sacred pomp descends the hill! yet wee
May for thy daughter to the Temple go   4550
Before they come: 'Devotion marches slow.

SCENA TERTIA.

Chorus of Shepherds, Chorus of Priests,
Montano, Mirtillo.

Cho. Sh. Sol's sister, Daughter of great Jupiter,
That shin'st a second Sun in the first Sphere
                     To the blind World!

   Cho. Pr. Thou whose life-giving, and more temp'rate Ray   4555
Thy Brother's burning fury doth allay;
Whence bounteous Nature here produces after
All her blest off-springs, and Air, Earth, and Water
Enriches and augments with Vegetals,
With Creatures sensitive, with Rationals.   4560
Ah, pity thy Arcadia, and that rage
Thou dost in *others*, in thy self asswage!
   Cho. Sh. Sol's Sister, Daughter of great Jupiter,
That shin'st a second Sun in the first Sphere
                 To the blind world!   4565
   Mon. Now sacred Ministers the Altars dresse:
You likewise Swains, that shew your selves no lesse
Devout then they, your voyces all unite,
And once again invoke the Queen of Night.
   Cho. Sh. Sol's Sister, Daughter of great Jupiter,   4570
That shin'st a second Sun in the first Sphere
                 To the blind world!
   Mon. Now shepherds and my servants all,
Withdraw your selves, and come not till I call.
Valiant young man (who to bestow upon   4575
Another, *life*, abandonest thine owne)
Die with this comfort: For a puffe of breath
(Which by the abject spirit is call'd death)
Thou buy'st Eternity: and when the tooth
Of envious Time (consuming the world's youth)   4580
Millions of lesser names devoured hath,
Then thou shalt live the pattern of true faith.
But for the Law commands that thou shouldst die
A silent Sacrifice, before thou ply
Thy knee to earth, if thou wouldst ought deliver,   4585
Speak; and hereafter hold thy peace for ever.
   Mir. Father, (for though thou kill me, yet I must
Give thee that name) My body to the dust,
Whereof 'twas made and kneaded up, I give;
My Soule to her in whom alone I live.   4590
But if she die, (as she hath vow'd) of me
What part (alas!) will then surviving be?
How sweet will death be unto me, if I
In mine owne person, not in hers, may die!

And if he merit pity at his death   4595
Who for meer pity now resignes his breath,
Take care (deer Father) of her life, that I
Wing'd with that hope, t' a better life may fly.
Let my Fate rest at my destruction,
Stop at my ruine; but when I am gone,   4600
Let my divorced soul in her survive,
Although from her I was divorc'd alive.
  Mon. (Scarcely can I refrain from weeping now:
O our mortality how frail art thou!)
Son be of comfort, for I promise thee   4605
I will perform all thou desir'st of me:
Here's my hand on't, and solemnly I swear,
Ev'n by this Miter'd head.
  Mir.   Then vanish fear.
And now for the most faithfull soul make room,
For (*Amarillis*) unto thee I come.   4610
With the sweet name of *Amarillis* I
Close up my mouth, and silent kneel to die.
  Mon. Now sacred Ministers, the Rites begin;
With liquid odoriferous Gumms keep in
The flame, and strowing frankincense and mirrhe,   4615
Whole clouds of perfume to the Gods preferre.
  Cho. Sh. Sol's Sister, Daughter of great Jupiter,
That shin'st a second Sun in the first Sphere
                            To the blind world!

                        SCENA QUARTA.

                   Carino, Montano, Nicandro,
                   Mirtillo, *Chorus of Shepherds.*

  Car. Did ever man so many houses view,   4620
And the inhabitants thereof so few?
But see the cause! If I mistake me not,
They're gotten all together here: O what
A troop! how rich! how solemn! It is sure
Some Sacrifice.
  Mon.   Give me the golden Ewre   4625
With the red wine, *Nicandro.*

        4602. from her I was] 47/48 (*c*); I was from her 47/48 (*u*).

Nic.   There.

Mon.   *So may*

Soft pity in thy brest revive to day
By this unguilty blood (Goddesse divine)
As by the sprinkling of these drops of wine
This pale and dying flame revives. Set up   4630
The golden Ewre. Reach mee the silver cup.
So may the burning wrath be quencht, which in
Thy brest was kindled by a false Maid's sinne,
As with this water (powr'd out like our tears)
I quench this flame.

     Car.   'T's a Sacrifice: but where's   4635
The offering?

     Mon.   Now all's prepar'd, there lacks
Onely the fatall stroak. Lend me the Axe.

     Car. I see a thing (unlesse my eyes mistake)
Like a man kneeling this way with his back.
Is he the offering? 'Tis so: Ah wretch!   4640
And o're his head the Priest his hand doth stretch.
O my poor Country! after all these years
Is not Heav'ns wrath yet quencht with blood and tears?

     Cho. Sh. Sol's Sister, Daughter of great Jupiter,
That shin'st a second Sun in the first Sphere   4645
                  To the blind world!

     Mon. Revengefull Goddesse, who a private fault
With publick rod dost punish: (Thou hast thought
Fit so to doe, and so in the Abysse
Of Providence eternall fixt it is)   4650
Since faithlesse Lucrin's *tainted blood was thought*
For thy nice Justice too impure a draught:
Carouse the guiltlesse blood then of this Swain,
By me now at thy Altar to be slain
A willing Sacrifice, and to his Lasse   4655
As true a Lover as Aminta *was.*

     Cho. Shep. Sol's Sister, Daughter of great Jupiter,
That shin'st a second Sun in the first Sphere
                  To the blind world!

     Mon. Ah, how my brest with pity now relents!   4660
What sudden numnesse fetters every sense!
I ne're was so before; To lift this Axe

My hands lack strength, and my heart courage lacks.

Car. I'le see the wretches face, and so be gone:
For such dire sights I cannot look upon.   4665

Mon. Perhaps the Sun, though setting will not look
On humane Sacrifice, and I am strook
Therefore with horrour. Shepherd, change thy place,
And to the Mountain turn thy dying face.
So, now 'tis well.

Car.   (Alas, what gaze I at?   4670
Is't not my Son? Is't not *Mirtillo*, that?)

Mon. Now I can do't.

Car.   ('Tis he.)

Mon.   And aim my blow—

Car. Hold sacred Minister, what dost thou do?

Mon. Nay thou, profane rash man, how dar'st thou thus
Impose a sacrilegious hand on us?   4675

Car. O all my joy *Mirtillo*! I ne're thought—

Mon. (Avant old man, that dot'st, or art distraught,)

Car. T' imbrace thee in this sort.

Mon.   Avant, I say,
It is not lawfull impure hands to lay
Upon things sacred to the gods.

Car.   'Twas they   4680
That sent me to this place.

Mon.   *Nicandro*, stay,
We'l hear him, and then let him go his way.

Car. Ah, courteous Minister! before thy hand
Upon the life of this young man descend,
Tell me but why he dyes. This I implore   4685
By that Divinitie thou dost adore.

Mon. By such a Goddesse thou conjur'st me, that
I should be impious to deny. But what
Concerns it thee?

Car.   More then thou dost suppose.

Mon. Because to die he for another chose.   4690

Car. Then I will die for him: O, take in stead
Of his, this old already tott'ring head.

Mon. Thou rav'st friend.

Car.   Why am I deni'd that now
Which unto him was granted?

Mon.   Because thou
A stranger art.
Car.   And if I should prove none,   4695
What then?
Mon.   Although thou shouldst, it were all one;
Because *he cannot be exchang'd again*
Who for another in exchange was ta'ne.
But who art thou, if thou no stranger be?
Thy habit speaks thee not of Arcadie.   4700
Car. Yet am I an Arcadian.
Mon.   I did ne're
See thee before (to my remembrance) here.
Car. My name's *Carino*; I was born hard by:
(This wretche's Father who is now to die).
Mon. Hence, hence, lest through thy fond paternal love   4705
Our Sacrifice should vain and fruitlesse prove.
Car. O if thou wert a Father!
Mon.   I am one:
I, and the Father of an onely Son.
A tender Father too; yet if this were
My *Silvio*'s head (by *Silvio*'s head I swear)   4710
I would as forward be to do to his
What I must do to this. 'For no man is
'Worthy this sacred Robe, but he that can
'For publick good put off the private man.
Car. Yet let me kisse him 'ere he die.
Mon.   Nor touch.   4715
Car. O mine own flesh and blood! art thou so much
A tyrant to me too, as to afford
To thy afflicted Parent not one word?
Mir. Dear Father, Peace.
Mon.   (Alas! we are all spoild:
The sacrifice (O Heavens!) is defil'd.)   4720
Mir. That blood, that life which thou didst give to me,
Spent for a better cause can never be.
Mon. Did I not say his vow of silence hee
Would break, when he his Fathers tears should see?
Mir. That such a grosse mistake I should commit!   4725
My vow of silence I did quite forgit.

4712. this] 47/48 (*c*); thine 47/48 (*u*).

Mon. But Ministers, why do yee gazing stay?
Him to the Temple quickly reconvay.
There in the holy Cloister again take
The voluntary Oath of him: then back   4730
Returning him with pomp along with you
For a new Sacrifice bring all things new,
New fire, and new water, and new wine.
Quickly: for *Phoebus* doth apace decline.

SCENA QUINTA.
Montano, Carino, Dameta.

Mon. Now thou old doting fool: thank Heav'n thou art   4735
His Father; for (by Heav'n) unlesse thou wert,
To day I'd made thee feel my fury, since
Thou hast so much abus'd my Patience.
Knowst thou who I am? Knowst thou that this wand
Doth both Divine and Humane things command?   4740
     Car. 'Let not the Priest of Heav'n offended be
'For begging mercy.
     Mon.   I have sufferd thee
Too long, and that hath made thee insolent.
Dost thou not know, 'when anger wanteth vent
'In a just bosome, it is gathering strength   4745
'Within, and bursts out with more force at length?
     Car. 'Anger was never in a noble mind
'A furious tempest: but a gentle wind
'Of Passion onely, which but stirs the soul,
'(Where Reason still doth keep her due comptroll)   4750
'Lest it should grow a standing pool, unfit
'For vertuous action. If I cannot get
Thee to extend that mercy which I crave,
Afford me justice; this I ought to have
From thee. 'For they who lawes to others give,   4755
'Ought not themselves without all law to live.
'And he that is advanc'd to greatest sway,
'Him that requireth Justice must obey.
And (Witnesse) I require it now of thee;
Do't for thy self, if thou wilt not for me.   4760
Thou art unjust if thou *Mirtillo* slay.

4757. greatest] 47/48 (*c*); greater 47/48 (*u*).

Mon. I prethee how?

Car.   To me didst thou not say,
Thou mightst not offer here a strangers blood?

Mon. I did: and said what Heav'n commanded.

Car.   Good:
This is a stranger then.

Mon.   A stranger? what?   4765
Is he not then thy Son?

Car.   All's one for that.

Mon. Is't 'cause thou gott'st him in a forraign land?

Car. The more thou seek'st, the lesse thou't understand.

Mon. It skils not here, *where*, but by *whom* hee's got.

Car. I call him stranger, cause I got him not.   4770

Mon. Is hee thy Son then, and not got by thee?

Car. I said he was my Son; not born of me.

Mon. Thy grief hath made thee mad.

Car.   I would it had!
I should not feel my grief, if I were mad.

Mon. Thou art or mad, or impious, chuse thou whether.   4775

Car. For telling the truth to thee I am neither.

Mon. How can both these (son and not son) be true?

Car. Son of my Love, not of my Loins.

Mon.   Go to;
He is no stranger, if he be thy Son:
If he be not, to thee no harm is done.   4780
So Father, or not Father, th' art confuted.

Car. 'Truth is truth still: though it be ill disputed.

Mon. 'That man that utters contradictions must
'Speak one untruth.

Car.   Thy action is unjust,
I say again.

Mon.   Let all this action's guilt   4785
Light on my head, and on my Son's.

Car.   Thou wilt
Repent it.

Mon.   Thou shalt, if thou wilt not take
Thy hands from off me.

Car.   My appeal I make
To men and Gods.

4767. 'cause] 47/48 (*c*); that 47/48 (*u*).

Mon.   To God, despis'd by thee?

Car. And if thou wilt not hear, hearken to me   4790
O Heav'n and Earth! and thou great Goddesse here
Ador'd! *Mirtillo* is a Forraigner,
No Son of mine: the holy Sacrifice
Thou dost profane.

Mon.   Blesse me good Heav'ns from this
Strange man! Say then, if he be not thy Son,   4795
Who is his Father?

Car.   'Tis to me unknown.

Mon. Is he thy kinsman?

Car.   Neither.

Mon.   Why dost thou then
Call him thy Son?

Car.   'Cause from the instant when
I had him first, I bred him as mine own
Still with a fatherly affection.   4800

Mon. Didst buy him? steal him? from whence hadst him?

Car. From *Elis* (the gift of a strange man).

Mon.   From whom
Had that strange man him?

Car.   That strange man? why he
Had him of me before.

Mon.   Thou mov'st in me
At the same time both laughter and disdain: 4805
What thou gav'st him, did he give thee again?

Car. I gave to him what was his own; then he
Return'd it as his courteous gift to me.

Mon. And whence hadst thou (since thou wilt make me mad
For company) that which from thee he had?   4810

Car. Within a thicket of sweet Mirtle, I
Had newly found him accidentally,
Neer to *Alfeo*'s mouth, and call'd him thence
Mirtillo.

Mon. With what likely circumstance
Thou dost thy lye embroider? Are there any   4815
Wild beasts within that Forrest?

Car.   Very many.

Mon. Why did not they devour him?

Car.   A strong flood

Had carry'd him into that tuft of wood,
And left him in the lap of a small Isle
Defended round with water.
 Mon.   Thou dost file   4820
One Lye upon another well. And was
The flood so pitifull to let him passe
Undrown'd? Such nurses in thy Country are
The Brooks, to foster infants with such care?
 Car. He lay within a cradle, which with mud 4825
And other matter gather'd by the flood
Calk't (to keep out the water) like a Boat
Had to that thicket carry'd him afloat.
 Mon. Within a cradle lay he?
 Car.   Yes.
 Mon.   A child
In swathing bands?
 Car.   A sweet one; and it smil'd.   4830
 Mon. How long ago might this be?
 Car.   'Tis soon cast:
Since the great Flood some twenty yeers are past,
And then it was.
 Mon.   What horrour do I feel
Creep thorow my veins!
 Car.   He's silenc'd, and yet will
Be obstinate. 'O the strange pride of those   4835
'In place! who conquer'd, yeeld not: but suppose,
'Because that they have all the wealth, with it
'They must be Masters too of all the wit.
Sure hee's convinc'd; and it doth vex him too,
As by his mutt'ring he doth plainly show: 4840
And one may see some colour he would find
To hide the errour of a haughty mind.
 Mon. But that strange man of whom thou tel'st me, what
Was he unto the child? his father?
 Car.   That
I do not know.
 Mon.   Nor didst thou ever know   4845
More of the man then thou hast told mee?
 Car.   No.
Why all these Questions?

Mon.   If thou saw'st him now,
Should'st know him?
Car.   Yes; he had a beetle-brow,
A down-look, middle-stature, with black hair,
His beard and eye-browes did with bristles stare.   4850
Mon. Shepherds & servants mine, approach.
Dam.   W' are here.
Mon. Which of these shepherds who do now appear,
To him thou talk'st of likest seems to thee?
Car. Not onely like him, but the same is hee
Whom thou talkst with: and still the man doth show   4855
The same he did some twenty yeers agoe,
For he hath chang'd no hair, though I am gray.
Mon. Withdraw, and let *Dameta* onely stay.
Tell me, dost thou know him?
Dam.   I think I doe:
But where, or how I know not.
Car.   I'le renew   4860
Thy memory by tokens.
Mon.   Let me talk
First with him if thou please, and do thou walk
Aside a while.
Car.   Most willingly what thou
Command'st I'le doe.
Mon.   Tell me *Dameta* now,
And do not lie.
Dam.   (O Gods, what storm comes here!)   4865
Mon. When thou cam'st back ('tis since some twenty yeer)
From seeking of my child, which the swoln Brook
Away together with its cradle took,
Didst thou not tell me thou hadst sought with pain
All that *Alpheo* bathes, and all in vain?   4870
Dam. Why dost thou ask it me?
Mon.   Answer me this:
Didst thou not say thou couldst not find him?
Dam.   Yes.
Mon. What was that little infant then which thou
In *Elis* gav'st to him that knows thee now?
Dam. 'Twas twenty yeers ago; and wouldst thou have   4875
An old man now remember what he gave?

Mon. Hee is old too, and yet remembers it.
Dam. Rather is come into his doting fit.
Mon. That we shall quickly see: Where art thou stranger?
Car. Here.
Dam.   Would thou wert interr'd, & I from danger!   4880
Mon. Is this the Shepherd that bestow'd on thee
The present, art thou sure?
　　Car.   I'm sure 'tis hee.
Dam. What present?
　　Car.   Dost thou not remember when
In *Jove Olympicks* Fane, thou having then
Newly receiv'd the Oracles reply,   4885
And being just on thy departure, I
Encountered thee, and asking then of thee
The signes of what th' adst lost, thou toldst them mee;
Then I did take thee to my house, and there
Shew'd thee thy child laid in a cradle; where   4890
Thou gav'st him me.
　　Dam.   What is inferr'd from hence?
Car. The child thou gav'st me then, and whom I since
Have brought up, as a tender Father doth
An onely Son, is this unhappy youth
Who on this Altar now is doom'd to die   4895
A Sacrifice.
　　Dam.   O force of Destinie!
Mon. Art studying for more lyes? Hath this man sed
The truth or not?
　　Dam.   Would I were but as dead
As all is true!
　　Mon.   That thou shalt quickly be
If the whole truth thou dost not tell to me.   4900
Why didst thou give unto another what
Was not thine own?
　　Dam.   Dear Master, ask not that;
For Heav'n's sake do not: too much thou dost know
Already.
　　Mon.   This makes me more eager grow.
Wilt not speak yet? Still keepst thou me in pain?   4905
Th' art dead if I demand it once again.
Dam. Because the Oracle foretold me there,

That *if the child then found returned e're*
To his own home, he should be like to die
By's Father's hand.
    Car.   'Tis true, my self was by.   4910
    Mon. Ay me! now all is cleer: This act of mine
The Dream and Oracle did well Divine.
    Car. What wouldst thou more? can ought behind remain?
Is it not plain enough?
    Mon.   'Tis but too plain.
I know, and thou hast said too much; I would   4915
I had search'd lesse, or thou lesse understood.
How (O) *Carino*, have I ta'ne from thee
At once thy Son, and thy Calamitie!
How are thy passions become mine! this is
My Son: O too unhappy Son, of this   4920
Unhappy man! O Son preserv'd and kept
More cruelly, then thou from hence wert swept
By the wild flood, to fall by the Sires hand,
And stain the Altars of thy native Land!
    Car. Thou Father to *Mirtillo*? Wondrous! How   4925
Didst lose him?
    Mon.   By that horrid flood which thou
Hast mention'd. O deer pledge! thou wert safe then
When thou wert lost: And now I lose thee, when
I finde thee.
    Car.   O eternall Providence!
For what deep end have all these Accidents   4930
Lain hid so long, and now break forth together?
Some mighty thing thou hast conceived, either
For good or evill: some unwonted birth
Thou art big with, which must be brought on earth.
    Mon. This was the thing my Dream foretold me; too   4935
Prophetick in the bad, but most untrue
In the good part: This 'twas which made me melt
So strangely; this, that horrour which I felt
Creep through my bones, when I heav'd up my hand.
For Nature's self seem'd to recoil, or stand   4940
Astonished, to see a Father go
To give that horrid and forbidden blow.
    Car. Thou art resolved then not to go on

With this dire Sacrifice?
Mon.   No other man
May do it here.
  Car.   Shall the Son then be slain   4945
By his own Sire?
  Mon.   'Tis law: and who dare strain
His charity to save another man,
When true *Aminta* with himself began?
  Car. O my sad Fate! what am I brought to see?
  Mon. Two Fathers over-acted Pietie   4950
Murther their son; Thine to *Mirtillo*; mine
To Heav'n. Thou by denying he was thine,
Thought'st to preserve him, and hast lost him; I
(Searching with too much curiosity)
Whilst I was to have sacrific'd thy son   4955
(As I suppos'd) find and must slay my own.
  Car. Behold the horrid Monster Fate hath teem'd!
O Cruell! O *Mirtillo*! more esteem'd
By me then life: Was this it which to me
The Oracle foretold concerning thee?   4960
Thus dost thou make me *in my Country blest*?
O my deer Son, whilome the hope and rest,
But now the grief and bane of these gray hairs!
  Mon. Prethee *Carino* lend to me those tears:
I weep for mine own blood. (Ah! why, if I   4965
Must spill it, is it mine?) Poor son! but why
Did I beget thee?—(Why was I got rather?)
The pitying deluge sav'd thee, and thy Father
Will cruelly destroy thee. Holy Pow'rs
Immortall (without some command of yours   4970
Not the least wave stirs in the Sea, breath in
The Air, nor leaf on Earth) what monstrous sin
Hath been by me committed 'gainst your Law,
This heavie Judgement on my head to draw?
Or if I have transgress'd so much; wherein   4975
Sinn'd my Son so, ye will not pardon him?
And thou with one blast of thy Anger kill
Me, thundring *Jove*? But if thy bolts lie still,
My blade shall not: I will repeat the sad
Example of *Aminta*, and the Lad   4980

Shall see his Father through his own heart run
His reeking blade, rather then kill his Son.
Dye then *Montano*; Age should lead the way:
And willingly I do't. Pow'rs (shall I say
Of Heav'n or Hell?) that do with anguish drive   4985
Men to despair; Behold, I do conceive
(Since you will have it so) your fury! I
Desire no greater blessing then to dye.
A kind of dire love to my naturall Gole
Doth lash me on, and hallow to my soul,   4990
To death, To death.
   Car.   'Las poor old man! in troth
I pity thee: for though we need it both,
Yet as by day the Starrs forbear to shine,
My grief is nothing, if compar'd with thine.

SCENA SEXTA.
Tirenio, Montano, Carino.

   Tir. Make haste my Son; yet tread secure, that I   4995
May without stumbling trace thee through this wry
And craggy way, with my old feet and blind.
Thou art their eyes, as I am to thy mind.
And when thou comest where the Priest is, there
Arrest thy pace.
   Mon.   Hah! whom do I see here?   5000
Is't not our Reverend *Tirenio*? hee
Whose eyes are seel'd up earthward, but heav'n see?
Some great thing draws him from his sacred Cell,
Whence to behold him is a miracle.
   Car. May the good Gods pleas'd in their bounty be   5005
To make his coming prosperous to thee.
   Mon. Father *Tirenio*, what miracle
Is this? What mak'st thou from thy holy Cell?
Whom dost thou seek? what news?
   Tir.   I come to speak
With thee: and news I bring, and news I seek.   5010
   Mon. But why comes not the holy Order back
With the purg'd offering, and what doth lack
Besides to th' interrupted Sacrifice?

4982. reeking] 47/48; reeling 64, 76/92.   5000. do] 47/48, 64; *omitted* 76/92.

Tir. 'O how much often doth the want of eyes
'Adde to the inward sight! for then the soul   5015
'Not gadding forth, but recollected whole
'Into it self, is wont to recompence
'With the mind's eyes the blindness of the sense!
'It is not good to passe so slightly over
'Some great events unlookt for which discover   5020
'In humane businesses an hand Divine,
'Which through a cloud of seeming chance doth shine.
'For Heav'n with Earth will not familiar be,
'Nor face to face talk with Mortality.
'But those great wondrous things which us amaze,   5025
'And on blind chance the more blind vulgar layes,
'Are but Heav'ns voice: the deathlesse Gods affect
'To speak to mortals in that Dialect.
'It is their language; mute unto our ears,
'But loud to him whose understanding hears.   5030
(A thousand times most happy is that wight
That hath an understanding pitcht so right).
The good *Nicandro* (as thou gav'st command)
Was ready now to bring the sacred Band,
Whom I withheld by reason of a change   5035
That fell out in the Temple. Which so strange
Event, comparing with what happen'd here
At the same time to thee, 'twixt hope and fear
I know not how, strook and amaz'd I stand:
Whereof by how much lesse I understand   5040
The cause, so much the more I hope and fear
Some happinesse, or some great danger neer.
Mon. That which thou understandest not, I do
Too well, and to my sorrow feel it too.
But is there ought in hidden Fate can shun   5045
Thy all divining Spirit?
    Tir.   O my Son!
'If the Divine use of prophetick light
'Were arbitrary, it would then be hight
'The gift of Nature, not of Heav'n. I find
(Tis true) within my undigested mind   5050
That there is something hidden in the deep
Bosome of Fate, which she from me doth keep,

And this hath mov'd me to come now to thee
To be inform'd more cleerly who is he
That's found to be the Father of the youth   5055
To dye now; if *Nicandro* told us truth.
 Mon. Thou knowst him but too well, *Tirenio*:
How wilt thou wish anon that thou didst know
Or love him lesse?
 Tir.   'I praise thee O my Son,
'For taking pity and compassion   5060
'On the afflicted: 'tis humanity.
How-ere let me speak with him.
 Mon.   Now I see
Heav'n hath suspended in thee all that skill
In Prophecie, which it was wont t' instill.
That Father whom thou seek'st to speak withall,   5065
Am I.
 Tir. Art thou his Father, that should fall
To *Dian* now an Immolation?
 Mon. The wretched Father of that wretched Son.
 Tir. Of that same *Faithfull Shepherd*, who to give
Life to another, would himself not live?   5070
 Mon. Of him who dies his Murthresse life to save,
And Murthers me, who unto him life gave.
 Tir. But is this true?
 Mon.   Behold the witnesse.
 Car.   That
Which he hath told thee is most true.
 Tir.   And what
Art thou that speak'st?
 Car.   *Carino*, thought to be   5075
Till now the young mans Father.
 Tir.   Was that he
The Flood took from thee long agoe?
 Mon.   Yes, yes,
Tirenio.
 Tir. And dost thou stile for this
Thy self a wretched Father? 'O how blind
'Is an unhallow'd and terrestriall mind!   5080
'In what thick mists of errour, how profound
'A night of Ignorance are our souls drown'd,

'Till thou enlighten them, from whom the Sun
'Receives his lustre, as from him the Moon!
Vain men, how can you boast of knowledge so?   5085
'That part of us by which we see and know,
'Is not our vertue, but deriv'd from Heav'n,
'That gives it, and can take what it hath giv'n.
O in thy mind, *Montano*, blinder far,
Then I am in mine eyes! What Juggler,   5090
What dazeling Divell will not let thee see
That if this noble youth was born of thee,
Thou art the happiest Father and most deer
To the immortall Deities, that e're
Begot Son in the world? Behold the deep   5095
Secret, which Fate did from my knowledge keep!
Behold the happy day, with such a flood
Expected of our tears, and of our blood!
Behold the blessed end of all our pain!
Where art thou man? come to thy self again.   5100
How is it that thou onely dost forget
That famous happy Oracle that's writ
In all Arcadian hearts? How can it be
That with thy deer son's lightning upon thee
This day, thy sense is not prepar'd and cleer   5105
The thunder of that heav'nly voice to hear;

Your Woe shall end when two of Race Divine
        Love shall Combine:—

(Tears of delight in such abundance flow
Out of my heart, I cannot speak.) *Your Woe—*   5110

Your Woe shall end when two of Race Divine
        Love shall Combine:
And for a faithlesse Nymph's apostate state
A Faithfull Shepherd supererogate.

Now tell me thou: This Shepherd here of whom   5115
We speak, and that should dye, is he not come
Of Divine Race (*Montano*) if hee's thine?
And *Amarillis* too *of Race Divine?*
Then who I pray but *Love hath them combin'd?*
Silvio by parents and by force was joyn'd   5120

       5099. blessed] 64, 76/92; bessed 47/48.

To *Amarillis*, and is yet as far
From loving her, as Love and Hatred are.
Then scan the rest, and't will be evident,
The fatall voice none but *Mirtillo* meant.
For who indeed, since slain *Aminta*, hath   5125
Express'd such *Love* as he? such constant *Faith*?
Who but *Mirtillo* for his Mistresse wou'd
Since true *Aminta*, spend his deerest bloud?
This is that work of *Supererogation*:
This is that *faithfull Shepherds* expiation   5130
For the *Apostate* false *Lucrina*'s fact.
By this admir'd and most stupendious Act
More then with humane blood the wrath of heav'n
Is pacifi'ed, and satisfaction giv'n
Unto eternall Justice for th' offence   5135
Committed 'gainst it by a woman. Hence
It was, that he no sooner came to pay
Devotions in the Temple, but streightway
All monstrous omens ceas'd; *No longer stood*
Th' eternall Image in a sweat of blood,   5140
The earth no longer shook, the holy Cave
No longer stank, and shrikes no longer gave:
But such sweet harmony and redolence
As Heav'n affords (if Heav'n affect the sense).
O Providence eternall! O ye Powers   5145
That look upon us from yon azure Towers!
If all my words were souls, and every soule
Were sacrific'd upon your Altars whole,
It were too poor a Hecatombe to pay
So great a blessing with: but as I may   5150
(Behold!) I tender thanks, and with my knee
Touching the earth in all humilitie
Look up on you that sit inthron'd in heav'n.
How much am I your debtor, that have giv'n
Me leave to live till now! I have run o're   5155
Of my life's race a hundred yeers and more,
Yet never liv'd till now, could never deem
My life worth keeping till this instant time.
Now I begin my life, am born to day.
But why in words do I consume away   5160

That time that should be spent in works? Help Son
To lift me up: Thou art the motion
Of my decayed limbs.

    Mon.   *Tirenio,*
I have a lightnesse in my bosom so
Lock't in, and petrifi'd with wonder, that   5165
I find I'm glad, yet scarcely know at what.
My greedy soule unto her self alone
Keeps all her joy, and lets my sense have none.
O miracle of Heav'n! farre, farre beyond
All we have seen, or e're did understand!   5170
O unexampled Bounty! O the great
Great mercy of the Gods! O fortunate
Arcadia! O earth, of all that e're
The Sun beheld or warm'd, most blest, most deer
To Heav'n! Thy weal's so deer to me, mine own   5175
I cannot feel, nor think upon my Son
(Twice lost and found) nor of my self buoy'd up
Out of the depth of sorrow, to the top
Of blisse, when I consider thee: but all
My private joy, set by the generall,   5180
Is like a little drop in a great stream
Shuffled and lost. O happy dream! (no dream,
But a Celestiall vision.) *Now agin*
Shall my Arcadia (as thou said'st) *be in*
A flourishing Estate: But why doest thou   5185
Stay here, *Montano?* Heav'n expects not now
More humane Sacrifice from us. No more
Th' are times of wrath and vengeance (as before)
But times of grace and love; glad nuptiall bands,
Not horrid Sacrifices at our hands   5190
Our Goddesse now requires.

    Tir.   How long to night?
    Mon. An hour, or little more.
    Tir.   We burn day-light:
Back to the holy Temple let us go;
There let the daughter of old *Titiro*
And thy Son interchange their Marriage vow   5195
To become Man and Wife, of Lovers now.
Then let him bring her to his Father's straight,

Where 'tis Heav'ns pleasure, that these fortunate
Descendents of two Gods, should henceforth run
United in one stream.—Lead me back, Son: 5200
And thou *Montano*, follow me.
    Mon.   But stay:
That faith which formerly she gave away
To *Silvio*, she cannot now withdraw
And give *Mirtillo*, without breach of Law.
    Car. 'Tis *Silvio* still, *Mirtillo* was call'd so   5205
At first (thy man told me) and *Silvio*
By mee chang'd to *Mirtillo*, to which hee
Consented.
    Mon.   True: (now I remember me)
And the same name I gave unto the other,
To keep alive the memory of 's Brother.   5210
    Tir. 'Twas an important doubt. Follow me now.
    Mon. Carino, to the temple too come thou.
Henceforth *Mirtillo* shall two Fathers own:
Thou hast a Brother found, and I a Son.
    Car. To thee a Brother in his love, a Father   5215
To him, a Servant (in respect) to either
Carino will be alwayes: And since I
Find thee to me so full of courtesie,
I will the boldnesse take to recommend
Unto thy love my second self, my friend.   5220
    Mon. Share me between you.
    Car.   O eternall Gods,
'Between our pray'rs slow-winding paths, what odds
'There is (by which we climb to Heav'n) and those
'Directer lines by which to us Heav'n bowes!

SCENA SEPTIMA.

Corisca, Linco.

    Cor. So it seems, *Linco*, that coy *Silvio*   5225
When least expected, did a Lover grow.
But what became of her?
    Lin.   We carry'd her
To *Silvio*'s dwelling, where with many a tear
(Whether of joy or grief, I cannot tell)

His Mother welcom'd her. It pleas'd her well   5230
To see her Son now marryed, and a Lover;
But for the Nymph great grief she did discover.
Poor Mother-in-law! ill sped, though doubly sped:
One Daughter-in-law being hurt, the other dead.
  Cor. Is *Amarillis* dead?
  Lin.   'Tis rumour'd so: 5235
That's now the cause I to the temple go,
To comfort old *Montano* with this newes,
One Daughter-in-law he gains, if one he lose.
  Cor. Is not *Dorinda* dead then?
  Lin.   Dead? would thou
Wert half so live and jocund as Shee's now!   5240
  Cor. Was't not a mortal wound?
  Lin.   Had she been slain,
With *Silvio*'s pity she had liv'd again.
  Cor. What Art so soon could cure her?
  Lin.   I will tell
Thee all the cure. Listen t' a miracle.
With trembling hearts, and hands prepar'd to aid,   5245
Women and men stood round the wounded Maid;
But she would suffer none to touch her save
Her *Silvio*; for the same hand which gave,
She said, should cure the wound. So all withdrew
Except my self, he, and his Mother: two   5250
T' advise, the third to act. Then *Silvio*
Removing first from her blood-dapled snow
Gently the cleaving garments, strove to pluck
The arrow out, which in her deep wound stuck.
But the false wood (forth coming) gave the slip   5255
To th' iron head, and left it in her Hip.
Here, here the lamentable cryes began:
It was not possible by hand of man,
Or iron instrument, or ought beside
To get it out. Perchance t' ave open'd wide   5260
The wound b' a greater wound, and so have made
One iron dive after another, had
Effected the great cure. But *Silvio*'s hand,
Too pitifull, too much with Love unmann'd
The Surgeon was, so cruelly to heal.   5265

Love searches not with instruments of steel
The wounds he makes. As for the love-sick Maid,
In *Silvio*'s hands her wounds grew sweet, she said.
And *Silvio* said (not yet discouraged)
Thou shalt out too, thou shalt, curst Arrow-head,   5270
And with lesse pain then is believ'd: the same
Who thrust thee in, can pull thee out again.
By using hunting I have learn'd to cure
This mischief which my hunting did procure.
A plant there is much us'd by the wild Goat   5275
When there's a shaft into her body shot:
She shew'd it us, and Nature shew'd it her:
(Remembred happily!) nor is it far
From hence. Streight went he to the neighb'ring hill,
And there a flasket with this Plant did fill;   5280
Then came again to us: thence squeesing out
The juice, and mingling it with Centry root
And Plantain leafe, thereof a pultise made.
O wonderfull! as soon as that was laid
Upon the sore, the blood was stanched streight,   5285
And the pain ceased; and soon after that,
The iron coming without pain away,
Did the first summons of the hand obey:
The Maid was now as vigorous and sound,
As if she never had receiv'd the wound.   5290
Nor mortall was't; for th' arrow having flown
(As hapt) betwixt the muscles and the bone,
Pierc'd but the fleshy part.
     Cor.   Thou hast displaid
Much vertue in a plant, more in a Maid.
     Lin. What afterwards between 'em happened   5295
May better be imagined then sed:
This I am sure, *Dorinda*'s well again,
And now can stir her body without pain:
Though thou believ'st, *Corisca*, I suppose
H' ath giv'n her since more wounds then that: but those,   5300
As they are made b' a diffrent weapon, so
Themselves are of a diffrent nature too.
And such a trick this cruell Archer has,
Of hitting all he shoots at since he was

A Huntsman; that to shew hee's still the same,   5305
Now hee's a Lover too, he hits the Game.
   Cor. Old *Linco* still!
   Lin.   Faith, my *Corisca*, still
If not in strength, I'm *Linco* in my will.
Nor yet, though my leafe's witherd, am I dead:
But all my sap into the root is fled.   5310
   Cor. My Rivall thus dispatch'd, I'le now go see
If I can get my deer *Mirtillo* free.

SCENA OCTAVA.

Ergasto, Corisca.

Erg. O Day with wonders fraught! O day of mirth!
All Love! and blessings all! O happy earth!
O bounteous heav'n!
   Cor.   But see! *Ergasto*'s here: 5315
How opportunely doth he now appear!
   Erg. At such a time let every living thing,
Heav'n, Earth, Air, Fire, the whole world laugh and sing.
To hell it self let our full joyes extend,
And there the torments of the damn'd suspend.   5320
   Cor. What rapture's this!
   Erg.   Blest woods! whose murmuring voyce
When we lamented did lament, rejoyce
At our joyes too, and wag as many tongues
As you have leaves now dancing to the songs
Of the pleas'd Birds, and musick of the Air   5325
Which rings with our delight. Sing of a pair
Of noble Lovers the felicitie
Unparalell'd.
   Cor.   He doth speak certainly
Of *Silvio* and *Dorinda*? Every thing
I see, would live. 'How soon the shallow spring   5330
'Of tears dryes up with us! but the swoln river
'Of gladnesse tarries with the longer liver.
Of *Amarillis*, who is dead, there's now
No more discourse: the only care is how
'To laugh with them that laugh; and tis well done: 5335

5324. to] 47/48, 76/92; no 64.

'Each man hath too much sorrow of his own.
Whither (so glad) *Ergasto* dost thou go?
Unto a Wedding happily?
 Erg.   I do
Indeed. Hast heard *Corisca* then, the wonder
O' th' two blest Lovers? was't not strange?
 Cor.   I under-   5340
Stood it of *Linco* now with joy of heart,
Which my great grief doth mitigate in part
For the sad death of *Amarillis.*
 Erg.   How!
Whom dost thou speak of, or speak I thinkst thou?
 Cor. Why, of *Dorinda*, and of *Silvio.* 5345
 Erg. What *Silvio*? what *Dorinda*? Dost not know
Then what hath past? My joy its linage drawes
From a more high, stupendious, noble Cause.
Of *Amarillis* and *Mirtillo* I
Discourse (the happiest Pair that this day frye 5350
Under the torrid Zone of Love).
 Cor.   Is not
Then *Amarillis* dead, *Ergasto*?
 Erg.   What
Death? She's alive, glad, beauteous, and a Wife.
 Cor. Thou mock'st me Shepherd.
 Erg.   No, upon my life.
 Cor. Was she not then condemn'd?
 Erg.   She was, 'tis true: 5355
But presently she was acquitted too.
 Cor. Do I dream this? or dost thou dreams relate? ⎫
 Erg. Stay here a little, thou shalt see her straight ⎬
Come with her faithfull and most fortunate ⎭
Mirtillo, from the temple (where they're now, 5360
And interchanged have their Nuptiall vow)
Towards *Montano*'s: of the bitter root
Of their long Loves to gather the sweet fruit.
O hadst thou seen mens joyes spring in their eyes!
If thou hadst heard the musick of their cryes! 5365
The temple's still as full as it can hold
Of numbers numberlesse: Men, women, old,
Young, Prelates, Laymen, are confounded there

Together, and distracted cannot bear
Their joy. With wonder every one doth run   5370
To see the happy couple, every one
Adores them, every one embraces them.
Their pity one extols, another's theme
Their constant faith is, or those graces giv'n
To them by Nature, or infus'd from Heav'n.   5375
The laund, the dale, the mountain, and the plain
Resound *the faithfull Shepherd*'s glorious name,
O happy, happy Lover, to become
From a poor Swain, almost a God so soon;
From death to life (whilst I speak this) to passe, 5380
And change a winding-sheet (which ready was)
For a remote despair'd-of Nuptiall,
Though it be much, *Corisca*, is not all.
But to enjoy her, whom he seem'd t' injoy
In dying for her, her who would destroy   5385
Her selfe, not to excuse, but share his Fate,
(His Mate in life, and not in death his Mate!)
This is such joy, such ravishing joy is this
As doth exceed all we can fancie Blisse.
And dost not thou rejoyce? and apprehend   5390
A joy for *Amarillis*, that's thy Friend
As great as that which I doe for my true
Mirtillo?
     Cor.   Yes, dost thou not see I doe?
     Erg.   O! if thou hadst present been
Amarillis to have seen,   5395
As the pledge of Faith when she
Gave her hand to him, and he
As the pledge of Love did either
Give or receive (I know not whether)
A sweet inestimable kisse,   5400
Surely thou hadst dy'd of blisse.
There was Scarlet, there were Roses,
All the colours, all the posies
Art or Nature ere did mix
Were excell'd by her pure cheeks,   5405
Cover'd with a waving shield
By her blushing Beauty held,

Stain'd with blood, which did provoke
From the striker a new stroke.
And shee coy and nice in show,   5410
Seem'd to shun, that shee might so ⎱
With more pleasure meet the blow, ⎰
Leaving it in doubt, if that
Kisse were ravished, or not.
With such admirable Art,   5415
'Twas in part bestow'd, in part
Snatch'd from her: And that disdain
Which she did so sweetly fain,
Was a willing No; an Act
Mixt of Conquest and Compact.   5420
Such a coming in her flying
As shew'd yeelding in denying.
Such sweet anger at th' abuse
In forcing her, as forc'd him use
That force again; such art to crave   5425
The thing she would not, yet would have,
As drew him the faster on
To snatch that which would be gone.
O heav'nly kisse! *Corisca*, I
Can no longer hold; God bu'y.   5430
'I'le marry too, The Pow'rs above
'Give no true joy to men, but Love.
   Cor. If he (*Corisca*) have told truth, this day
Quite cures thy wits, or takes them quite away.

SCENA NONA.

Chorus of Shepherds, Corisca,
Amarillis, Mirtillo.

   Cho. Holy Hymen hear our pray'r   5435
And our Song! The Earth hath not
A more happy loving pair:
Both of them Divinely got;
Pull holy Hymen, pull the destin'd knot.
   Cor. Ay me! *Ergasto* told me true (I see)   5440
This is the fruits (wretch) of thy vanitie.

<hr>

5414. Kisse were ravished] 47/48 (*c*); kisses were ravish'd 47/48 (*u*).

O thoughts! O wishes! as unjust, as vain
And fond. Would I an innocent have slain
To compasse my unbridled will! So blind,
So cruell was I? Who doth now unbind   5445
Mine eyes? Ah wretch! what do I see? my sin
With the mask off just as 'tis here within.
    Cho. Holy Hymen hear our pray'r
And our song! The Earth hath not
A more happy loving Pair: 5450
Both of them divinely got:
Pull holy Hymen, pull the destin'd knot.
See (thou *Faithfull Shepherd*) where
After many a briny tear,
After many a stormy blast,   5455
Thou art landed now at last!
Is not this (behold her!) shee
Heav'n and Earth deny'd to thee?
And thy cruell Destinie?
And her Icie Chastitie?   5460
And thy degree so far beneath?
And her Contract? and thy Death?
Yet *Mirtillo* (loe!) shee's thine.
That sweet face, those eyes divine,
Brest and hands, and all that thou   5465
See'st and hear'st, and touchest now,
And so often hast in vain
Sigh'd for, now thou dost obtain,
As thy constant Love's reward:
Yet thy lips hath silence barr'd?   5470
    Mir. 'Cannot speak: I do not know
Whether I'm alive or no.
Or if these things reall be
Which I seem to hear and see.
Sweetest *Amarillis* mine,   5475
(For my soul is lodg'd in thine)
I from thee would gladly know,
(Tell me Love) are these things so?
    Cho. Holy Hymen hear our pray'r
And our song! The Earth hath not   5480
A more happy loving Pair:

Both of them divinely got:
Pull holy Hymen, pull the destin'd knot.
 Cor. But why do you, you still about me stay,
Arts to deceive the world, arts to betray? 5485
(The body's robes, but the souls rags.) For one,
I'm sure shee's cousen'd by you, and undone.
Pack hence: and as from worms ye had your birth,
Return to worms, and strew your grandame earth.
Once ye were weapons of lascivious Love: 5490
But now the trophies of fair Vertue prove.
 Cho. *Holy Hymen hear our pray'r*
And our Song! The Earth hath not
A more happy loving pair:
Both of them Divinely got; 5495
Pull holy Hymen, pull the destin'd knot.
 Cor. What stick'st thou at *Corisca?* 'tis a day
Of Pardons this: then ask without dismay.
What dost thou dread? no punishment what-ere
Can fall so heavie, as thy fault lies here. 5500
Fair, and happy pair (the Love
Of us here, and those above)
If all earthly Pow'r this day
To your conquering Fates give way,
Let her likewise Homage doe 5505
To your conquering Fates, and you,
Who all earthly Pow'r imploy'd
To have made their Ord'nance voyd.
Amarillis (true it is)
He had mine, who had thy heart: 5510
But thou onely hast gain'd his,
'Cause thou onely worthy art.
Thou enjoy'st the loyall'st Lad
Living; and *Mirtillo* thou
The best Nymph the world ere had 5515
From the birth of Time till now:
I the touch-stone was to both,
Try'd her chastitie, his troth.
But thou (Courteous Nymph) before
Thou on me thy anger powre, 5520
Look but on thy Bridegrooms Face:

Something thou wilt spy therein
That will force thee to shew grace,
As it forced mee to sin.
For so sweet a Lovers sake   5525
Upon love no vengeance take;
But since thou the flames dost prove,
Pardon thou the fault of Love.

 Am. I do not onely pardon, but respect
Thee as my friend, regarding the effect,   5530
And not the cause. 'For poysons if they make
'Us well, the name of soveraign Med'cines take;
'And painfull lancings for that cause are dear:
So whether friend or foe, or whatso e're
Thou wert to me in purpose and intent;   5535
Yet my Fate us'd thee as her instrument
To work my blisse, and that's enough: for me
'Twas a good Treason, a blest Fallacy
I'm sure. And if thou please to grace our Feast,
And to rejoyce with us, thou art my guest.   5540

 Cor. Thy pardon is to me a better feast:
A greater joy, my conscience now at rest.

 Mir. And I all faults 'gainst me can pardon wel,
But this long stop.

 Cor.   Joys on you both! Farewell.

 Cho. Holy Hymen hear our pray'r   5545
And our Song! The Earth hath not
A more happy loving Pair:
Both of them divinely got:
Pull holy Hymen, pull the destin'd knot.

SCENA DECIMA.

Mirtillo, Amarillis.
Chorus of Shepherds.

 Mir. Am I so wedded then to grief and anguish,   5550
That in the midst of joy too I must languish?
Was not this tedious pomp enough delay,
But I must meet too my old Remora
Corisca?

 Am. Thou art wondrous hasty.

Mir.   O

My treasure! yet I am not sure; but go   5555
In fear of robbing still, till as my Spouse
I doe possesse thee in my Fathers house.
To tell thee true, me thinks I fare like one
Who dreams of wealth, and ever and anon
Fears that his golden sleep will break, and he   5560
Be wak'd a beggar. I would gladly be
Resolv'd by some more pregnant proof, that this
Sweet waking now is not a dream of blisse.

    Cho. Holy Hymen hear our pray'r
And our Song! The earth hath not   5565
A more happy loving pair:
Both of them divinely got:
Pull holy Hymen, pull the destin'd knot.

CHORUS.

O Happy couple! that hath sown in Tears
And reaps in Comfort! What a foil your fears   5570
Prove to your joyes! Blind Mortals, learn from hence,
Learn (yee effeminate) the difference
Betwixt true goods and false. All is not joy
That tickles us: Nor is all that annoy
That goes down bitter. 'True joy is a thing   5575
'That springs from Vertue after suffering.

FINIS.

CRITICAL NOTES

PROLOGUE. The prologue was written for a performance at Turin, celebrating the marriage of Carlo Emanuele I, Duke of Savoy, to Catherine of Austria, daughter of Philip II of Spain, in 1585. There is some doubt whether this performance actually took place (see Introduction).

14–22. Translation is inaccurate and confusing; literally: 'Behold, leaving my ancient and well-known course, through an unknown sea, meeting the wave of the proud king of rivers [i.e. the Po], here I rise and I come here happy to see again that ancient land of mine whence I derive, as free and beautiful as it used to be, now desolate and enslaved.'

37–38. Amphion's playing of the lyre caused the stones to build themselves into a wall around Thebes.

69–70. Turin is at the confluence of the Po and the Dora Riparia.

116. *silver*, not in G.

ACT I, SCENE I

127. *lodg'd*, Italian is *chiudeste*, i.e. 'enclosed'.

136. *grove*, Italian is *giro*, i.e. 'circle'.

239–43. Cf. Seneca, *Hippolytus*, ll. 451–3 (G.'s note).

249. *yon star*, Venus.

277–8. Cf. Terence, *The Self-Tormenter*, Act I, scene i (G.'s note).

ACT I, SCENE II

341–3. The adders stop their ears so that they cannot be charmed; see (Vulgate) Psalm lviii. 4.

355–6. Cf. Petrarch, *Rime*, ccvii. 66 (G.'s note).

365–6. Cf. Petrarch, *Trionfo d'amore*, ii. 63. 'All this part of Mirtillo is pathetic, genteel, full of strong love, and in good taste' (G.'s note).

376. *qualifi'd*, Italian is *gentile*, i.e. 'well-born'.

379–80. Cf. Shakespeare, Sonnet cxvi.

395 ff. 'This dialogue is all sententious as is fitting to whoever persuades and consoles' (G.'s note).

444–5. Cf. Virgil, *Aeneid*, I. 11 (G.'s note).

445 ff. 'This tragic story is taken from Pausanius.' (G.'s note.) See *Description of Greece*, Bk. VII, ch. XIX.

486. *fence*, defence.

536. *lightning before death*, probably a reminiscence of *Romeo and Juliet*, v. iii. 90; G. has simply, 'and felt perhaps that blow'.

571. *And for a . . . state*, G. has 'For the ancient error of that unfaithful woman', clearly referring to Lucrina.

572. *supererogate*, to make up by excess of merit for the failing of another (*OED*).

586. *all this do*, all this ado.

ACT I, SCENE III

619–20. *possible . . . in me*, literally: 'It seems impossible that an amorous flame ever burned for him in my breast.'

ACT I, SCENE IV

762. *not yet seventeen*, G. has 'not yet eighteen'.

768–9. Literally: '*Mon.* It is possible to have a flower without fruit. *Tit.* With flowers, maturity always brings love as a fruit.'

834. *Beech*, here and in l. 850 G. has 'plane-tree'.

848–9. *signes . . . vengeance*, not in G.

907–8. Cf. *Twelfth Night*, II. iv. 45–46.

ACT I, SCENE V

935–8. Cf. Theocritus, *Idylls*, viii; Virgil, *Eclogues*, v (G.'s note).

979. *hatch*, to lay strips or plates of gold or silver in or on (a surface) by way of ornament (*OED*).

986. *feulemort*, of the colour of a dead or faded leaf, brown or yellowish brown (*OED*).

989–96. 'A very fine figure, which Aristotle in *Rhetoric*, iii, calls "energeian" but which I think should be called "enargeian" as Quintilian calls it in Book VI' (G.'s note). The fact that the 1602 English translator omitted this passage and cut the whole scene much more heavily than any other suggests that he may have found neither *enargeian* nor the *satiro buffo* to his taste.

1020. *Argos*, 'It came to be called wicked because it was the birthplace of Helen' (G.'s note).

1022. *from tracing out*, from being traced out or discovered.

1023. *jettst*, thou struttest, swaggerest (*OED*).

1030. *There's . . . sainted*, literally: 'A woman adored is a god from Hell.'

1068–9. Fishing image not in G.

1070. *Rellief*, (hunting term) of the hare or the hart: the act of seeking food; feeding or pasturing (*OED*).

FIRST CHORUS

1079–90. An exact and literal translation of the important first stanza of this chorus would run: 'O high and powerful law, written or rather born in the breast of Jove, whose sweet and amorous force bends minds and compels nature toward that good which all created things feel though they do not understand! Not the frail shell [of things] which the sense hardly sees, and which is born and dies with the changing of the hours, but the hidden seeds and the internal cause which has eternal force, move and govern.' G. says in his note that the subject of this chorus is fate, but adds that he equates fate with the law of nature and thus with the governing intelligence of God.

1093–1100. Cf. Virgil, *Aeneid*, vi. 724–32 (G.'s note).

1113. *Soul of the World*, in the Italian, *O detto inevitabile*, literally, 'O inevitable word'. 'I mean "Fate" which in Latin is "Fatum", that is to say "detto"' (G.'s note).

1135–42. This stanza, which G. in his note calls a digression, compares Silvio and Mirtillo struggling against Fate in different directions with the fabled giants who tried to storm heaven. Fanshawe has condensed slightly.

ACT II, SCENE I

1162–5. Literally: 'But do not let yourself so haughtily be mastered by your sorrow; master yourself if you want to conquer others; live and breathe sometimes.'

1222–7. *At the first view . . . Mirtillo*. G. has simply 'And without making any defence at the first glance which she directed into my eyes, I felt an imperious beauty enter my breast and say to me—Give me your heart, Mirtillo.'

1238. *imps*, to eke out, lengthen out, or enlarge something (*OED*). See also l. 2020.

1242. *footsteps*, vestiges.

1245. In his note G. cites Theocritus, *Idylls*, xii, as his source for the Megarensian custom of kissing contests.

1304–6. The military image is not in G.

1325. *dart*, i.e. the bee's sting, continuing the image of the bee and the rose from l. 1318; the incongruous similes in ll. 1321–2 are Fanshawe's additions.

1337. *Remora*, impediment or hindrance; see also ll. 3809, 5553.

1345. *Syrian dog*, the constellation of Sirius.

1369. *use*, usury.

1404–6. Fanshawe's rendering is awkward; literally: 'But the only safety for the desperate is the despairing of safety.' G. is imitating Virgil's famous line, 'Una salus victis, nullam sperare salutem', *Aeneid*, ii. 354.

ACT II, SCENE II

1426–7. Cf. Petrarch, *Rime*, ccviii (G.'s note).

1481. *Shittle-cock*, variant of 'shuttle-cock', used for Silvio because he changes his tone so frequently.

1516. Fanshawe omits G.'s next line: 'If your heart didn't have ice in it.'

1568. *Setting by*, literally: 'holding dear'.

ACT II, SCENE III

1601–6. Cf. Seneca, *Hippolytus*, 613–16, 700–2 (G.'s note).

ACT II, SCENE V

1653. *horrors*, used in archaic sense, 'roughness, raggedness', as a metonym for 'trees'; here it translates G.'s *orrori*, but above, l. 723, Fanshawe's *gloomy horrors* translates G.'s *ombrose selve*. Cf. Milton, *Comus*, l. 37.

1738-9. Literally: '*Am.* And did he consent to your breaking it? *Cor.* Gladly!'

1800. *God bu'y*, common old variant of 'goodbye', i.e. 'God be with you'.

1824-5. Fanshawe names eight nymphs where G. has five; he adds Celia, Daphne, Silvia, and Laura and omits Licoris; the change is doubtless introduced for metrical reasons, since Licoris inconsistently appears below, l. 2187.

1850. *'natomie*, i.e. 'anatomy', a body or model of a body showing the parts in dissection; the image is not in G.

ACT II, SCENE VI

1857. *quick*, pun on 'alive' and 'swift'.

1917. *kerve*, carve.

1966-7. *that grave . . . in't*, literally: 'That putrid, slobbering, toothless cavern.' The reference is to the Satyr's mouth; cf. below, ll. 1977-8.

1970. *pincers*, literally, 'hands'.

2027. *Come by his owne*, i.e. get his own heart back.

2028. *that hair*, Berenice's.

SECOND CHORUS

2048. *carcasse of their coffin'd gold*, literally, 'a corpse of gold'. De Sanctis took this for a reference to Corisca's hair, but this seems unwarranted; see *History of Italian Literature*, ii. 680.

2057 ff. Besides this passage, that in Act II, scene i, and that in Act V, scene viii, G. has two madrigals that expatiate sensuously on kissing. Tasso has a similar passage in *Aminta*. These passages are generally cited as signs of decadence, or as the Italians say, *secentismo*.

2066. *sound at the loose*, sound at the discharging of an arrow (*OED*).

ACT III, SCENE I

2089-98. Cf. Petrarch, *Trionfo d'amore*, i. 1-3 (G.'s note).

ACT III, SCENE II

2135 ff. G.'s notes on the play of blindman's buff in this scene are worth quoting at length:

It is necessary to warn the reader that all the movements that are customary in such a disordered and casual game are, in this scene, studied with metre and harmony, in such a way that it is not less a dance than a game, which imitates the ancient custom of the Greeks and Romans, as Lucian clearly shows in his excellent treatise on the art of dancing. . . . Nor can I pass over in silence the way in which our poet composed the words of this dance, which was thus: First, he had the dance composed by an expert in such exercises, he devising a way of imitating the motions and gestures that are customarily used in an ordinary game of blindman's buff. The dance done, it was put to music by Luzzasco, the most excellent musician of our time. Then the poet wrote the words under the notes of the music, which caused the diversity of the verses, now of five syllables, now of seven, now of eight, now of eleven, according to what satisfied the requirements of the notes. It was a thing that appeared impossible; and if he had not done it many other times with so much greater difficulty when in other dances he was not master of the invention as he was in this one, he would not have believed it possible. For in those dances he had not only the trouble of putting the words under the notes, but of inventing the dance movements which they would fit and managing the plot as well.... The subject of all this dance, that is to say of the words made for it, is nothing but the scorning of Love and showing that it has no power over the heart that resists it, and therefore it was said that 'a free heart makes a nimble heel', because whoever wants to avoid amorous practices must begin with the heart, freeing it from disturbing affections. And therefore [the speaker of the chorus] says that in vain he is pursued, because he has a free heart, thus informing us that the blindman represents Love and those who jest all around him are like the hearts which he seeks to capture.

2212. *mouth*, G. has 'arms'.

2236-8. In the 1602 English translation, these lines do not appear; instead there are the following:

> Catch how thou will thou getst not mee,
> The reason is my hart is free.
> > (Amarillis takes Mirtillo now.)
> Him thou hast caught it is no wonder
> For loue holds all his senses under.

ACT III, SCENE III

2248. *short hair*, because the Satyr has taken her hair.

2250-1. *thus*, apparently she strikes him.

2327. *stock*, piece of wood; G. has *sterpi*, 'twigs'.

2410-11. Cf. Theocritus, *Idylls*, xx (G.'s note).

2440. Literally: 'It is not in the power of him who has lost his soul not to die.'

ACT III, SCENE IV

2500-4. Literally: 'Holy virtue, who alone art the inviolable guardian spirit of a well-born soul, to you I consecrate as an innocent victim this amorous desire which I have stabbed with the steel of your holy rigour.' Cf. the translations in Appendix II.

ACT III, SCENE V

2543-9. 'All this amplification is taken from the charge of Marcus Tullius in his *Pro Milone* to which passage, because it is so good, I should like to refer: "For this, judges, is not a written law, but a native law, which we did not learn but we received, we collected: indeed from nature itself we snatched it, drank it, squeezed it out: to this we were not taught but created, not instituted but imbued as with our very life"'(G.'s note).

2556–7. *if to be . . . mind*, G. has here 'If all the guilty ones should die, believe me, the country would remain womanless'.

2575–8. Literally: 'Let the men chatter, Amarillis, as they do not know nor cannot feel the tribulations of women, and very different from the condition of the man is that of the poor woman.'

2593–600. Cf. Catullus, 'Vivamus mea Lesbia' (G.'s note).

2615. *the still sow*, cf. 'The styll sowe eath all thy draffe, my sowe eath none', Epigram 142, *John Heywoodes Woorkes* (London, 1562).

2651–4. Fanshawe's *Phillida* substitutes for G.'s *Leucippe*, a substitution made for metrical reasons, one would suppose. Cf. note on ll. 1824–5. These names are common pastoral ones and have, we believe, no specific references; Egle, for example, does not refer to Giraldi Cinthio's character of that name.

ACT III, SCENE VI

2743–5. Bears were believed to be born in shapeless lumps which the mother must lick into the form of a cub; see *Dictionary of Folklore, Myth, and Legend*, ed. Maria Leach (New York, 1949), i. 124.

ACT III, SCENE VII

2959. The third heaven in Dante's *Paradiso* is that of Venus.

ACT III, SCENE VIII

2982. *This wretched man*, Mirtillo refers to himself.

2988. *hath spu'd*, the subject is *which* in l. 2983.

ACT III, SCENE IX

3109. Refers to Pan's punishing Syrinx's coldness by turning her into a reed pipe.

THIRD CHORUS

3141. *fairer*, than heaven.

3167. *Reason*, more exactly, 'human nature'. The great miracle that love has wrought is to make Mirtillo love even without hope and thus to transcend human nature.

ACT IV, SCENE II

3308. *knapt*, broken into parts or pieces with a sharp cracking sound (*OED*).

ACT IV, SCENE III

3425. The line is from Ovid, *Amores*, I. viii. 43. The form *akst*, for *asked*, though common before 1600, was archaic by Fanshawe's time; see *OED*.

3439. *sincere*, pure, clear in colour (*OED*).

ACT IV, SCENE IV

3554. The military image is not in G.

ACT IV, SCENE V

3598–9. This broken-off sentence, indicating hysteria or faintness in Amarillis, is Fanshawe's own invention; G. does, however, use the device at l. 3720.

3630–1. Literally: '*Am.* If reason does not govern the sense is wrong./ *Nic.* And the reason is wrong if the fact is doubtful.' On Nicandro's answer G. notes: 'Legal term. *Ex facto ius oritur.*'

3681–6. 'There rises in her greatly the fear of death which is made with art: first to move compassion in this tragic part; and then to make so much greater the miracle of her courage when she elects to die for Mirtillo, with the purpose of showing the greatness of her love for him; but much more the constancy and the honesty which she has always maintained in her words and which have never allowed her to cross the bounds of decorum are the prime object and, so to speak, the architectonic of our poet in her character' (G.'s note). Cf. the remarks on this passage in Sir Walter Wilson Greg, *Pastoral Poetry and Pastoral Drama* (London, 1906), pp. 200–1.

3720. As his precedent for the broken-off speech, G. cites Ariosto, *Orlando Furioso*, Canto 42, stanza 14.

ACT IV, SCENE VII

3805. *tumbling cast*, extremity, near to death or ruin (*OED*).

3838. *can't*, can it.

3856. *Aspine*, of or pertaining to an asp.

ACT IV, SCENE VIII

3907. *hers*, i.e. Adonis.

3926. *I glow*, means that since he glows he is the son of Vulcan, the smith-god. This awkwardness is in the Italian; Fanshawe's translation is very close throughout this scene.

ACT IV, SCENE IX

4005. Following this speech of Linco's, there is a one-line speech of Silvio's, 'O Earth, why do you not open up and engulf me?' which Fanshawe has omitted. The omission could have been an accident, or the line could have been missing in the Italian edition which Fanshawe used. Of some fifty Italian editions, or more probably issues, which were available to Fanshawe, we have checked without positive results the following: G. B. Brifadino, Venice, 1590; Franceschi Senese, Venice, 1596; V. Boldini, Ferrara, 1596; G. B. Ciotti, Venice, 1602; G. B. Ciotti, Venice, 1605; G. B. Ciotti, Venice, 1616; G. B. Ciotti, Venice, 1621.

4041. *at all adventures*, at any risk, whatever may be the consequences, recklessly (*OED*).

4109. *Alablaster*, the spelling in the sixteenth and seventeenth centuries is almost always this (*OED*).

FOURTH CHORUS

4217. *cels*, this word, *chiostri*, which does not make much sense here, is forced on Guarini because it is one of Tasso's rhyme-words (see Introd.).

ACT V, SCENE I

4227. *Carino*, this character represents Guarini just as Tirsi represents Tasso in *Aminta*.

4315. *Egon*, represents Scipione Gonzaga (see Introd.).

4336. *Delphick iron, ferro* means here 'knife'; in his note G. cites, 'For she [Nature] is not niggardly, like the smith who fashions the Delphian knife for many uses.' Aristotle, *Politics*, Bk. I, ch. 2.

4405. Ariosto would have been the first Ferrarese poet crowned with laurel (G.'s note).

4419-20. *a traveller with language*, a traveller with ability to speak a foreign language (*OED*). The saying is proverbial.

4420-1. 'Uranio, not being obliged to appear any more, having only served as one of those persons whom the Greeks called *protatika*, with much judgement is provided with a hostel so that he may rest, having been shown above to have great need of the same' (G.'s note).

ACT V, SCENE II

4435. *sconce*, a small fort or earthwork.

4436-7. *A woman . . . companion*, literally, 'A woman unaccompanied is always badly guarded.'

ACT V, SCENE III

4559-60. *with Vegetals, with Creatures sensitive, with Rationals*, i.e. with plants, animals, and men; see Aristotle, *De Anima*, Bk. II, esp. chs. 3-4.

4570-3. This refrain is assigned without annotation to the Chorus of Priests by L. Fasso in his 1950 edition; the 1602 Venice edition, however, gives it to the Chorus of Shepherds as Fanshawe does.

4617-19. 'While the ministers excite the flame and strew over it that material which will produce the smoke which the sacrificial ceremony demands, the stage does not remain destitute of words, which would be a very great fault in a dramatic poem; but the chorus of shepherds sings the three intercalary verses, which finished, Carino enters and speaks and after him Montano begins, so that the stage is never without words' (G.'s note).

ACT V, SCENE V

4742. 'Here begins the very fine and artistic recognition in this plot, which has all those elements which Aristotle teaches us belong to the more perfect and notable plots. These are three: that it be both necessary and realistic; that it be made not through signs [see *Poetics*, ch. 16] but through reasoning; and that it produce a change either from happy to sad or from sad to happy fortune—

which conditions are all clearly present in this recognition . . . Above all it is so like that of the *Oedipus Tyrannis*, truly marvellous and greatly celebrated by the Philosopher, that it could not be more so, the messenger in the work having carried over the very terms and words of Sophocles. . . . Thus Sophocles did it also that while the messenger seeks to console Oedipus and to persuade him that he should not fear having to fall into the sin of parricide and incest with his mother he happens to reveal the one and the other in such a way that it seemed impossible that the recognition could have come about better in any other way' (G.'s note).

4884. *Jove Olympicks Fane*, the temple of Olympian Jove.

ACT V, SCENE VI

5048. *arbitrary*, the Italian is *voluntario*; he means that, if he had prophetic power whenever he wanted it, it would be a natural phenomenon.

ACT V, SCENE VII

5251–88. Cf. *Aeneid*, xii. 387–424; *Gerusalemme Liberata*, xi, stanzas 67–74 (G.'s note).

5295–6. So the union of Aminta and Silvia is described in Tasso's play, Act v, scene i, near the end.

ACT V, SCENE VIII

5381–2. Cf. Dryden, 'Elegy on the Death of the Lord Hastings', l. 4.

ACT V, SCENE IX

5453. 'The song of the chorus having ended, one alone speaks, as an actor, just as was seen in iv. iii, of this same play' (G.'s note).

APPENDIXES

APPENDIX I

GUARINI'S PREFACE TO THE 1602 EDITION

[NOTE: The following statement appears as a preface to the 1602 edition of *Il Pastor Fido*, which has the annotations printed after each scene. In the 1737 edition it appeared at the beginning of the notes, which in that edition are gathered together with separate pagination at the end of the play. Since *Il Compendio* was written by 1601, this statement probably postdates it and thus represents Guarini's last word on his play. In general this preface summarizes what Guarini says in the two *Verati* and *Il Compendio*. Like any good critic Guarini attempts to state his ideas in the critical language current in his day, so that he should be read in the context of sixteenth-century Italian criticism. Madeleine Doran's comment on Guarini (*Endeavors of Art*, pp. 203–8 *et passim*) and the selections in Allan Gilbert's anthology will prove helpful in this respect.]

THE name of 'Faithful Shepherd' has been given to this fable with good reason and judgement, being taken from that role which acts out its precise and true aspect. That is to say from Mirtillo, a sort of noble centre around whom all the intrigues of the present fable revolve. The subject of the oracle is his faith. And he with his faith endures the difficulties, resists the flatteries, conquers the impediments, spurns death, comes to his marriage, possesses the lady he loves, liberates his country, than which nothing in the world can be more glorious. He is worthily called 'Faithful' and faithfully has he loved his lady, with such faith indeed that, when he did not believe she loved him and was certain not to have her for his own, he loved her all the more ardently. Thus Petrarch called his love for Laura 'Faith' in his sonnet 'S'onesto amor' [cccxxxiv]. And he more than any other deserves the title of 'Faithful' because he not only conquered grief but even pleasure, with which no one else in the play is tempted. It is an adjunct which fits the name 'shepherd' as well as the one Petrarch calls 'faithful', the pilot in the 'Canzone della Vergine' [*Rime*, ccclxvi] and in many other places in the *Canzoniere*. And so much for the name.

As for the fable, it is certainly dramatic in kind; but in constitution it is not double but mixed, and in subject it is not simple but composite. The mixture is of tragic and comic characters; it is not like that which is enumerated by the Philosopher among the tragedies with a double ending, in which the good characters come to a good end and the bad characters come to a bad end.[1] But it is mixed in such a way that tragic and comic roles, having been well harmonized together and reformed, are led to a single comic end. And for this reason it is more like to the *Amphytrion* of Plautus, from which the name of tragicomedy was taken, than it is to the *Cyclops* of Euripides, which can rather be called double in constitution, being befouled with blood and having diverse conclusions, which deal out good to the better characters and bad to the worse, which is not the case in the *Amphytrion*. I said further that in subject it is not simple but composite, in this respect more like those of Terence in which one subject acts as the principal and the other as the episode, but the latter is so well fitted in that it does not injure the unity of the fable. The principal is the love of Mirtillo and Amarilli from which arises basically the knot, the denouement, the interpretation of the oracle, the necessity of the marriage, and the happy issue. The other, which acts as episode, is built around the characters of Silvio and Dorinda, and it also ends in marriage. The other roles, then, are the means and the instruments necessary to lead all things with verisimilitude and with decorum to their proper conclusions. That the tragicomic mixture may produce a praiseworthy poem it is not necessary for me to show, because this is of itself eminently clear to anyone who is not completely ignorant of belles lettres, and because, moreover, *Il Verato* has defended it and has proved the point sufficiently. Let whoever wishes to be fully informed read it.

And because it could happen that the name 'tragicomedy' might suggest to the reader an urban fable, the provident author thought to clear up the ambiguity with the adjunct 'pastoral', in order that it might be known that the characters introduced are not urban, but only shepherds—from which, since some are noble and some base (the former fitting for tragedy and the latter for comedy), united together they can form a mixed drama in which both kinds participate. Thus to say 'pastoral tragicomedy' is as much as to say a fable about shepherds ordered in the form of tragicomedy. For the name of shepherd in the title alone is not sufficient to show this since it could easily happen in an urban fable that one might find a faithful shepherd from whom it took its name, titles of comic fables being simply designed to please, as is well known to almost everyone however indifferently learned he may be. That the pastoral condition may contain personages worthy of tragic poetry is a thing so clear to nearly all authors, Hebrew, Greek, and Latin, that to make a long discourse about it would be excessive, it being my purpose here to comment, not to discourse.

Now, there are to be found two kinds of simple fables: one which is considered simple in subject, of which I have spoken above with the

---

[1] Aristotle, *Poetics*, ch. 13. In *Il Compendio* Guarini relates tragicomedy to Aristotle's 'plot with a double story and an opposite issue for the good and bad personages'. His denial of this relationship here is a sounder position; cf. Doran, *Endeavors of Art*, pp. 196–7.

authority of Terence: the other which regards the form and was called by the Philosopher ἁπλῆ, that is, simple, because it lacks change of fortune and recognition; the contrary of this is the 'knotted' kind, called in Greek πεπλεγμένη.[1] Without any doubt *Il Pastor Fido* should be put in the second class, whence it becomes a noble type of fable, having the most esteemed condition which a dramatic poem may have and a recognition very similar to that of *Œdipus Tyrannis*, which was most highly praised by the afore-mentioned Philosopher, a recognition by means of which the state of the fable is unexpectedly changed from sad to happy fortune.

The scene is figured in Arcadia, a province of Peloponnesus, which to-day is called the Morea. And I should give notice that the site is entirely feigned, just as the whole fable and all the incidents are feigned, which is permitted for a comic or tragicomic poet as contrariwise it is not permitted in tragedy. With good judgement, then, is the action feigned in Arcadia to give more verisimilitude to the beauties which are in it: because anciently the Arcadians held no study nor exercise more noble nor more frequently than poetry, as Polybius has shown in the fourth book of his history, to which place as notable and worthy to be seen the reader is referred. Concerning this subject Virgil said in one of his eclogues:

> Arcades ambo
> Et cantare pares, & respondere parati.[2]

which shows us the natural aptitude and the great promptness of that people in improvising. And although it is granted to the comic poet to invent all things for the sake of verisimilitude whether or not they exist or ever have existed, whether places, times, people, cities, forms of govern-ment, names, and all other things in nature, for the sake of verisimilitude, nevertheless our poet has many things which are supported by the verity of history. And as in this he has done well, so he has not erred when he has done the contrary.

And in order not to depart from the custom of the ancient approved grammarians[3] in dividing the fables of Terence, we shall divide this of *Pastor Fido* also into the customary four parts, namely prologue, protasis, epitasis, and catastrophe. The prologue will be discussed below. In the protasis is contained the marriage arranged by Montano, father of Silvio, and by Titiro, father of Amarilli, in the hope of liberating by this means their country from the horrible sacrifice; the abhorrence of Silvio and Amarilli toward this match; the plot of Corisca to lead into misfortune the enamoured and incautious girl. In the epitasis is contained the taking of Amarilli as a condemned adulteress, the marriage upset, Mirtillo offered in

---

[1] *Poetics*, ch. 10. [2] *Eclogues*, VII. 4–5.
[3] Especially Donatus; text and translation of the passage in question are given in H. W. Lawton, *Handbook of French Renaissance Dramatic Theory* (Manchester, 1949), pp. 12–17.

sacrifice, the arrival of Carino, Amarilli unhappy, Titiro tearful, Montano afflicted, and the province grieving.

In the catastrophe is contained the agon between Montano and Carino, the recognition of Mirtillo, the interpretation of the oracle, the death of Mirtillo converted to marriage, all things which had a moment ago been tearful made joyful, the lovers who had up to then been miserable espoused, the province freed from the horrible tribute, and the fable happily changed from very sad to very joyful fortune only through the recognition of the Faithful Shepherd. I do not speak of Silvio nor of Dorinda, because they do not enter into the principal knot of the fable, being the episodic part and therefore independent, as one says.

And it is necessary to say that tragedy is divided into its own parts: that is, prologue, episode, exode, chorus, and commos,[1] which are thus different from those of comedy, as the comic order is much different from the tragic. And because *Il Pastor Fido* is of the comic order, I have divided it comically, because that part which Aristotle called 'episode' in tragedies becomes another thing in comedies, which cannot be regulated by the practice of tragedies in their management, the knot of comedy being full of many intrigues, which are not suitable to the gravity and the context of tragedy.

---

[1] *Poetics*, ch. 12, where 'episode' apparently means the part between two choruses. Guarini is evading an issue here, since Aristotle's division cannot be reasonably applied to any Renaissance drama, tragedy or comedy.

SCENES FROM THE TWO EARLIER ENGLISH TRANSLATIONS

WE include two scenes, in which are represented most of the types of writing to be found in Guarini's text, from the two earlier English translations, i.e. from:

(1) Il Pastor Fido: | OR | The faithfull Shepheard. | Translated out of Italian into | *English.* | [device] | London | Printed for Simon Waterson. | 1602.

The dedication to this volume reads: 'To the Right Worthy and learned Knight, Syr *Edward Dymock, Champion to her Maiestie.* Syr, this worke was committed to me to publish to the world, and by reason of the nearnesse of kinne to the deceased Translator, and the good knowledge of the great worth of the Italian Author; I knew none fitter to Patronize the same then your worthinesse, to whom I wish all happinesse, and a prosperous new yeare. London this last of December, 1601. *Your Worships euer to be commaunded.* Simon Waterson.'

(2) Il | Pastor Fido | OR | The Faithfull Sheapheard | An Excellent Pastorall | Written | In Italian by | Battista Guarini | And translated into English | By | Jonathan Sidnam Esq | Anno. 1630
[This translation is contained in B.M. Add. MS. 29,493.]

From

IL PASTOR FIDO (London, 1602)

ACT III, SCENE 4. *Amarillis.*

Oh *Mirtillo*! oh my dearest soule
Could'st thou but see into her hart whom thou
Call'st cruell *Amarillis*, then wouldst thou say
Thou hadst that pittie which thy hart desires.
Oh mindes too much infortunate in loue!
What bootes it thee my hart to be belou'd?   5
What bootes it me to haue so deare a Loue?
Why should the cruell fates so disvnite
Whō loue conioines? and why should traiterous loue
Conioyne them whom the destenies do part?
Oh happie sauadge beasts whom nature giues   10
No lawes in loue, saue verie loue it selfe.

Inhumane humane lawe, that punish'st
This loue with death, if't be so sweet to sin,
And not to sin so necessary bee,   15
Imperfect nature that repugneth law,
Or law too hard that nature doth offend.
But tush, she loues too litle that feares death,
Would gods death were the worst that's due to sin.
Deare chastitie, th' inviolable powre   20
Of soules well-borne that hast my amorous will
Retein'd in chaines of holy rigour still:
To thee I consecrate my harmelesse sacrifize.
And thou my soule (*Mirtillo*) pardon me,
That cruell am where I should piteous bee.   25
Pardon her that in lookes and onely words
Doth seeme thy foe, but in my heart thy friend.
If thou wouldst be reueng'd, what greater paine
Wouldst thou inflict, then this my cruel griefe?
Thou art my heart, and shalt be spite of heauen   30
And earth, when thou dost plaine & sigh, and weep,
Thy teares become my bloud, thy sighes my breath:
And all thy paines they are not onely thine,
For I them feele, and they are turned mine.

SCE. 5. *Corisca. Amarillis.*

Hide you no more my *Amarillis* now.   35
    Ama. Wretch I discouered am. (*Co.*) I all haue heard,
Be not afraid, did I not say I lou'd you,
And yet you are afraid? and hides your selfe
From her that loues you so. Why do you blush?
This blushing is a common fault.   40
    Ama. Corisca I am conquer'd *I* confesse.
    Co. That which you cannot hide you wil confesse.
    Ama. And now *I* see too weake a thing doth proue
A womans heart t' encounter mightie loue.
    Co. Cruel vnto *Mirtillo*, but more cruel to your selfe.   45
    Ama. It is no crueltie that springs of pitie.
    Co. Cicute and *Aconite* do grow from holsome rootes.
I see no difference twixt this crueltie
That doth offend, and pitie helping not.
    Ama. Ah me *Corisca*! (*Co.*) These sighes good sister   50
Are but weakenesse of your heart. Th' are fit
For women of small worth. (*Ama.*) *I* could not be
Thus cruell but I should loue cherish hopelesly.

Therefore to shun him shewes *I* haue compassion
Of his ill and mine. (*Co.*) Why hopelesly?   55
   Ama. Do you not know *I* am espows'd to *Siluio*,
And that the law each woman doomes to death
That violates her faith? (*Co.*) Oh simple foole,
Is this the let? Which is more auncient among vs,
Dianaes lawe or loues? this in our breasts   60
Is bred and growes with vs, *Nature* her selfe
With her owne hands imprints in our hearts breasts:
And where this law commands, both heau'n & earth obey.
   Ama. But if the other law do take my life,
How can loues lawe restore it me againe?   65
   Co. You are too nice, were eu'ry woman so,
Had all such straight respects. Good times farewell,
Small practisers are subiect to this paine.
The lawe doth neuer stretch vnto the wise.
Beleeue me should blame-worthy all be slaine,   70
The countre then would soone prooue womanlesse.
It needfull was, theft should forbidden bee
To them that closely could not couer theft.
This honestie is but an art to seeme so,
Let others as they list beleeue, Ile thinke so still.   75
   Ama. These are but vanities (*Corisca*) 'twere best
Quickly to leaue that which we cannot hold.
   Co. And who forbids thee foole? This life's too short
To passe it ouer with one onely loue:
Men are too sparing of their fauours now,   80
(Whether't be for want, or else for frowardnesse)
The fresher that we are, the dearer still:
Beautie and youth once gone w' are like Bee hiues
That hath no honey, no nor yet no waxe.
Let men prate on they do not feele our woes,   85
For their condition differs much from ours,
The elder that they grow, they grow the perfecter:
If they loose beautie, yet they wisedome gaine:
But when our beautie fades that oftentimes
Conquers their greatest witts, strait fadeth all our good,   90
There cannot be a vilder thing to see
Then an old woman. Therefore ere thou age attaine,
Know me thy selfe, and vse it as thou shouldst.
What were a Lion worth did he not vse his strength?
What's a mans wit worth that lies idly by?   95
Eu'n so our beautie proper strength to vs,

As force to Lyons, wisedome vnto men,
We ought to vse whilst it we haue. Time flies
Away and yeares come on, our youth once lost
We like cut flowres neuer grow fresh againe.   100
And to our hoary haires loue well may runne,
But Louers will our wrinkled skinnes still shunne.
  Ama. Thou speakest this (*Corisca*) me to trie,
Not as thou think'st I am sure. But be assur'd
Except thou show'st some meanes how I may shun   105
This marriage bonds, my thought's irreuocable,
And I resolued am rather to die
Then any way to spot my chastitie.
  Co. I haue not seene so obstinate a foole,
But since you are resolu'd I am agreed.   110
But tell me do you thinke your *Siluio* is
As true a friend to faith as you to chastitie?
  Ama. Thou mak'st me smile. *Siluio* a friend to faith?
How can that be? hee's enemy to loue.
  Co. Siluio an enemy to loue? O foole,   115
These that are nice put thou no trust in them:
Loues theft is neuer so securely done
As hidden vnder vaile of honestie,
Thy *Siluio* loues (good *Sister*) but not thee.
  Ama. What goddesse is she? for she cannot bee   120
A mortall wight that lighted hath his loue.
  Co. Nor goddesse, nor a Nimph. (*Ama.*) What do you tell?
  Co. Know you *Lisetta*? (*Ama.*) She that your cattell keeps?
  Co. Eu'n she. (*Ama.*) Can it be true? (*Co.*) That same's his hart.
  Ama. Sure hee's prouided of a daintie Loue.   125
  Co. Each day he faines that he on hunting goes.
  Ama. I eu'ry morning heare his cursed horne.
  Co. About noone-time when others busie are,
He his companions shuns, and comes alone
By a backe way, vnto my garden there,   130
Where a shadow hedge doth close it in,
There doth she heare his burning sighes his vowes,
And then she tells me all, and laughes at him.
Now heare what I thinke good to doo. Nay I
Haue don't for you alreadie. You know the law   135
That tyes vs to our faith, doth giue vs leaue
Finding our spowses in the act of perfidie,
Spite of our friends the marriage to denie,
And to prouide vs of an other if we list.

Ama. That know I well, I haue examples two,   140
Leucipp to *Ligurine, Armilla* to *Turingo,*
Their faith once broke, they tooke their owne again.
    Co. Now heare! *Lisetta* by my appointment hath
Promist to meet th' vnwary Louer here
In this same Caue, and now he is the best   145
Contented youth that liues, attending but the houre
There would I haue you take him. Ile be there
To beare you witnesse oft't, for else we worke
In vaine, so are you free from this same noisome knot
Both with your honour, and your fathers too.   150
    Ama. Oh braue inuentiō, good *Corisca* what's to do?
    Co. Obserue my words. In midst of this same caue
Vpon the right hand is a hollow stone,
I know not if by Art or nature made,
A litle Caue all linde with Iuy leaues,   155
To which a little hole aloft giues light,
A fit and thankfull receptacle for loues theft.
Preuent their comming and attend them there:
Ile haste *Lisetta* forward, and as soone
As I perceiue your *Siluio* enter, so will I: 160
Step you to her, and as the custome is,
Weele carry both vnto the Priest, and there dissolue
This marriage knot. (*Ama.*) What to his father?
    Co. What matter's that? Think you *Montanus* dare
His priuate to a publike good compare?   165
    Ama. Then closing vp mine eyes, I let my selfe
Be ledde by thee my deare, my faithfull guide.
    Co. But do not stay now, enter me betime.
    Ama. I'le to the Temple first, and to the Gods
My prayers make, without whose aide no happy end   170
Can euer sort to mortall enterprise.
    Co. All places (*Amarillis*) temples are,
To hearts deuout, you'le slacke your time too much.
    Ama. Time's neuer lost in praying vnto them
That do commaund the time. (*Co.*) Go then dispatch.   175
Now if I erre not, am I at good passe,
Onely this staying troubles me, yet may it helpe,
I must goe make new snares to traine in *Coridon.*
Ile make him thinke that I will meet him there,
And after *Amarillis* send him soone,   180
Then by a secret way Ile bring *Dianaes* Priests:
Her shall they finde, and guiltie doome to death.

My riuall gone (*Mirtillo*) sure is mine,
See where he comes. Whilst *Amarillis* stayes
Ile somewhat trie him. Loue now once inspire   185
My tongue with words, my face with heau'nly fire.

FROM THE UNPUBLISHED MS. OF A TRANSLATION OF *IL PASTOR FIDO* BY JONATHAN SIDNAM

Act: 3. Scena 4ª./

Amarillis/

O Mirtillo Mirtillo. my deare Soule,
Couldst thou but looke into her hart wth in
Whom now thou calst thy cruell Amarillis,
I knowe thou then wouldst pittie her sadd case
From whom thou seekst for pittie,   5
O wretched Soules, vnhappie in your loues,
What bootes yt thee (my hart) to be beloud,
Or me to haue a loue soe truelie true?
Why doe you separate you cruell fates,
Those whom true loue hath joynd soe faithfullie?   10
And cruell loue why dost thou tie soe fast,
Those whom the heauens seperate?
O happie creatures, happie sauage beastes
On whom kinde nature hath imposd noe law
In loue, but loue yt selfe,   15
Inhumane, humane law, that dost reward
True loue in men wth death,
'If sinn be in yt selfe soe sweete,
'And not to sinn be of necessitie,
'O nature too imperfect then,   20
'That dost contend against soe stricke a lawe,
'O lawe too too seuere, that dost
'Oppose the rules of nature/
But thats a fainte weake loue that feares to die:
O my Mirtillo would the Godds were pleasd.   25
That death alone might expiate the fault
Of loueing thee./
Religious chastitie, that onelie art
Th' inuiolable Godhead of an hart
Incensd wth noble flames/   30
To thee I consecrate the sacrifice
Of all my amorous thoughts.

Slaine on thine altar, wth the piercing sword
Of thy most Sacred rigour/
And thou Mirtillo (my deare hart) forgiue   35
Her that is forc't to use thee cruellie,
Onelie because shee dares not pittie thee
Pardon her fault that onelie in her wordes,
And in her lookes is thy fierce enemie,
But in her hart a loue as pittifull   40
As thine owne Soule can wishe:
But yf thy minde can thinke of a reuenge,
Ay-me what greater vengeance canst thou haue
Then thine owne priuate sorrowe?
For yf thou be my hart as in despight   45
Of earth and heauen too thou needes must be,
When thou dost weepe and sigh, those teares of thine,
Come from my dearest blood,
Those sighes, spend my best spiritts, and that paine
W^{ch} thy greefe feeles, doth cleaue my hart in twaine.   50

Act: 3. Scena. 5.^{a}/

Corisca. Amarillis./

Corisca   O sister now conceale thy selfe noe more
Amarillis Alas I am discouered/
Corisca   I understand too well whats past,
           Did I not saie she loues? and now tis plaine,
           And dost thou then conceale thy thoughts from me?   55
           Dost thou hide ought from her that loues thee soe?
           Blush not, be not asham'd, tis a disease
           Comõn to all.
Amarillis I am conuict Corisca, I confesse
Corisca   Yes now confesse when't cannot be denied./   60
Amarillis And too too well I finde, wretch that I am
           A feeble hart too weake a vessell is
           To stand against loues furious assaultes,
Corisca.   O cruell to thy deare Mirtillo, but
           Vnto thy selfe more Cruell   65
Amarillis Cruell that cannot be wch springs from pietie
Corisca   Did euer Aconite or poison spring
           From anie holesome roote? what difference
           Is there twixt crueltie that injures vs,
           And pietie that will not helpe at neede?   70
Amarillis Ay-me Corisca

Corisca To sigh my sister is the vanitie
Of a fainte hart, and onelie fitt for them
That want both witt and courage:
Amarillis Were yt not greater crueltie 75
If I should feede his loue w^{th}out all hope?
That I auoide him, is a certaine signe
I pittie both his fortune, and mine owne,
Corisca Why w^{th}out hope?
Amarillis Knowst thou not I am promisd vnto Siluio? 80
Knowst thou not that the Law Condemnes to death
Her that doth violate her faith?
Corisca O simple that thou art, doth noething else
Hinder thy full Content?
W^{ch} of those Lawes hath more antiquitie 85
That wch Diana, or wch loue Com̃andes?
This is borne wth our selues, my Amarillis
And growes vpp wth our age,
Tis neither taught, nor learn't, but natures selfe
W^{th} her owne handes imprintes yt in our Soules, 90
W^{th} out a Master, and where shee Com̃andes,
Not onelie Earth, but heauen must obey:
Amarillis. But yf Dianas law cutt short my life,
Tis not this law of loue can succour mee:
Corisca Thou art too warie, yf all woemen else, 95
Were such as thou, and had the same respectes,
Good daies adieu: This law was onelie made,
For sillie fooles that want experience,
Such as are wise, owe noe subjection to yt:
If all should die that haue offended yt, 100
Beleeue me woemen would be scarce ere long,
And yf none else but fooles fall under yt,
'Tis reason theft should be forbidd to those,
'That know not cuninglie how to conueigh
'The art of stealing/ 105
In fine our chastitie is noething else,
But a nice studdie of appearing chast,
Each one maie thinke as likes them best
For my part this is my beleefe./
Amarillis. O my Corisca these are vanities, 110
'Tis wisedome soone to leaue, what long wee cannot hold.
Corisca. What hinders thee poore foole?
Life is too short to be consum'd awaie
W^{th} onelie one loue and noe more,

And wicked men (whether yt be defect   115
Or cuñing in them yt is hard to saie)
Are too too sparing in disposing of
Their fauours to vs./
'Make this account, wee are noe longer deare,
'Nor pleasing to them, then whilst we are yong,   120
'Take youth and beautie from vs, and wee rest
'Like drie neglected Bee hiues, that containe
'Nor combes nor hony./
Giue men my Amarillis leaue to talke,
Yet neither knowe they, nor can apprehend   125
The discomodities that woemen feele.
For our Condition (heauen knowes) is farr,
Farr different from that of theirs:
'Age giues a man his full perfection,
'For losse of beautie, judgmͭ is acquir'd,   130
'But in a woeman when her youth is gone,
'When beautie failes, by wᶜʰ the witt of man
'And all his wisedome is oft ouercome,
'All that was good in her is gone,
'Nor can wee speake, or thinke a thinge more vile,   135
'Then an old doating woman is/
Ere then this vniuersall miserie,
Proper vnto our sexe, shall seise on thee,
Know thine owne worth, and yf thy life be yet
Strong on the right hand, reach not forth the left,   140
'What were the lyon better for his strength
'If hee should neuer vse yt?
'What should man doe wᵗʰ all the witt he hath,
'If he should not imploie yt for his good?
'Soe wee our beautie, (wᶜʰ a vertue is   145
'To vs as propper, as the lyons strength
'Or witt to man) must vse yt while wee maie,
'Or else wee loose yt: Let vs then enjoye
Deare Sister, letts enjoye, the sweetes yt bringes
Time will awaie; and yeares perhapps to them   150
Maie yet restore the losses of their cold
By past infirmities./
But yf in vs youth once be withered,
Tis sure inough yt never growes greene againe,
And to graie haires, a pale and wrinckled face,   155
Loue maie returne, but a true louer neuer/

Amarillis   Surelie thou speakest this rather to trie

What my thoughts are, then wth intent to shew,
Either what thou dost thinke, or dost desire:
Take this for certaine then, vnlesse thou knowe   160
An easie waie, but aboue all, a waie
Vertuous and honest, to breake off this Match,
My hart wth an irreuocable vow,
Resolues to die Corisca, rather then
To bring a staine vppon myne honestie:/   165

Corisca   I neuer yet sawe one more obstinate,
             Then this fond woman is/
             If that be then thy resolucõn
             Lett vs thinke on't;
             Tell me sweete Amarillis canst thou deeme   170
             Thy Siluio as true a frend to faith,
             As thou art to thine honestie/

Amarillis   Why dost thou aske: can Siluio be
             A friend to faith that euer was to loue
             Soe greate an Enemie?   175

Corisca.   Siluio to loue an enemie? O simple wench!
             Thou knowst him not: but he knowes how to doe
             And keepe his councell too: that I can tell.
             Learne this of me these nice, coye, wayward fooles
             Trust not, yf thou be wise: 180
             Theres not an amorous stealth they cannot hide,
             Nor a dissembling slight they cannot cloake,
             Vnder the vaile of honestie,
             Thy Siluio loues my sister, but not thee/

Amarillis   What Goddesse is yt then/. for sure inough   185
             Tis not a mortall wight that can incense
             His hart to loue./

Corisca   Nor Goddesse, nor yet Nymph/
Amarillis   Whats that thou saist?
Corisca.   Know'st thou my maide Lisetta?   190
Amarillis   What not Lisetta that lookes to thy flock?
Corisca   Thats shee that hath his hart
Amarillis   See yf the coye yong man,
             Bee not prouided of a louelie peece/

Corisca.   And dost thou know what toile and paines he takes? 195
             Each daie on hunting he pretendes to goe
Amarillis   Tis true each morning by the breake of daie
             I heare his cursed horne./

Corisca.   And about noone when all the rest are most
             Busie about the chace, he steales awaie   200

From his camrades, and by an vnknowne path,
Comes all alone into my garden, where
Shee in the thickest of those shadie bowres,
Giues audience to his praiers and amorous sighes,
And after tells them me, and laughs a good./   205
Now then ile tell thee what I thinke to doe
Naie what I haue as good as done alreadie
For thy aduantage/
I doubt not but thou knowst the selfe same law,
W.^{ch} hath impos'd on vs fidelitie,   210
To our espoused loues: Comandes as well,
That yf they ere be taken in an act,
Of falsehood vnto us: wee maie
Against the will of all our freindes denie
To marrie them, and gett vs other loues/   215

Amarillis This I know verie well, and in my time,
Haue seene examples of yt:
Leucippa did yt vnto Ligurino, Egla vnto Licotas
And Armilla to Turingo:
For falsehood vnto them, all these recouered   220
The faith they had ingadg'd

Corisca Marke what I saie then,
By me Lisetta therevnto aduis'd,
This daie hath promisd in that Caue to meete,
Her heedlesse youthfull louer: who remaines   225
The most contented man aliue, and onelie waites,
The happie wisht for houre:
There I would haue thee take him, and my selfe,
Will there be for a wittnesse of the fact,
For w.thout that our labours but in vaine,   230
Thus w.thout danger either to thine owne
Or to thy fathers honour thou shalt be,
Free from this wofull bondage./

Amarillis O how discreetelie has thou laide, thy plott
What haue wee more to doe?   235

Corisca That wch ile tell thee now,: obserue me then,
W.th in the middle of that Caue wch is
Sufficientlie long, but narrow fram'd,
Vppon the right hand side, there is a vault,
A little hollow vault, wrought in the stone,   240
Whether by nature, or by humane art,
Tis hard to tell: and this is all adornd,
One euerie side w.th twinning Iuie round:

And from the topp a little crevise sendes,
A darksome light into yt: all wch makes 245
The place, a receptacle fitt for loue,
And amorous encounters./
There I would haue thee then preuent,
These two fond louers, and there hide thy selfe,
To waite their Coming: thither will I send, 250
Lisetta out of hand: and I my selfe,
Waiting a prettie distance off will marke,
When Siluio enters in, and follow him,
Where staieing him from flight, Ile straight crie out
(For soe I wth Lisetta haue agreed) 255
Thou at the noise shalt then come running in
And thus according to the lawe pursue,
His breach of faith: Lisetta and wee two,
Complaining to the Priest shall soe dissolue
This knott that thus afflicts vs./ 260

Amarillis Before his father:? Cor: That importes not much
Thinkst thou Montano dare preferr his owne
Priuate respects, before the publique good
Or neglect holie thinges, to saue profane?

Amarillis Wth blinded eyes I then permitt my selfe 265
To be ledd by thee O my happie guide./

Corisca But staie not then my hart: Amar: I first will goe
Vnto the temple to adore the Godds
Happie successe cannot attend the Care
Of mortall wights, vnlesse they can obtaine 270
A blessing first from heauen./

Corisca. All places Amarillis are alike,
All holie temples, to an hart deuout:
Wee shall loose too much time./

Amarillis Time is not lost in praieing vnto those 275
That can Comand our time./

Corisca. Goe then and come againe wth speede:
If I be not deceiud, I now haue found,
A readie waie vnto my wishes, where
Nothing afflicts me, but this short delaie, 280
And this perhapps maie further my deseignes/
But I must now goe spinn another webb,
And make my louer Coridon beleeue,
That I will meete him in the selfe same Caue
And send him after Amarillis, then 285
By the most secrett path, Ile cause to come